JUVENILE DELINQUENTS
GROWN UP

LONDON
GEOFFREY CUMBERLEGE
OXFORD UNIVERSITY PRESS

JUVENILE DELINQUENTS
GROWN UP

SHELDON and ELEANOR GLUECK

1940
NEW YORK · THE COMMONWEALTH FUND

PUBLISHED BY THE COMMONWEALTH FUND

41 EAST 57TH STREET, NEW YORK, N.Y.

———

LITHOGRAPHED IN THE UNITED STATES OF AMERICA

TO THE MEMORY OF OUR FRIENDS
ELLA LYMAN CABOT
RICHARD CLARKE CABOT

AUTHORS' PREFACE

OUR first study of juvenile delinquents, published in 1934, reported what had happened to a thousand boys during a five-year period immediately following "treatment" for a specific offense for which they had been brought before a juvenile court.[1] At that time there was no plan for following their careers further, but the interest aroused by the report, and the fact that it was of use to those concerned with the problems of delinquency, suggested that valuable additional information might be obtained if the behavior of the boys were studied during another ten years, at the end of which time most of them would be grown up. The generosity of the Commonwealth Fund has made this follow-up possible.

We cannot list in detail all the individuals, institutions, and public and private welfare agencies in Massachusetts and in other states who have assisted us in one way or another in this work, and without whose ready cooperation it would have been impossible for us to carry through this research. We must, however, particularly mention Dr. William A. Healy and Dr. Augusta Bronner of the Judge Baker Guidance Center of Boston; Mr. Roscoe C. Hill and Miss Carrie V. Moyer of the Bureau of Criminal Identification of the Massachusetts Department of Public Safety; Miss Laura G. Woodberry of the Boston Social Service Index, whose files were consulted for information about the contacts of social agencies with our youths and their families; Hon. Albert Carter, Commissioner of Probation of Massachusetts, who, like his predecessor, Mr. Herbert C. Parsons, facilitated the clearance of our cases through the files of the Board of Probation, where the criminal records of offenders committing crimes in Massachusetts are centralized; Hon. Arthur T. Lyman, Commissioner of Correction of Massachusetts, who permitted us to consult records in the files of the department; Mr. Richard Winslow, until recently Director of the Personnel De-

---

[1] Sheldon and Eleanor T. Glueck, *One Thousand Juvenile Delinquents,* Volume I of Harvard Law School Survey of Crime and Criminal Justice in Boston, Cambridge, Harvard University Press, 1934.

partment of the Massachusetts State Prison, and the members of his staff; Mr. Charles A. Du Bois, Superintendent of the Lyman School for Boys, Mr. George P. Campbell, Superintendent of the Shirley School for Boys, Mr. C. Frederick Gilmore, Superintendent of the Boys' Parole Branch of the Massachusetts Department of Public Welfare, and Mr. Walter C. Bell, Executive Secretary of the Division of Juvenile Training of the Massachusetts Department of Public Welfare, all of whom made it possible for us to secure data concerning the behavior of our youths while they were under the supervision of these various agencies and institutions; and Judge John F. Perkins of the Boston Juvenile Court, who allowed us to consult the records of the court when we found it necessary.

Our thanks go, as always, to Professor Earnest A. Hooton of Harvard University for his ready counsel, and to the members of his statistical staff, particularly Mrs. Sarah R. Cotton, for very able assistance in the tabulation and statistical handling of our data.

Our indebtedness is acknowledged also to Dean James M. Landis of the Harvard Law School, who, like his predecessor, Dean Roscoe Pound, is giving us the utmost encouragement in our researches.

For the skilful handling of the manuscript, including various constructive suggestions for revision, we express our appreciation to the Division of Publications of the Commonwealth Fund.

And, finally, we are, as always, grateful to the members of our staff who have given loyally of themselves in one or another phase of this research: Mr. Samuel C. Lawrence, Mrs. Mildred P. Cunningham, Mr. Stacy C. Saunders, Mrs. Beatrice H. Scheff, and Mrs. Virginia A. Maddux. For able part-time assistance during a portion of the work, our thanks are due to Mrs. Miriam B. Sachs, Mrs. Marion Billings, and Mr. Emanuel Borenstein.

It is our sincere hope that the data contained in this further study of the careers of *One Thousand Juvenile Delinquents* will add to the growing store of accurate knowledge and fruitful theory regarding the administration of criminal justice.

E. T. G. and S. G.

Harvard Law School, December 1939

CONTENTS

Chapter I

INTRODUCTION

THE significance of follow-up studies of the results of peno-correctional treatment need no longer be labored. Not only do such researches furnish a gauge of the effectiveness of social institutions developed for coping with the problems of delinquency and crime, but they furnish an insight into the natural history of delinquents and criminals, into the changes in their behavior with advancing years and under the impact of different environmental stimuli.

In 1934 we published the results of an investigation of a thousand boy delinquents who had been brought into the Boston Juvenile Court and who had been examined, at the request of the Court, in the Clinic of the Judge Baker Foundation[1] during the years 1917–1922, when they were of an average age of thirteen and a half years.[2] The major emphasis in that work was on the amount of recidivism among these youths during a five-year period following the completion of the treatment that had been carried out by the Court and its affiliated community agencies. It was concerned, also, with the effectiveness of the coordination of the Court and Clinic in following the prescribed treatment, and with an analysis of the reasons why many of the Clinic's recommendations to the Court had not been followed.

As part of that study the personal traits and environmental backgrounds of the juvenile offenders were analyzed, not only to describe the delinquents in some detail but also to determine whether there are constellations of traits on the basis of which the future behavior of delinquents can be predicted.

Some ten years have elapsed since the end of the first five-year follow-up period. What has happened to these one thousand juvenile delinquents during this time? Have they gone from bad to

---

[1] Now known as the Judge Baker Guidance Center.

[2] *One Thousand Juvenile Delinquents*, Cambridge, Harvard University Press, 1934.

worse, or has the picture brightened? How account for the changes in behavior that have occurred with the passing of the years? Can the future behavior of such lads be foretold? What lessons can be learned from the manner of their development as they passed from childhood into adolescence and adulthood? How did they respond to the various types of peno-correctional treatment to which society subjected them in the course of their antisocial careers? Such questions impelled us to check the behavior of these youths as they stumbled down the corridor of time.

In this work the searchlight is focused on the behavior of the delinquent boys during the second and third five-year periods that have elapsed since the original study was completed, and on their conduct during the various peno-correctional treatments to which they have been subjected since first coming into contact with agencies of the law.[3] The study probes also into the reasons for such changes in conduct as have occurred in the group. It develops further than did the prior work our method of forecasting the behavior of offenders. Until now, the predictive technique has been limited to foretelling the conduct of different types of offenders *following* peno-correctional treatment; in the present work the prediction method is also applied to the response of the men *during* their subjection to varieties of treatment.

One of the most challenging aspects of such a follow-up study has to do with *finding* the men about whom we were seeking information. Criminals and ex-criminals as a group represent a highly mobile part of the population; and although many of them formerly lived in Boston and Massachusetts, they have since wandered to many corners of the United States and even to foreign countries.

---

[3] It should be emphasized that the nature and length of the treatment accorded by the Boston Juvenile Court and its affiliated agencies is of no further concern to us. For practical purposes it has seemed best to continue to utilize the time of appearance of these lads in the Boston Juvenile Court as the point of departure for a continuing investigation, but we could just as well have taken as the starting point of the present research any other time in their early delinquent careers. As long as we consider each successive five-year span in relation to the age of the group at the beginning and end of that particular period, we need not for present purposes attach any significance to the point from which the first five-year period was measured.

The task of locating them, therefore, was an exciting and absorbing one; that of interviewing them a delicate one, because by now so many of these former juvenile delinquents, already of an average age of twenty-nine years, are married and have children. In proceeding on the assumption that their wives might not know of their earlier delinquencies we had to be particularly careful not to make revelation of this fact or to interview the men in the presence of their children; and if we found them living in small towns or rural districts we had to be particularly watchful not to reveal the nature of our quest to neighbors, local officials, or employers, for obviously in smaller towns the position of a man might be endangered by such knowledge.

Over the years we have developed a technique of tracing and interviewing delinquents, of gathering data about them from innumerable sources, and of verifying these data. Because the validity of the findings of a research of this nature depends on the method by which the data are gathered and upon their accuracy, we have considered it necessary to make a detailed accounting of our procedures. These are described in Chapter XXI. Meanwhile we shall set down the findings themselves. After considering these, the reader may be interested to know just how we assembled and verified the data upon which they are based.

Chapter II

CHARACTERISTICS OF THE DELINQUENTS

PRELIMINARY to an analysis of the findings of the present inquiry, it is necessary to review the background of the thousand juvenile delinquents as reported in the original volume entitled *One Thousand Juvenile Delinquents*. It should be emphasized that in this summary, as in all the statistical data in succeeding chapters, it was not always possible to obtain full and reliable data on all the points under consideration. Hence the percentages, although statistically valid, are not necessarily based on the full thousand cases.

NATIVITY, BIRTHPLACE, AND RELIGION OF PARENTS

Some 80 per cent of the parents of the 1,000 juvenile delinquents were born in foreign countries, while a like proportion of the boys themselves were born in the United States. It seems obvious that these children were to a considerable extent subjected to conflicting cultures; for in 70 per cent of the cases one or both of their parents was foreign born while the boys themselves were born in the United States. In addition, 17 per cent of the boys were foreign born as were their parents, and they also had to undergo a cultural adaptation but of a somewhat different character; at least, in being transplanted from a foreign country to American soil they shared with their parents the difficulty involved in the adaptation. In only 13 per cent of the cases were both parents and boys born in this country.

What was the native land of these foreign-born parents? What national cultures did they bring into the stream of American life? In 40 per cent of the cases of foreign-born fathers, the country of origin was Italy; in 23 per cent, Russia, Poland, or Lithuania; in 16 per cent, Ireland; in 9 per cent, Canada. The remaining 12 per cent came from various other European countries. From the fact that so large a proportion of the parents were of Italian origin, it may reasonably be inferred that the culture conflict to which their sons were subjected was probably especially intense; for Italians cling strongly to their native customs and traditions and their children are therefore likely to be torn between loyalty to the ways of the parents and to those of the American environment in which they find themselves.

As to religious backgrounds, in 74 per cent of the cases both parents were Catholic, in 13 per cent they were Hebrew, and in 10 per cent they were Protestant. There were a few mixed marriages among the parents but on the whole it is evident that conflicting religious backgrounds were inconsequential in number.

SOCIO-ECONOMIC STATUS OF FAMILIES

In what socio-economic level of society had these boys been reared? One indirect answer to this question lies in the educational attainments of their parents, which may be used as a rough index of economic capacity.

In only 50 per cent of the cases did one or both of the parents have any formal schooling whatsoever, and in most of these cases it did not extend beyond grammar school. Only a few of the parents attended high school, and in but 5 cases did one of the parents enter college. Obviously, these young delinquents were reared in homes of relative ignorance.

But the actual financial condition of these families more pointedly discloses their place on the lowest rung of the socio-economic ladder; for, even in a period of normal employment, 68 per cent of them hovered precariously on the margin between self-support and dependency, living on the daily earnings of the breadwinner and accumulating little or nothing for a critical period of unemployment or illness. In case of any cessation of employment they had to resort immediately to aid from social agencies or relatives. Eight per cent of the families were constantly dependent on public or private social welfare agencies for support. Even the fourth of the families who were not, strictly speaking, in the class of the "poverty stricken," were nevertheless only a little better off, for they had savings sufficient to tide them over a period of only four months of stress without resort to outside aid.

The fact that social welfare agencies gave assistance of one kind or another to the families of 87 per cent of the youths is further evidence of their inadequate socio-economic status. The assistance given these families by over 2,300 welfare organizations was not limited to rendering financial help. Much aid had to be given in coping with the problems of rearing the children, in dealing with the physical and mental health of both parents and children, in straightening out domestic difficulties, and the like. But much of the aid was necessitated by essentially economic problems.

The sub-standard economic position of these families is further evidenced by the fact that a large proportion of the mothers of the boys (41 per cent) were compelled to work in order to supplement the family income, and by the nature of the father's employment. A fifth of the fathers worked in the building trades as plumbers, electricians, mechanics, carpenters, bricklayers, stonecutters, tinsmiths, and so on; another fifth were day laborers; 4 per cent were policemen, firemen, motormen; another 4 per cent were bakers, chefs, or cooks; 3 per cent were peddlers; 9 per cent were small shopkeepers; 6 per cent were factory hands; 7 per cent were teamsters or truck drivers; 6 per cent were restaurant workers, janitors, or watchmen; 4 per cent were clerks or bond salesmen; 10 per cent were engaged in such trades as tailoring, but working for others; only one per cent were engaged in what might be considered professional occupations—a few musicians and a few photographers.

In view of the low economic status of these families it is not surprising to find that most of the fathers of the delinquents were not highly skilled workers; nor were they very steadily employed. The families were large, and obviously the earnings of one breadwinner were not enough to take care of all the needs of growing families. Even at the time when these juvenile delinquents appeared before the Boston Juvenile Court, when the families were still uncompleted, there was an average of five children per family.

HOME AND NEIGHBORHOOD CONDITIONS

The basic inadequacy of the physical aspects of the homes in which these youths were reared can readily be surmised from the low economic status of the families. In 62 per cent of the cases the homes had to be characterized as unwholesome, being overcrowded (more than two persons sharing a bedroom), very disorderly, and poorly ventilated; in an additional 25 per cent at least one of these disadvantageous conditions was present, even though in certain respects there was more comfort in the physical arrangements.

It is not surprising to find that homes devoid to so large an extent of physical comforts were set in districts unfavorable to the rearing of children. The neighborhoods in which 86 per cent of the families resided were the locales of street and alleyway gangs, and contained centers of vice and crime within a radius of two blocks of the home. It is hardly likely that in such areas boys could find decent recreations and out-of-school interests. About this more will be said later.

FAMILY RELATIONSHIPS

It might be surmised that, though the physical aspects of the homes and neighborhoods in which our lads were reared presented many conditions inimical to the wholesome development of youngsters, there were certain saving graces in the psychological configuration of the family group, as reflected in the relationship of the parents to each other and to the boys, or in their disciplinary practices, and the supervision given the children. The facts, however, only serve to add to the already discouraging picture of the atmosphere surrounding these boys.

First it should be noted that in 16 per cent of the cases the parents were grossly incompatible in their conjugal relationships, even though they continued to live together; certainly the frictions engendered in such a situation must have had an unwholesome effect upon the children. In another 22 per cent the parents had been separated or divorced. Thus almost 40 per cent of the youngsters were reared in an atmosphere of parental bickerings, dissatisfactions, and unhappiness.

Nor was the relationship of the parents to the boys conducive to sound development from childhood into manhood. In 32 per cent of the cases the fathers were either wholly indifferent to their sons or showed unmistakably their lack of affection and even hostility. This may likewise be said of 18 per cent of the mothers.

Although it may be inferred from the above figures that a goodly proportion of these boys enjoyed some affection from one or the other parent, this must have been materially counteracted by very erratic disciplinary practices. In 96 per cent of the cases the fathers either wavered between firm and lax discipline or were always excessively easy-going or excessively strict. This was likewise true of 97 per cent of the mothers. Such practices frequently result either in open rebellion against parental authority or in complete license. Either situation leads to well-recognized evils.

Certainly the psychological atmosphere of the homes in which these boys were reared was inimical to the development of a sense of security. No fewer than 92 per cent of the homes either were "broken" by the death of one or both parents, by desertion, separation, or divorce, or by the prolonged absence of one or both parents owing to imprisonment or mental illness, or were otherwise clearly unsuited to the rearing of children, even though both parents were in the home, for they were households in which one or both of the parents were criminalistic or markedly incompatible or poor disciplinarians or careless supervisors of the lives of growing children.

DELINQUENCY AND MENTAL ABNORMALITIES IN THE FAMILY

Even more suggestive of the unwholesome atmosphere in which these boys were reared is the amount of delinquency and mental abnormality among the members of the family group. The high proportion of 70 per cent of the boys were brought up in households in which there was delinquency or criminality on the part of either parents or brothers and sisters. In a considerable fraction of these cases, one or both parents actually had some criminal record or were known to have committed offenses for which they might at any time have come to the attention of the police. Thus, the pattern of delinquency as a way of life was often substituted for the traditional wholesomeness and innocence of childhood.

Still further emphasizing the disadvantages suffered by these youths are the facts pertaining to the presence of mental defect, disease, and other mental abnormalities and peculiarities of their parents or brothers and sisters. Such conditions—ranging from extreme aberration to mild handicaps—were known to be present in 81 per cent of the families.

Such, then, is the burdened background of these 1,000 boys. What of the boys themselves?

EARLY ENVIRONMENTAL EXPERIENCES

When these youths appeared before the Boston Juvenile Court at the average age of thirteen and a half years, 57 per cent of them were living with both their parents, while the remainder were making their homes with one parent, with a parent and a step-parent, or with relatives or foster parents, and a few of them (1.2 per cent) were living in institutions. In the 464 cases in which the homes had been broken by the death, desertion, divorce, separation, or prolonged absence of one or both parents, the average age of the lads was six and a half years when the breach in the normal family situation occurred, so they had been subjected to unwholesome environmental experiences very early in life.

Half the thousand boys had left or had been taken from their parental homes at one time or another prior to their appearance before the Court. In 27 per cent of these cases the precipitating cause of this first breach with home ties was the death, separation, divorce, or desertion of the parents; the illness of a parent in 3.5 per cent; the delinquency of the boys themselves in 18 per cent; the unsuitability of the home because of neglect by the parents or their inability to provide properly in 4.5 per cent. In 11 per cent of the cases the boys ran away from home for one reason or another, and were thus at an early age shifting about and readily exposed to possible vicious influences. Some of them also had the unstabilizing experience of excessive moving about (more than once a year), thus having little opportunity to strike root in any one neighborhood. Still others had been brought to the United States from foreign countries and so had to adapt themselves to life in a new world. Thus, in at least 50 per cent of the cases, the early lives of these boys did not run a smooth course. They were subjected to experiences of a kind which could only add to their feelings of insecurity. It must also be remembered that, even though the remaining half of the group were not thus shuttled about from pillar to post, the homes of most of them were inadequate in one way or another for the proper rearing of children. Finally, it should be pointed out that 323 of the boys had already, prior to their appearance in the Boston Juvenile Court, been in orphanages, and a few had been in correctional schools.

Thus, fully half the entire group of juvenile delinquents had experienced abnormal living conditions, while the childhood environment of an even more substantial proportion of them was far from wholesome.

SCHOOLING OF OFFENDERS

When these 1,000 boys were brought before the Boston Juvenile Court and referred to the Judge Baker Foundation for examination, 59 per cent of them were still attending school. But in the achievement of the 41 per cent who had already completed their formal schooling, we get a picture of the educational limitations of all the boys. Of this group, 11 per cent had left school in the fifth grade, 16 per cent in the sixth, 31 per cent in the seventh, 25 per cent in the eighth; while only 17 per cent began but did not complete high school. Although the reason for withdrawal from school in 66 per cent of the cases was represented to be economic need (the children having to work to supplement the family's meager resources), it would seem evident that this reason was not unmixed with a strong desire to escape the discipline of school life.

Even more significant, perhaps, than the limited schooling of the group is the fact that so many of the boys were behind grade for their age. Only 15 per cent were not retarded in school, and if a retardation of one year is not to be considered serious, we can add to this figure 23 per cent more, making a total of only 38 per cent who were not more than one year behind class for their age and leaving 62 per cent who were two or more years behind grade. This not only indicates lack of ability to do school work but often reflects various intellectual and personality difficulties. In fact, 59 per cent of the boys were below normal intelligence as determined by standard tests, 13 per cent of them being definitely feebleminded. Obviously, therefore, a large proportion of these young offenders were not readily "teachable" and were destined to failure in school work. That many of them shunned the classroom and found it difficult to make a happy adjustment to school life is reflected in the fact that 64 per cent were truants.

EMPLOYMENT HISTORY

In the light of their brief schooling and the great economic stress of their homes, it is not surprising to find these lads seeking work at an early age. Two-thirds of the group had already been gainfully employed at the time of their appearance before the Boston Juvenile Court, 37 per cent having started to work when they were under thirteen, and 54 per cent when they were thirteen or fourteen years old. Their average age on entering employment was thirteen years. The highest proportion of the group (58 per cent) were engaged in street trades, as newsboys, bootblacks, errand boys, or messengers; 15 per cent worked as store boys, bellboys, or clerks; 11 per cent were employed in factories; 13 per cent were general helpers or restaurant hands, or engaged in various other kinds of unskilled work. And even at this early age a few of these boys (seventeen) had already ventured into illegitimate activities, such as selling stolen goods.

This analysis of the early occupational experiences of the boys includes Saturday and after-school work as well as full-time employment, because, as has already been pointed out, 59 per cent of them were still attending school at the time of their appearance before the Boston Juvenile Court. This has some relation to, but does not completely account for, the fact that 80 per cent of those youths who had full-time jobs were "irregular" workers, changing jobs frequently, going from one "blind-alley job" into another without any constructive plan for vocational advancement.

USE OF LEISURE

The hazards of street trades and of unskilled boys' jobs during the years of puberty and adolescence are well known. The uncontrolled street life, the early contact with undesirable and even dangerous companions which such work often entails, are bound to take their toll in the development of antisocial attitudes and of petty forms of misconduct that often lead to more serious offenses. In fact, 93 per cent of these young boys indulged in harmful recreations, such as hanging about the streets and associating with undesirable companions with whom they gambled or engaged in illicit sex practices and developed other vicious habits. The counterpoise of legitimate and healthful recreational outlets was too often missing; for most of these boys were never absorbed into organized programs for the use of leisure. Thus, 75 per cent of them never belonged to any organizations or clubs such as the Scouts, YMCA, settlement houses, and the numerous other organizations which operate in crowded areas for the benefit of the neighborhood children.

The extent to which these boys were gregarious is partially reflected in the fact that 35 per cent of them were either members of gangs or hung around street corners and poolrooms with groups of youngsters. It is also indicated in the fact that while only 30 per cent were without accomplices in the commission of the particular offenses for which they were brought into the Juvenile Court, 28 per cent committed such offenses in the company of one other boy, and 43 per cent had the companionship of two or more other youngsters in their illegal escapades.

EARLY ANTISOCIAL BEHAVIOR

Enmeshed in a complex web of poor biologic and social conditions, it is little wonder that all but a few of these 1,000 boys had seriously misbehaved in one way or another prior to the arrest which brought them into the Boston Juvenile Court; little wonder, too, that on the average they were of the immature age of nine and a half years when their antisocial conduct first became clearly evident, and only twelve years old when first arrested.

The early antisocial behavior of these boys will be described in some detail in the following chapter.

MENTAL AND PHYSICAL CONDITION

Examination of the boys in the Clinic of the Judge Baker Foundation revealed not only all the conditions and circumstances already reviewed in this chapter, but also some factors about their physical and mental condition which should be mentioned before leaving this description of their early life. The doctors at the clinic found that 57 per cent of the lads were in sound physical condition, meaning that their general development was good and that they had only minor ailments (such as carious teeth, defects of nose and throat, and the like) which did not directly interfere with their activities. Thirty per cent were only in fair condition; while not showing evidence of disease or serious handicaps, their general development was below standard. Some 13 per cent were found to be suffering from serious physical diseases, handicaps, or deficiencies, such as epilepsy, tuberculosis, syphilis, marked defects of vision or hearing, partial paralysis, serious heart lesions, and the like.

The examination by the psychiatrists at the clinic further revealed that 557 (56 per cent) of these boys had marked mental, emotional, or personality distortions, a diagnosis having been made in 137 instances of constitutionally inferior personality, psychopathy, "peculiar personality," epilepsy, traumatic constitution, psychosis or "question of psychosis"; in 70 of the cases the diagnosis was "marked adolescent instability"; while in 350 cases there were manifested, to a degree noted by the psychiatrists as excessive, various deviant personality traits, such as great impulsiveness, over-suggestibility, marked sensitiveness, and the like.

*   *   *   *   *

That our juvenile delinquents were heavily handicapped by both Nature and Nurture is evident. Throughout this analysis the assumption has been implicit that these various obstacles to wholesome development must somehow, in most instances, have been related to the delinquencies of the boys. Without equally thorough comparative data respecting non-delinquent boys, it is of course not strictly justifiable to arrive at such a conclusion. On the other hand, it seems incredible that the multiple incidence of so many factors which in other fields of human experience are readily regarded as unwholesome and deteriorative had no bearing whatsoever on the etiology of these delinquent careers. It seems sounder to say that the *degree* of causal relation cannot be absolutely known without a "control" group. It will not be amiss in this connection to reproduce some remarks made in *One Thousand Juvenile Delinquents* (page 63):

Perhaps the chief obstacle to adequate studies into the causation of crime is the absence of reliable comparable data about the characteristics of the general population. The relatively few subjects covered by the government census publications and the occasional studies made by school authorities and other officials do not afford an adequate basis for comparison with the more detailed and accurate descriptions already available of special populations, such as delinquents. Were the chief objective of this descriptive portion of our study a determination of the *causes* of juvenile delinquency, the information would not be complete, because of the lack of comparable data with respect to the general population. Descriptions of the non-criminal population are as yet so imperfect as to permit of only very cautious comparisons with delinquents and criminals.

The absence of reliable comparable data regarding the non-delinquent population does not, however, as some have inferred, vitiate all research into the makeup of delinquents. Even without information on certain characteristics of the non-delinquent population, a descriptive account of the makeup of offenders is of value in the practical task of understanding delinquent careers and determining upon modes of attack on the problems they present.

Chapter III

DELINQUENCY PRIOR TO APPEARANCE IN BOSTON
JUVENILE COURT

CONTINUING our description of the salient characteristics of
the thousand juvenile delinquents, we here present data indicating the widespread and varied antisocial and illegal acts of these
boys even before they were brought into the Boston Juvenile Court.
In this connection, the present investigation made it possible to supplement the data regarding the delinquencies of the boys as presented in the original work.[1] That many lads brought into court as
"first offenders" or "good boys suddenly gone wrong" are found,
upon careful scrutiny of their careers, to have been offenders of
long standing, is a fact of the utmost significance both in making
generalizations about the etiology of delinquency and in planning
means of treatment and rehabilitation.

Since we wish to free of tables this and the three succeeding chapters, the reader is asked to refer to Appendix B from which the descriptive data have been drawn, where fuller details than were considered necessary for the text are given.

All percentages in the text are of course based on "known and
applicable" totals. Where the number of unknown or inapplicable

---

[1] In *One Thousand Juvenile Delinquents,* the information regarding early criminal careers of the boys was narrower in scope and scantier in detail than that obtained in the
present investigation. In the earlier work, little more than the number of arrests was presented. We have now managed to secure data on the frequency of arrests, the number, kind,
and frequency of convictions, the number and nature of peno-correctional experiences, the
length of time spent in institutions. It has also been possible to determine the predominant
character of the offenses of individual youths, as well as the number of months they were
at large in the community. In the course of this more penetrating investigation, additional
arrests were found in a few cases, thus increasing the total number of arrests originally reported on for the group as a whole; and in a very few cases, a court record previously reported as belonging to a particular boy was found to have been an error, either because of
confusion of an early record with that of another boy of like name or because court appearances were found to have been "informal" or non-official. It should be emphasized,
however, that these slight changes make practically no difference in the general description
of the group as originally reported.

cases is so small that the findings are not affected, no mention is made of the size of the particular sample. However, instances in which the "unknown" or "inapplicable" groups are sufficiently large to warrant comment are discussed in the text. The number of cases in the unknown or inapplicable categories will be found in Appendix B.

NUMBER AND NATURE OF ARRESTS

Our delinquents were arrested an average of 2.28 ($\pm$.04) times prior to the arrest which brought them before the Boston Juvenile Court. Of the 624 who had been previously arrested, 294 were apprehended once, 151 twice, 130 three or four times, and 49 five or more times; 374 boys had not been arrested at all.[2]

These 624 boys were apprehended 1,333 times, 62.9 per cent of the arrests being for offenses against property (breaking and entering, larceny, pickpocketing, receiving stolen goods, forgery, and the like); 21.7 per cent for petty statutory offenses against the public peace, morals, or order (disturbing the peace, gaming or being present at gaming, peddling without a license, trespassing, vagrancy, loitering, begging, and similar offenses[3]); 12.6 per cent for distinctly juvenile offenses such as "stubbornness," waywardness, disobedience, truancy, and malicious mischief; while 2.5 per cent of the arrests were for offenses against the person (assault, assault and battery); and 4 arrests were for offenses against chastity (lewdness, unnatural acts). It should be mentioned that during the period prior to the appearance of the boys in the Boston Juvenile Court, there were for obvious reasons no arrests for drunkenness or drug using or selling, nor were there any arrests which might be classified

---

[2] Appendix B, 11. In *One Thousand Juvenile Delinquents* it was reported that 364 boys were not previously arrested, while 305 were arrested once, 152 twice, 114 three or four times, and 64 on five or more occasions. Despite these slight changes in the classification, the average number of arrests for the group was likewise 2.3. It should be noted that there are now ten fewer boys reported as being arrested. This is due to the fact that upon careful rechecking of the data the supposed court records in ten cases represented informal court appearances or were found not to belong to the boy to whom they had been originally assigned.

[3] These will for brevity be referred to as offenses against the public welfare.

as "against family and children" since these youths were then not old enough to have any families of their own. It will be recalled that they were of an average age of thirteen and a half years when they appeared before the Boston Juvenile Court on the particular offense which furnished the point of departure for *One Thousand Juvenile Delinquents*.[4]

Considering now the nature of their arrests from the point of view of the proportion of boys who were arrested for each type of offense, it appears that, of the 624 lads who were apprehended, 76.6 per cent were arrested for the commission of offenses against property; 32.7 per cent for offenses against the public welfare; 21.2 per cent for delinquencies such as stubbornness, truancy, malicious mischief, or running away from home; 4.8 per cent for crimes against the person; and 4 boys (.6 per cent) for offenses against chastity.[5]

FREQUENCY OF ARRESTS

Of the 329 boys who were arrested more than once,[6] 8.8 per cent had been arrested as frequently as once in less than 3 months, 14.9 per cent as often as once in 3 to 6 months, 21.6 per cent once in 6 to 9 months, 18.2 per cent once in 9 to 12 months, 10 per cent once in 12 to 15 months, 9.4 per cent once in 15 to 18 months, 6.1 per cent in 18 to 21 months, 11 per cent less frequently than once in 21 or more months.[7] The average frequency of arrests of those arrested more than once in the period prior to the appearance of these boys before the Boston Juvenile Court was one arrest in 10.57 months ($\pm$.25).[8]

---

[4] Appendix B, 12.

[5] Appendix B, 14.

[6] Actually 330 boys were arrested more than once, but in one instance it was impossible to establish the frequency of his arrests.

[7] Since, of course, it was not possible to calculate frequency of arrests for a boy who had been arrested only once, this group of cases was eliminated from consideration. Of the boys arrested more than once the frequency of their arrests was calculated on the basis of the number of months from the date of the first arrest to the date of arrest for the offense which brought them to the attention of the Boston Juvenile Court. From this period was subtracted the number of months during which the boy was in peno-correctional institutions, and the remaining total of months was divided by the number of arrests which had occurred within the period.

[8] Appendix B, 13.

NUMBER AND NATURE OF DISPOSITIONS BY COURT

The 1,333 arrests of 624 boys were followed by commitments in 7.6 per cent, while 44.6 per cent of the arrests resulted in "straight probation" and 6 per cent in probation under suspended sentence; 5.2 per cent of the total number of arrests were disposed of by fines or restitution, 27.8 per cent by placing the case on file; 8.3 per cent of the arrests resulted in a finding of "not guilty"; while 3 arrests (.2 per cent) were nol prossed.[9]

Almost nine-tenths (87.5 per cent) of the 1,333 arrests resulted in convictions (or findings of delinquency). Of the boys convicted, 48.5 per cent had one conviction, 23.9 per cent two, 14 per cent three, 8.1 per cent four, and 5.5 per cent five or more. The average number of convictions among the 624 arrested boys was 2.18 ($\pm$.03).[10] Only 42 of the 624 boys arrested were not convicted.

Turning now to the types of disposition made by courts of the arrests of the 624 boys, it is found that 11.2 per cent of the boys were committed to peno-correctional institutions on new sentences, while 2.9 per cent were recommitted on revoked paroles on old sentences, 63 per cent experienced straight probation, 11.9 per cent were placed on probation under suspended sentence at one time or another prior to their appearance before the Boston Juvenile Court, 9.6 per cent were fined or compelled to make restitution, while 32.4 per cent had charges against them filed. Less than a sixth of the group (14.9 per cent) had at one time or another been found non-delinquent or not guilty, while 3 boys (.5 per cent) had charges against them nol prossed.[11]

FREQUENCY OF CONVICTIONS

Frequency of convictions was calculated in the same manner as frequency of arrests,[12] and is applicable to 326 of 330 boys who were arrested more than once. On this basis, 5.8 per cent of the boys who were arrested more than once were convicted as often as once in less

---

[9] Appendix B, 16.   [10] Appendix B, 15.   [11] Appendix B, 18.
[12] See note 7 for method of calculating frequency of arrests. In four cases it was, for one reason or another, not possible to calculate frequency of convictions.

than 3 months, 15 per cent once in 3 to 6 months, 20.6 per cent once in 6 to 9 months, 16.6 per cent once in 9 to 12 months, 11 per cent once in 12 to 15 months, 9.5 per cent once in 15 to 18 months, 8.3 per cent once in 18 to 21 months, and 13.2 per cent less frequently than once in 21 or more months.

The average frequency of convictions among those arrested more than once prior to the arrest which brought them before the Boston Juvenile Court was one in 11.44 months ($\pm$.25).[13] It will be recalled that the average frequency of arrests was one in 10.5 months.

NUMBER, NATURE, AND LENGTH OF PENO-CORRECTIONAL EXPERIENCES

Prior to their appearance in the Boston Juvenile Court, 930 of the boys had never been inmates of correctional institutions. Of the 70 boys who had been committed to such institutions, 47 had served one commitment, 16 had been twice incarcerated, 5 three times, one on four occasions, and one five times. The average number of penal experiences among those who had been previously committed was 1.72 ($\pm$.06).[14] With four exceptions these commitments were to truant and correctional schools; two of the four were to reformatories and two to schools for the feebleminded.[15]

Of the boys who had been in correctional establishments prior to their appearance before the Boston Juvenile Court, 10.6 per cent were incarcerated for less than 6 months, 15.2 per cent for 6 to 12 months, 27.3 per cent for 12 to 18 months, 16.7 per cent for 18 to 24 months, 16.7 per cent for 24 to 30 months, and 13.5 per cent for 30 months or longer. The average length of time spent in correctional schools by this small group of young delinquents was 18.82 months ($\pm$.85).[16]

OFFICIAL AND UNOFFICIAL DELINQUENCY

It has already been stated that 624 of our 1,000 young delinquents had been arrested one or more times. It is not sufficient, however, to consider the delinquency of the group merely in terms of their official court records. In addition to the 624 boys whose offenses had

[13] Appendix B, 17.   [14] Appendix B, 19.   [15] Appendix B, 20.   [16] Appendix B, 21.

been "officially" recognized, 364 boys had committed offenses of one sort or another for which they might well have come to the attention of the police and courts.

This information about their early antisocial behavior was gathered in connection with *One Thousand Juvenile Delinquents,* by analyzing the case histories which had been assembled by the Judge Baker Foundation at the time the boys were referred to that Clinic for examination. These "unofficial" delinquencies included such offenses as stealing, bunking out, running away from home, truancy, sex delinquencies, "stubbornness," and similar offenses for which boys are not infrequently brought to the attention of police and court. Thus of the 988 boys who had to be considered delinquent prior to their contact with the Boston Juvenile Court, 63.3 per cent had already had official court records while 36.7 per cent, though clearly delinquent, had not actually been arrested.

Only seven of the 1,000 boys were definitely known not to have committed any offenses previous to the arrest which brought them to the Boston Juvenile Court. In 5 cases it was not possible to determine whether the boys had been delinquent.[17]

PREDOMINANT OFFENSE

Considering next the major type of delinquency committed by each one of the 988 offenders from the onset of their delinquent careers to the time of their appearance in the Boston Juvenile Court, it was found that in 71.1 per cent of the cases the most characteristic offenses were crimes against property; in 1.2 per cent, offenses against chastity; in 2.2 per cent, offenses against the public welfare; in 2 cases (.2 per cent), crimes against the person. In 6.5 per cent of the cases no one type of antisocial behavior was predominant, two or more kinds of offenses appearing to be of equal weight in their early criminal careers. In 18.8 per cent of the cases the most frequent offenses were not classifiable in any of the above categories, being of the kind typically designated as juvenile offenses—stubbornness, malicious mischief, running away from home, school truancy, and the like.[18]

[17] Appendix B, 23.   [18] Appendix B, 24.

Obviously we are dealing here mainly with a group of young thieves and burglars, many of them in search of adventure, some of them expressing an apparently uncontrollable desire to pilfer.

SERIOUS AND MINOR DELINQUENCY

In addition to the detailed account of the specific offenses committed by the youths, it is useful to classify them as serious or minor offenders. For that purpose we have designated as serious offenders those who were convicted of crimes regarded as major (essentially felonies). We also classified as serious offenders a few boys who were not arrested for major crimes and a few who, though arrested, were not convicted but whose guilt was clearly indicated.

Youths who committed only petty offenses (misdemeanors and violations of ordinances) were designated minor offenders.

Among serious offenses are included all crimes against property, assault with intent to rape, murder, or rob, and pathological sex offenses. Crimes classified as minor are those described as offenses against the public welfare, simple assault, drunkenness, fornication, neglect of family, non-support, and so on. On this basis, 24.4 per cent of the 988 offenders could be classified as minor delinquents and 75.6 per cent as serious offenders.[19]

PRINCIPAL COMPONENT OF MISCONDUCT

In determining whether a boy was a serious or a minor offender we first took into account the offenses for which he was actually arrested. However, if he was arrested only for minor offenses but was known to have committed serious offenses for which he did not come to the attention of police and courts, he was designated a serious offender. If he was convicted for minor offenses but was arrested and not convicted for serious offenses, he was likewise designated a serious offender.

On such a basis of judging delinquent behavior, 45.6 per cent of the group classed as serious offenders prior to their appearance in the Boston Juvenile Court were so categorized because they had been convicted for serious offenses, and 3.2 per cent were so desig-

[19] Appendix B, 26.

nated by reason of the fact that they were arrested for serious offenses even though not convicted. Since most of these boys had also committed "unofficial" serious offenses (i.e., those not discovered by police authorities), there was no question about the fact that they were actually serious offenders. A fourth (26.7 per cent) of the boys were classed as serious offenders on the basis of their commission of grave crimes for which they were for one reason or another not arrested. Some of them may well have been arrested or convicted for minor offenses also.

As to minor offenders, 7.5 per cent of the group were so judged on the basis of conviction for petty offenses and 1.1 per cent because they had been arrested for petty offenses but not convicted. The boys in these two groups did not commit any serious offenses for which they might have come to the attention of officials. An additional 15.8 per cent of the 988 boys were considered minor delinquents on the basis of their commission of petty offenses for which they were not arrested.[20]

MONTHS IN COMMUNITY

All but 6.8 per cent of the 1,000 boys had lived in the community throughout the period prior to their court appearance; the remainder had been incarcerated in correctional establishments or confined in institutions for the mentally ill or the chronically disabled, a situation which made it difficult, if not impossible, to commit offenses in the community.[21]

OFFENSES FOR WHICH SENT TO BOSTON JUVENILE COURT

We have presented a picture of the early criminal careers of these 1,000 delinquents up to the arrest which brought them into the Boston Juvenile Court, by which they were in turn referred to the Clinic of the Judge Baker Foundation for examination. It should be added that 55 per cent of the boys had previously been before this same court. We are concerned, however, only with the offenses for which they were taken to the Boston Juvenile Court on the particu-

[20] Appendix B, 25.   [21] Appendix B, 22.

lar occasion which furnished the point of departure for the study of
One Thousand Juvenile Delinquents.

At that contact with society's official agency for dealing with delinquents, 736 of the boys appeared in the Court for the commission
of property crimes (larceny, burglary, and similar offenses), 107
for "stubbornness" (waywardness and disobedience), 46 for running away from home, 30 for truancy, 24 for assault and battery or
disturbing the peace, 10 for trespassing and similar offenses, 9 for
sex offenses (fornication, indecent assault, lewdness, unnatural
acts), 7 for gaming or being present at gaming. And 31 boys were
taken to the Court on the occasion in question for various other
minor offenses such as vagrancy, begging, peddling without a license, drunkenness, and the like.[22]

Thus, 73.6 per cent of these boys appeared before the Boston Juvenile Court for the commission of serious offenses, which, it
should be noted, is about the same proportion as of the boys who
were serious delinquents in the period prior to the arrest under consideration (75.6 per cent).

TREATMENT GIVEN

There is no need to repeat in any detail what has already been presented in Chapter VII of *One Thousand Juvenile Delinquents* concerning the recommendations made by the Judge Baker Foundation to the Boston Juvenile Court for the treatment of these young
offenders. It needs only to be emphasized that the recommendations of the Clinic to the Court dealt primarily with suggestions as
to where the offenders should live during the period of oversight—
that is, on probation at home, in a foster home, with relatives, or in
the country; or in a correctional institution, a school for the feebleminded, or some non-penal institution. In three-fourths of the cases,
suggestions were also made concerning the physical care of the
boys, their educational and vocational adjustments, and their recreational activities. Recommendations were also often made concerning their discipline, and in some cases it was advised that these

---

[22] See *One Thousand Juvenile Delinquents*, page 100.

boys be studied further so that treatment might be modified from time to time.[23]

The actual "treatment period" was interpreted, for the purposes of *One Thousand Juvenile Delinquents,* as the length of time during which the Court kept the particular form of supervision over a boy which had been recommended by the Clinic. For example, in cases in which probation had been recommended, the "treatment period" extended to the termination of probation by the Court. If the recommendation was that the delinquent be placed on a farm or in a foster home or with relatives, the actual duration of such placement was considered the treatment period. If the recommendation was that the delinquent should be placed in some institution, the period of time up to his first release (whether on parole in the regular course or by expiration of sentence or by discharge upon request of relatives) was deemed the treatment period. If the Clinic had recommended another type of placement to follow immediately upon release from the institution, the duration of this second experience was included in the treatment period.

On this basis, the average length of the treatment period was 6.3 months in those cases in which the recommendations of the Clinic as to where the offender should live were carried out. Apparently, in many cases the length of the treatment period was insufficient to effect any fundamental change in attitudes, habits, and conduct. For example, in half (53.5 per cent) the cases in which the Court followed the Clinic's recommendation that the young offender should be placed on probation at home, such oversight lasted no more than six months. An equally brief period of supervision was applied to almost a third (31.8 per cent) of the cases in which the recommendation was for placement in a foster-home (not with relatives). In a third (35.5 per cent) of the cases in which the Clinic's recommendation carried out by the Court involved placement with relatives, the treatment period lasted six months or less.

[23] For details concerning the nature of the Clinic's recommendations to the Court and the extent to which they were carried out, the interested reader is referred to *One Thousand Juvenile Delinquents,* Chapter VII.

An equally brief time was involved in a third (34.5 per cent) of the cases in which the Clinic recommended placement in the country for an indefinite time.

On the other hand, the duration of some of the forms of recommended treatment was for a more substantial period. Thus, commitment to a correctional institution lasted for more than six months in three-fourths (75.8 per cent) of the cases; commitment to a school for the feebleminded lasted for more than six months in 43.6 per cent. It should be remembered that determination of the length of such types of treatment was not within the power of the Court but rather in that of the institution's authorities.

In a fifth of the cases there was no treatment period, since the Court did not follow the recommendations of the Clinic as to where the offender should live;[24] in another fifth the offender was under treatment for a very short time (a few weeks to three months); but in three-fifths of the cases treatment extended for three months to over a year.

All the recommendations made by the Clinic for the treatment of individual delinquents were carried out in only 21 per cent of the cases.

That the coordination of treatment between the Clinic, Court, and community was not as close as it might be was amply brought out in Chapter VIII of *One Thousand Juvenile Delinquents*. In the present work, we are not concerned with the reasons for this lack of coordination, our purpose being rather to trace the criminal careers of these 1,000 delinquents over three five-year follow-up periods after the termination of their management by the Court and its affiliated agencies, in order to determine what changes, if any, occurred in the behavior of these offenders with the passing of the years.

---

[24] In such cases the first follow-up period extended over five years from the date of the boy's appearance in Court.

Chapter IV

DELINQUENCY IN FIRST FOLLOW-UP PERIOD

WE now proceed to a consideration of the behavior of our juvenile delinquents during the first five-year span following their treatment by the Boston Juvenile Court.[1] At the end of this first follow-up period, 9.1 per cent of the youths were still under sixteen years of age, 61.7 per cent were between sixteen and twenty, 29 per cent were between twenty-one and twenty-five, and .2 per cent were between twenty-six and thirty. Their average age was nineteen years.[2] Twenty-one of the lads had died before the end of this follow-up period, and are therefore excluded from this calculation of age.

NUMBER AND NATURE OF ARRESTS

A fifth of the youths were not arrested at all during the first five-year follow-up period. Of those who were apprehended, 42.9 per cent were arrested once or twice, 29.6 per cent three or four times, 15.9 per cent five or six times, and 11.6 per cent seven or more times.[3] The average number of arrests was 3.42 ($\pm$.05).

The 749 who were arrested were apprehended 2,719 times.[4] Of

---

[1] In *One Thousand Juvenile Delinquents*, "treatment" was interpreted as the carrying out of recommendations made by the Judge Baker Foundation Clinic to the Boston Juvenile Court. If the major recommendation, which dealt with whether or not a delinquent boy should be placed on probation, sent to a correctional institution, placed in a foster home, sent to live with relatives or on a farm, and the like, was not carried out by the Court, he was regarded as not having had any treatment; and in that event the follow-up period was regarded as extending over five years from the date of the lad's appearance in the Court.

[2] Appendix B, 7.

[3] Appendix B, 27. In *One Thousand Juvenile Delinquents*, 79 men were reported as "unknown if arrested." As a result of the amplification of the data for the present investigation this group was reduced to 51, which partly accounts for the change in the distribution of the cases. It should be noted, however, that the average number of arrests for the entire group who were arrested remains about the same, the average originally reported being 3.6, and now 3.4.

[4] In the original study, 776 youths were reported as having been arrested 2,523 times during the first five-year period. A careful rechecking of all these data has now revealed the increased number of arrests, but for a slightly smaller group. In many cases our search

these arrests, 48.7 per cent were for offenses against property, 22.2 per cent for offenses against the public welfare, 9.3 per cent for drunkenness, 4.4 per cent for offenses against the person, 1.6 per cent for offenses against chastity; 14 (.5 per cent) were offenses against family and children (largely charges of neglect and non-support), one arrest was for using drugs; 13.2 per cent were for various other offenses (largely stubbornness, truancy, malicious mischief, running away, and the like),[5] a finding related to the fact that 150 of the boys were still under seventeen years of age at the end of the first follow-up period and the average age for the whole group was but nineteen.[6]

Considering now the arrests of these 749 youths by type of offense, we find that 74.8 per cent were arrested one or more times during this first follow-up period for crimes against property; 43.7 per cent for crimes against the public welfare; 31.6 per cent for offenses such as stubbornness, truancy, running away, malicious mischief; 13.4 per cent for drunkenness; 12.4 per cent for crimes against the person; 4.7 per cent for offenses against chastity. Seven youths (.9 per cent) were apprehended for offenses against family and children, and one for using drugs.[7]

It should be noted that the average number of arrests per boy increased during this first follow-up period as compared with the time preceding their appearance in the Boston Juvenile Court. During the preceding period those who were arrested were apprehended an average of 2.3 times, while during the first follow-up period those arrested were apprehended an average of 3.4 times.

for criminal records was aided by the use of fingerprints which had not been available to us in connection with the first research. The apparent decrease in the number of boys now reported as arrested is accounted for in footnote 36.

[5] Arrests which had to be designated "for violation of probation" are omitted from these percentages, since the actual nature of the offenses was unknown.

[6] Appendix B, 28. Despite the increase in the number of arrests reported for the group in the present work, the general distribution of the nature of arrests remains approximately the same. Of the 2,523 arrests previously reported, 52.1 per cent were for property crimes, 29.9 per cent for offenses against the public welfare, 11.7 per cent for drunkenness. The interested reader is invited to consult Table 14, page 155, of *One Thousand Juvenile Delinquents.*

[7] Appendix B, 30.

Not only was there an increase in the average number of arrests among those arrested but there was an increase from 62.5 to 79.8 per cent in the proportion of those arrested.[8]

Comparing next the nature of the arrests in the time preceding court appearance and in the first follow-up period, we find a decrease from 62.9 to 48.7 per cent in the proportion of arrests for offenses against property. Certain modifications in the proportion of other offenses are also to be noted. Previously there had been no arrests on charges of drunkenness, the boys having been hardly old enough in that period to drink, while during the first follow-up period 9.3 per cent of all the arrests were for drunkenness. As might be expected, however, some increase occurred, from .3 to 1.6 per cent, in arrests for sex offenses. Previously, also, there were no arrests for offenses against the family and children and for the illicit use of drugs; and during the first follow-up period there was an increase, from 2.5 to 4.4 per cent, in the proportion of crimes against the person. The proportion of offenses against the public welfare remained about stationary, as did also the ratio of distinctively juvenile offenses, such as stubbornness, running away from home, truancy, and the like.[9]

Considering now the change in the proportion arrested for each type of offense during the two periods under comparison, it appears that the percentage of youths apprehended for crimes against property remained stationary (76.6 per cent in the pre-court span and 74.8 per cent in the first follow-up period). There was, however, an increase (from 32.7 to 43.7 per cent) in the proportion arrested for offenses against the public welfare; and also in the proportion of lads arrested for crimes against the person (from 4.8 to 12.4 per cent). More boys, 31.6 per cent as compared to 21.2 per cent, were arrested during the first follow-up period for offenses like stubbornness, truancy, running away, malicious mischief. A proportional increase, readily explainable on the ground of age, occurred also in the number of boys arrested for offenses against chastity

[8] Appendix C, 2.   [9] Appendix C, 4.

(from .6 per cent in the prior period to 4.7 per cent in the first follow-up period). As already indicated, some of the youths were apprehended during the first follow-up span for offenses against family and children, for drunkenness, and for illicit use of drugs, whereas none had previously been apprehended for such offenses.[10]

Understanding of the changes which have occurred in the group with the passing of the years will be enhanced through a case-by-case comparison to supplement our picture of the mass statistics of changes already presented. Thus, of the 350 lads who had not previously been arrested,[11] 26.9 per cent were likewise not arrested during the first follow-up period, 19.7 per cent were arrested once, 18.3 per cent twice, 13.4 per cent three times, 12.6 per cent four or five times, and 9.1 per cent six or more times. Of the 587 youths who had already been arrested one or more times during the period prior to their appearance in the Boston Juvenile Court, all but 16.4 per cent were also arrested during the first five-year period.

FREQUENCY OF ARRESTS

Of 592 youths arrested more than once in the first follow-up period, the frequency of whose arrests could be estimated, 13.5 per cent were apprehended as often as once in less than 6 months, 16.9 per cent once in 6 to 9 months, 12.5 per cent once in 9 to 12 months, 11.1 per cent once in 12 to 15, 9.8 per cent once in 15 to 18, 13.7 per cent once in 18 to 21, and 22.5 per cent once in 21 or more months.

The average frequency of arrests in this group was one in 14.02 months ($\pm$.21).[12] This represents a decrease in frequency of arrests among those youths who were arrested more than once in each period, for previously arrests had occurred once in 10.5 months.[13] It should be borne in mind when interpreting this finding, however, that a greater proportion of youths were actually arrested

[10] Appendix C, 5.

[11] The number of cases does not represent all the boys who were not arrested during the prior period. Actually, 374 boys were not arrested at that time. Obviously, in case-by-case comparisons only those can be included about whom information is known and applicable in both periods under consideration.

[12] Appendix B, 29.   [13] Appendix C, 3.

during the first follow-up span than in the pre-court period, and that for the group as a whole the average number of arrests increased.

NUMBER AND NATURE OF DISPOSITIONS BY COURT

What dispositions did the courts make of the 2,719 arrests of the 749 youths known to have been arrested during this first follow-up span? A fifth of the arrests (19.3 per cent) resulted in new commitments to peno-correctional institutions, 11.3 per cent in re-commitments (by revocation of parole), 17.4 per cent in straight probation, and 9.4 per cent in probation under suspended sentence. A seventh (13.7 per cent) of the arrests resulted in fines, 16.6 per cent in the filing of charges, 1.9 per cent in release by probation officers without defendants' court appearance;[14] 8.9 per cent of the arrests were followed by a finding of "Not guilty," while 1.3 per cent resulted in nol-prossing or in a grand jury finding of "No bill."[15]

Of the 2,719 arrests, 2,340 were followed by convictions. Of 733 youths known to have been convicted one or more times during the follow-up period under discussion, 22.8 per cent were convicted once, 24.2 per cent twice, 18.7 per cent three times, 13.5 per cent four times, 8.9 per cent five times, and 11.9 per cent six or more times, the average number of convictions among those arrested one or more times being 3.12 (±.05).[16]

Half of the 749 youths (49.3 per cent) arrested during the first follow-up period were given new commitments to peno-correctional establishments, 24.3 per cent were returned to such institutions upon revocation of their paroles, 42.5 per cent were placed on ordinary probation, while 25.6 per cent were given probation under suspended sentences. A little over a fourth of the youths (26.8 per

---

[14] This refers to certain cases of drunkenness in which the probation officer is permitted to release the defendant without taking him to court.

[15] Appendix B, 32.

[16] Appendix B, 31. In *One Thousand Juvenile Delinquents* the average number of convictions of 757 men was reported as 3.3. It will be seen that the average remains practically the same. The explanation for the change in the number of youths arrested and convicted will be found in footnote 36.

cent) had to pay fines, almost two-fifths of them (38.1 per cent) had charges against them placed on file, a little over one-fifth (22.4 per cent) were found "Not guilty," 2.1 per cent had charges against them nol-prossed, the charges against 2 per cent resulted in a finding of "No bill," while 4.5 per cent were released by the probation officer on charges of drunkenness without having to appear in court.[17]

Considering now the differences in the nature of the dispositions of all the arrests in this first follow-up period and in the prior period, we find a marked increase (from 7.6 to 30.6 per cent) in the proportion that resulted in commitments to peno-correctional institutions, either under new sentences or by revocation. There was also an increase (from 6.3 to 9.4 per cent) in arrests disposed of by probation under suspended sentence, which carries with it the threat of commitment to a peno-correctional institution in the event of a violation of probation.

The increase in sentences of imprisonment is accompanied by a correlative decrease in the use of probation (from 44.6 per cent in the prior period to 17.4 per cent in the first follow-up span). During the latter period, also, the courts placed fewer of the charges against these youths on file than they had previously done (16.6 per cent as compared with 27.8 per cent). There was, however, a marked increase in the proportion of arrests resulting in fines (from 5.2 per cent to 13.9 per cent). There was also a slight increase in the nol-prossing of cases (from .2 per cent to .7 per cent). A finding of "Not guilty" disposed of a like proportion of arrests in both periods (8.3 per cent and 8.9 per cent).[18]

The above figures deal with cases rather than persons. A comparison, next, of the number of youths experiencing each type of disposition during the two periods under review reveals a very sharp increase, from 14.1 to 73.6 per cent, in the proportion whose convictions resulted in commitment to institutions either on new sentences or by revocation. There was also an increase, from 11.9 to 25.6 per

[17] Appendix B, 34.   [18] Appendix C, 9.

cent, in the proportion of boys treated by probation under suspended sentence, but a decrease in the proportion placed on straight probation, from 63.0 to 42.5 per cent. A very material increase, from 9.6 to 26.8 per cent, occurred in the proportion of youths who paid fines as a punishment for their arrests, and a slight increase, from 32.4 to 38.1 per cent, in the proportion of those against whom complaints were placed on file. The proportion of youths who were found "Not guilty" by the courts increased from 14.9 to 22.4 per cent. The cases of none of these boys had, during the prior period, resulted in a finding of "No bill" or "Release by a probation officer," while in the first follow-up span 2 per cent of the youths had their arrests followed by a finding of "No bill," and 4.5 per cent were released by the probation officer.[19]

Considering now the number of arrests followed by convictions, we find that the average number of convictions in the group as a whole rose from 2.18 during the period prior to the appearance of the boys in the Boston Juvenile Court to 3.12 in the first five-year follow-up span.[20]

The actual changes may be more clearly seen from the fact that of 389 youths who either were not arrested or were not found delinquent before their appearance in the Juvenile Court, 73.3 per cent were convicted one or more times during this first follow-up period; while of 543 boys who had been found delinquent one or more times prior to their appearance in the Juvenile Court, 81.4 per cent were convicted one or more times during the follow-up period.

FREQUENCY OF CONVICTIONS

Of 588 youths arrested more than once during the first follow-up period, the frequency of whose convictions could be estimated, one-tenth (10.1 per cent) were convicted as often as once in less than 6 months, 14.1 per cent once in 6 to 9 months, 12.2 per cent once in 9 to 12 months; another 12.1 per cent were convicted once in 12 to 15

[19] Appendix C, 10. The percentages total more than 100 because many of the boys experienced more than one type of disposition.
[20] Appendix C, 7.

months, 10.2 per cent once in 15 to 18 months, 16.8 per cent once in 18 to 24 months, and 24.5 per cent as infrequently as once in 24 or more months. The average frequency of convictions among the youths who were arrested more than once was once in 15.16 months (±.21),[21] a decrease in the frequency of convictions as compared to the pre-court period when the boys had been convicted as often as once in 11.4 months.

It should be remembered, however, that a considerable increase occurred in the proportion of youths who were convicted, the rise being from 58 per cent of the total number of boys in the pre-court span to 78 per cent in this first five-year follow-up period.[22]

NUMBER, NATURE, AND LENGTH OF PENO-CORRECTIONAL EXPERIENCES

More than half our youths (55 per cent) were not incarcerated during the follow-up period in question, that is, they did not receive new sentences to peno-correctional institutions, were not returned to peno-correctional institutions by revocation of parole, were not transferred from one institution to another, and did not finish service on sentences imposed during the previous period. Almost half the youths (45 per cent) served 836 periods in peno-correctional institutions[23] during the first follow-up period, the average number of peno-correctional experiences being 2.06 (±.04).

Three-fourths (76.4 per cent) of the 424 youths who served one or more terms in peno-correctional establishments during the five years involved spent some time in truant or correctional schools, 21.4 per cent served one or more sentences in reformatories, 21.2 per cent served sentences in jails, houses of correction, or state

---

[21] Appendix B, 33.

[22] Appendix C, 8.

[23] Appendix B, 35. In *One Thousand Juvenile Delinquents*, 654 commitments to penal institutions were recorded. The increase to 836 now reported is partly due to the fact that a different method of classification was used in the present research in order to make the materials comparable with our other researches, namely *500 Criminal Careers, Five Hundred Delinquent Women,* and *Later Criminal Careers.* Transfers from one institution to another have now been counted as separate penal experiences. In addition, some new commitments and returns to institutions by revocation (particularly to correctional schools) were discovered in this more thorough search for information.

farms, and 6.9 per cent were in prisons (including a few incarcerated in institutions for defective delinquents).[24]

During the first follow-up period an eighth (12.3 per cent) of these 424 youths spent less than 6 months in peno-correctional institutions, 21 per cent were incarcerated from 6 to 12 months, 24.5 per cent from 12 to 18 months, 16.5 per cent from 18 to 24 months, another 16.5 per cent from 24 to 36 months, and 9.2 per cent 36 or more months. The average number of months spent in punitive or correctional institutions was 17.98 ($\pm$.39).[25]

Comparing now the change in the incidence of peno-correctional experiences in the pre-court span and the first follow-up period, we find a marked increase, from 7 to 45 per cent, in the proportion of youths "serving time."[26] This increase is primarily reflected in commitments to correctional schools.

Although there was a striking increase over the prior period in the proportion of youths who experienced imprisonment, the average number of penal experiences (including new commitments, revocations, and transfers from one institution to another) of those confined during the two periods did not change markedly, being 1.7 in the pre-court span and 2.06 during the first follow-up period.[27]

Nor was there any marked change in the average length of incarceration, which during the prior period was 18.8 months and in the follow-up period 17.9 months.[28]

With the increase in the proportion of youths serving sentences, there occurred an understandable change in the character of their penal experiences. Prior to their contact with the Boston Juvenile Court, 95.7 per cent of those who had been in institutions had been confined in truant and correctional schools, 2.9 per cent in reformatories, and 2.9 per cent in schools for the feebleminded. During the first five-year follow-up period, 76.4 per cent of the boys served sentences in correctional schools, under the jurisdiction of which most of them remained until they were twenty-one years old. A marked

---

[24] Appendix B, 36.   [25] Appendix B, 37.   [26] Appendix C, 11.
[27] Appendix C, 12.   [28] Appendix C, 13.

increase, from 2.9 per cent to 21.9 per cent, occurred also in the proportion of offenders serving sentences in reformatories. This is of course largely explainable on the ground of age. During this period, also, many of our youths served sentences in prisons, jails, and institutions for defective delinquents but had had no such experiences previously because they were too young to be committed to such places.[29]

A case-by-case comparison of the boys whose records in both periods were known reveals that of 875 who had had no penal experiences before their appearance in the Boston Juvenile Court, 42.9 per cent spent some time in peno-correctional institutions during the first five-year follow-up period; while of 67 boys who had been in correctional institutions during the prior period, 73.1 per cent underwent imprisonment during the follow-up period.

OFFICIAL AND UNOFFICIAL DELINQUENCY

The 749 youths known to have been arrested during the first follow-up period may be considered "official" offenders. In addition to these, there were six boys who had to be so categorized because, even though they were not actually arrested, their offenses had been officially recognized by dishonorable discharge or desertion from the Army or Navy. There were, moreover, 49 youths who were definitely proven to be delinquents during this period even though they had not been arrested and had not otherwise come to the attention of agencies of the law. Of a total of 804 delinquents, therefore, 93.9 per cent committed offenses which had been noted and acted upon by the authorities, while only 6.1 per cent could be called "unofficial" offenders.[30]

There was a marked increase, from 63.3 to 93.9 per cent, in the proportion of delinquents who committed offenses for which they

[29] Appendix C, 15.

[30] Appendix B, 39. From Table 68–9 on page 318 of *One Thousand Juvenile Delinquents* it is determined that 774 youths were, in that research, categorized as "official" offenders as compared with 755 now; and 24 were categorized as unofficial delinquents as compared with 49 now. The explanation of this change will be found in footnote 4.

came to the attention of the authorities, and a dropping off, from 36.7 to 6.1 per cent, in the proportion of those who had to be classed as "unofficial" delinquents.[31]

A case-by-case comparison of the offenders in the two periods under comparison reveals that of 590 boys who had to be categorized as "official" delinquents prior to their Juvenile Court contact, 84.1 per cent continued to be so in the follow-up span, 4.5 per cent had become "unofficial" offenders, while 11.4 per cent had passed into the non-delinquent class. And of 339 boys who previously were "unofficial" delinquents, only 6.5 per cent could be so described in the first five-year follow-up period, 74.3 per cent had become officially recognized offenders, while 19.2 per cent had shifted to the non-offender category.

PREDOMINANT OFFENSE

At the beginning of this chapter we analyzed the offenses for which these youths were arrested during the first follow-up period. Turning now to the character of the delinquencies committed by the 804 youths who were delinquent during that period, we find that 65.5 per cent of them committed mainly offenses against property, 10.7 per cent committed chiefly offenses against the public welfare, 4.2 per cent were predominantly drunkards, 1.5 per cent committed mostly offenses against chastity, 4 youths were charged mainly with offenses such as neglect of family and non-support, one with using drugs, and 5 with offenses against the person. In a small proportion of cases (7.6 per cent), the crimes committed by our young men had to be characterized as "varied," because no particular offense appeared to predominate in their delinquent behavior. Some of them, although committing property crimes, were also marked drunkards or sex offenders. Some characteristically committed offenses both against the public welfare and against the person. And in 9.3 per cent of the cases, the offenses were typical juvenile delinquencies, such as stubbornness, running away

---

[31] Appendix C, 16.

from home, unmanageableness, and similar offenses not otherwise classifiable.[32]

A comparison of the nature of the predominant offenses committed by our youths in this period and in the period prior to their appearance in the Boston Juvenile Court shows a slight dropping off, from 71.1 to 65.5 per cent, in crimes against property as the most usual or distinctive offense. There was also a falling off, from 18.8 to 9.3 per cent, in the commission of distinctly "juvenile delinquencies," which is readily explainable on the ground of age. There was an increase, however, in the proportion of youths primarily classifiable as offenders against the public welfare, from 2.2 per cent in the prior period to 10.7 per cent in the follow-up period. The proportion classified as "varied" offenders remained about the same, 6.5 per cent in the prior period and 7.6 per cent in the first five-year period. It will be recalled that because of their youth none of the boys could, prior to appearance in the Boston Juvenile Court, be classified as an offender against family and children, or as a drunkard or drug user. During the first five-year follow-up span several youths could be thus categorized.[33]

Since property crimes continued to predominate during the first follow-up period, it is well to compare the changes which took place in the types of offenses committed by those youths who were primarily offenders against property during the pre-court years. Of 615 such boys, 7 of every 10 continued to be chiefly offenders against property, 7.4 per cent became mainly offenders against the public welfare, 3 per cent became "drunks," and 5.2 per cent committed varied offenses, 5 youths (.8 per cent) had to be designated offenders against chastity, 3 youths (.5 per cent) offenders against the family, one (.1 per cent) as an offender against the person, while 13 per cent became non-delinquents.

SERIOUS AND MINOR DELINQUENCY

It was impossible to determine whether or not 49 of our boys were

---

[32] Appendix B, 40.   [33] Appendix C, 16.

delinquent during the first follow-up period. Ten more, though not actually delinquent, had to be placed in the "inapplicable" category because they had been confined in non-penal institutions, such as mental hospitals or hospitals for the chronically ill, or had died very early in the period.

It will be recalled that 804 of the youths were delinquent during the first five-year follow-up span.[34] Of these, 622 (77.4 per cent) had to be regarded as serious offenders because they committed property crimes or pathological sex offenses or assaults with intent to rob, rape, or murder;[35] while 22.6 per cent could be classified as minor offenders. One hundred and thirty-seven of our youths were definitely found to be non-delinquent during this first five-year period. Eliminating from consideration the 49 whose behavior was unknown and the 10 regarding whose behavior during this period no determination could be reached for one reason or another, we find that 14.6 per cent of the remaining 941 youths were non-delinquents during this period, 19.3 per cent were minor offenders, and 66.1 per cent were serious offenders. Thus, *a total of 85.4 per cent were offenders during the first five-year follow-up period.*[36]

[34] 798 were reported delinquent in *One Thousand Juvenile Delinquents.* See table 67, page 317, of that work.

[35] See *500 Criminal Careers,* pages 141, 354–357, for detailed classification of serious and minor offenses.

[36] Appendix B, 42. It has already been indicated in several places in this chapter that some slight differences have occurred in the tabulations of delinquency for the group from those reported in *One Thousand Juvenile Delinquents.* It will be recalled that in that work 88.2 per cent of our juveniles were reported to have recidivated, while the proportion is now reported as 85.4 per cent. A comparison of the figures on delinquency as presented in *One Thousand Juvenile Delinquents* and in the present investigation, upon which hinge any differences already recorded in other parts of this chapter, will serve as a basis for indicating why the changes in the tabulation have occurred:

	One Thousand Juvenile Delinquents	Present investigation
Non-delinquent	107	137
Delinquent	798	804
Inapplicable (non-penal institution, chronic invalid, dead), or unknown whether delinquent	95	59

First, it should be noted that the *inapplicable* and *unknown* cases have been reduced from 95 to 59 by this more detailed study, thereby causing some shift in the distribution of the other classifications. However, this only partly explains the differences. It needs to be

If we compare the behavior of the group during this first follow-up span (at the end of which the average age of the boys was nineteen years) with their behavior prior to their appearance in the Boston Juvenile Court (when their average age was thirteen and a half years), we find a *considerable increase, from .7 to 14.6 per cent, in the proportion of non-delinquents.*[37]

Comparison of the delinquents in the two periods discloses practically no change in the proportion of serious and minor offenders among those who have in one way or another violated the law or who, though not arrested, have nevertheless committed offenses for which they might have been apprehended.[38]

The changes which occurred in the proportion of delinquents and non-delinquents in the two periods involved are more clearly seen from a case-by-case comparison. Of 701 youths who were designated serious delinquents prior to their appearance in the Boston Juvenile Court, and whose behavior in the first follow-up period could be ascertained, 72.3 per cent continued to be such in the first follow-up period, 15.4 per cent became minor offenders, and 12.3 per cent became non-delinquents. On the other hand, of 228 boys who previously had been minor offenders, 31.6 per cent continued as such in the first follow-up period; 48.2 per cent had to be classified as serious offenders; and 20.2 per cent became non-offenders.

pointed out that in the original tabulation there were 28 cases classified as delinquent which are now tabulated as non-delinquent. Actually they were non-delinquent during the first five-year follow-up span but they committed delinquencies very shortly after the end of the period. In view of the fact that there was no definite plan at the time of the original study for continued follow-up investigations and that it was the purpose of *One Thousand Juvenile Delinquents* to ascertain the proportion of recidivism following Court-Clinic treatment, it was felt that an incomplete picture of the recidivism of the group would be given if these 28 cases were called non-delinquents. Because in the present investigation we are able to divide the follow-up period into three five-year spans, we can now properly tabulate these 28 cases as non-delinquents in the first follow-up period but delinquents in the second. These 28 cases, previously included in the picture of recidivism of *One Thousand Juvenile Delinquents* following Court-Clinic treatment, are now categorized as follows: unknown in first five-year period, serious or minor offenders in second five-year period, 15 cases; non-delinquent in first five-year period, serious or minor offenders in second five-year period, 13 cases.

[37] Appendix C, 20.
[38] Appendix C, 18.

Of 7 boys who, in the period prior to their appearance in the Boston Juvenile Court, were non-delinquents, 5 continued to be non-delinquents during the follow-up period, while 2 became minor offenders.

PRINCIPAL COMPONENT OF MISCONDUCT

Classification as serious offenders of 67.5 per cent of the 804 delinquents was based upon their actual conviction for serious crimes, and of 3.3 per cent upon the commission of serious offenses which were not followed by conviction. Since all these men had pursued a proven course of serious misconduct, they could definitely be classed as serious offenders. In another 5.6 per cent of the cases the determination of behavior was based primarily upon the commission of serious offenses for which the men somehow escaped the attention of the police or courts. In 2 cases (.2 per cent) a judgment of serious delinquency resulted from the fact that commitment to a penal institution on a sentence imposed in the prior period was still being served at the beginning of the follow-up period. In 9 cases (1.1 per cent) the determination of delinquency was based upon dishonorable discharge from the Army or Navy, for such dismissal may reasonably be considered to follow the commission of a serious offense.

Almost a fifth (17.4 per cent) of the 804 delinquents were judged minor offenders because of conviction for minor crimes; while seven men (.9 per cent) were classified as minor offenders because they were arrested, though not convicted, for petty crimes. Their course of petty misconduct was clear, however. Finally, 4 per cent of the men were judged minor offenders on the basis of the commission of petty crimes for which they were not arrested.[39]

Comparing the two periods in respect to the major basis on which the delinquency of the youths was determined, we find an increase, from 45.6 per cent in the prior period to 67.7 per cent in the follow-up period, in the proportion judged delinquent because of conviction for serious offenses. There was likewise an increase, from 7.5

[39] Appendix B, 41.

to 17.5 per cent, in the proportion of youths classed as delinquents on the basis of actual convictions for minor offenses. However, a marked decrease occurred, from 26.7 to 5.6 per cent, in the proportion classified as delinquent mainly because of the commission of serious offenses for which they were not arrested; and there was a drop, from 15.8 to 4 per cent, in the proportion of youths who had to be judged delinquent by reason of the commission of minor offenses not resulting in arrest. The percentage of youths judged delinquent because of the commission of serious offenses not followed by convictions remained the same, as did also the small percentage of men whose delinquent status was based on the commission of minor offenses that were not followed by convictions.[40]

MONTHS IN COMMUNITY

Turning now to the length of time during which our youths were entirely "at liberty" during this first follow-up period, we find that, barring 63 men whose whereabouts were either partly or entirely unknown or who died during the five-year span, 512 (54.6 per cent) of 937 men lived in the community throughout the period—i.e., they were not incarcerated in peno-correctional institutions or compelled to spend any time in mental hospitals or in institutions for the chronically disabled. The remaining 425 spent an average of 41.5 months ($\pm$.41) in the community out of the 60-month period.[41]

A comparison with the length of time spent in the community in the period prior to the appearance of these boys in the Boston Juvenile Court is not valid, because that period covered many more years than the five-year follow-up span. It is sufficient to point out that 93.2 per cent of these youths had not been confined in peno-correctional or in non-penal institutions prior to their appearance in the Boston Juvenile Court as compared with 54.6 per cent thus confined during the first five-year follow-up period. It might also be pointed out that 56.7 per cent of 873 youths not confined in penal or non-penal institutions in the prior span were likewise not con-

[40] Appendix C, 17.   [41] Appendix B, 38.

fined during the first five-year follow-up period; while 75.4 per cent of 65 youths who were in penal or non-penal institutions for at least part of the prior period were likewise confined for part or all of the 60 months of the first five-year follow-up period.[42]

* * * * *

From this comparison of the behavior of our youths during the years preceding their appearance before the Boston Juvenile Court and during the first five-year period following their handling by the Court, it would appear that the changes that occurred among the delinquents are related to their emergence from childhood into adolescence, to their growing experience in the ways of crime, and to an increasing contact with police and other officials. Childhood delinquencies had not yet been entirely left behind, but officially recognized criminality had markedly increased. Most notable is the rise in the proportion of youths committed to peno-correctional institutions, the change in the type of their peno-correctional experiences, and a decrease in the percentage of offenders placed on probation. In all this it must be recalled that even by the end of this first follow-up span these youths were of an average age of but nineteen years. Clearly, the peak of their criminality had not yet been passed.

Thus far we have reviewed only a segment of the lives of our 1,000 juvenile delinquents. The story must be projected further into time if the true pattern of their conduct is to emerge. Therefore, we now turn our attention to their behavior during the second five-year period that elapsed since they were in the hands of the Boston Juvenile Court.

[42] Appendix C, 14.

Chapter V

DELINQUENCY IN SECOND FOLLOW-UP PERIOD

WITH the passage of five more years since the end of the first five-year follow-up period a total of 39 of the original one thousand youths had died. All but one of these have to be eliminated from any further consideration. This youth died so late in the second follow-up period that we could determine his conduct. Our concern in the present chapter, therefore, is with 962 of the original one thousand juvenile delinquents.

By the close of the second follow-up period the average age of the group was twenty-four years ($\pm$.06). Only 9.2 per cent were under twenty-one, 61.7 per cent were between twenty-one and twenty-five, 28.9 per cent were between twenty-six and thirty, and two had reached an age between thirty-one and thirty-five.[1]

NUMBER AND NATURE OF ARRESTS

In 85 instances it could not be determined whether the boys had been arrested or not during the second follow-up period. Of 877 whose behavior could be checked, 33.9 per cent had not been arrested, while 66.1 per cent had been apprehended one or more times. Of those arrested, 19.2 per cent had been apprehended once, 20.4 per cent twice, 13.0 per cent three times, 12.5 per cent four times, 16.9 per cent five or six times, and 18.0 per cent on seven or more occasions. The average number of arrests was 3.76 ($\pm$.06).[2]

The 580 youths arrested were apprehended a total of 2,547 times.

The nature of the offenses involved was known in 2,493 instances.[3] One-fourth (24.6 per cent) of them were for property crimes, 30.3 per cent for offenses against the public welfare, 29 per cent for drunkenness, 7.3 per cent for offenses against the person, 2.4 per cent for offenses against chastity, 1.6 per cent for offenses

---

[1] Appendix B, 8; Appendix C, 1.   [2] Appendix B, 43.

[3] Fifty-four arrests had to be tabulated as for "violation of probation," their exact nature being unknown.

against the family and children (neglect and non-support), 8 (.3 per cent) for drug using or selling, and 4.5 per cent for various other offenses not classifiable in any of the above categories, such as running away from home or from an institution.[4]

Turning from offenses to persons committing them, we find that of the 580 youths arrested during this period, 50.9 per cent were apprehended one or more times for property crimes, 58.8 per cent for offenses against the public welfare, 35.3 per cent for drunkenness, 24.3 per cent for crimes against the person, 7.9 per cent for offenses against chastity, 6 per cent for offenses against the family and children, and 1.4 per cent for drug using or selling.[5]

More significant, however, are the changes that occurred in the number and nature of arrests in the first and second follow-up periods. Though there was only a very slight increase in the average number of arrests, from 3.4 per cent during the first five-year period to 3.7 per cent in the second, it is to be noted that there was a considerable increase, from 20.2 to 33.9 per cent, in the proportion of youths not arrested at all.[6]

A considerable change also occurred in the nature of the offenses. First, there was a falling off, from 48.7 per cent in the first five years to 24.6 in the second, in the percentage of arrests for property crimes, in which category are included larceny, breaking and entering, pickpocketing, forgery, and similar offenses. There was likewise a diminution, from 13.2 to 4.5 per cent, in such offenses as running away, truancy, stubbornness, and malicious mischief. These decreases appear to have been absorbed by increases, from 22.2 to 30.3 per cent, in the percentage of offenses against the public welfare (such as vagrancy, gaming, violation of liquor laws, disturbing the peace) as well as in the proportion of arrests for drunkenness, which jumped from 9.3 per cent in the first follow-up period to 29 per cent in the second. The proportion of arrests rose, from 4.4 to 7.3 per cent, for offenses against the person, such as simple assault and assault and battery; there was an increase, from .5 to 1.6 per cent, in the percentage of arrests for offenses against the family and

---

[4] Appendix B, 44.   [5] Appendix B, 46.   [6] Appendix C, 2.

children, and an increase in arrests for offenses against chastity, from 1.6 to 2.4 per cent.[7]

Considering, now, those youths who were apprehended one or more times for each type of offense, we note substantial decreases among those arrested for property crimes (from 74.8 to 50.9 per cent) and among those arrested for such offenses as stubbornness, truancy, running away, and malicious mischief (from 31.6 to 14.3). These decreases were evidently absorbed by increases among those arrested for various offenses against the public welfare (from 43.7 to 58.8), for drunkenness (from 13.4 to 35.3), for offenses against the person (from 12.4 to 24.3), for offenses reflecting neglect or non-support of family (from .9 to 6.0), and for drug using or selling (from .2 to 1.4 per cent).[8]

A case-by-case comparison indicates that of 183 youths who had not been arrested at all during the first five-year period, 75.4 per cent were likewise not arrested during the second, 9.8 per cent were arrested once, 3.8 per cent twice, a like proportion three times, 3.4 per cent four or five times, and 3.8 per cent six or more times. On the other hand, of 674 youths who had been arrested during the first period, 76.9 per cent were also arrested during the second.

FREQUENCY OF ARRESTS

Of 464 youths arrested more than once during the second five-year follow-up span the frequency of whose arrests could be estimated, 19.2 per cent were apprehended as often as once in less than 6 months, 15.1 per cent once in 6 to 9 months, 13.4 per cent once in 9 to 12 months, 10.1 per cent once in 12 to 15 months, 10.6 per cent once in 15 to 18 months, 12.3 per cent once in 18 to 24 months, and 19.3 per cent as infrequently as once in 24 or more months. The average frequency of arrests among those arrested more than once was once in 13.21 months ($\pm$.24).[9]

Comparison of the frequency of the arrests of those arrested more than once during the first and second follow-up periods discloses a small increase in the average frequency of arrests—from one arrest

[7] Appendix C, 4.   [8] Appendix C, 5.   [9] Appendix B, 45.

in 14 months during the first five years to one arrest in 13.2 months during the second.[10]

NUMBER AND NATURE OF DISPOSITIONS BY COURT

How did the courts dispose of the 2,547 arrests of the 580 youths who were known to have been arrested during this second follow-up span? The disposition of 2,504 arrests was ascertainable. Of these, 17.2 per cent resulted in new commitments to peno-correctional institutions, 3 per cent in recommitments by revocation of parole, 8.7 per cent in probation, and 5.4 per cent in probation under suspended sentence. About a fourth of the arrests (27 per cent) were followed by fines, and 8 of the arrests (.3 per cent) resulted in commitments for non-payment of fine. In almost a sixth of the arrests (13.9 per cent) the charges were placed on file, in 15.9 per cent there was a finding of "Not guilty," 4.5 per cent resulted in release by the probation officer, 2 per cent in nol-prossing, and 1.9 per cent in a finding of "No bill."[11]

Convictions followed 1,894 of the 2,547 arrests. Of the 539 youths known to have been convicted one or more times during the second five-year span, 27.2 per cent were convicted once, 19.6 per cent twice, 15.5 per cent three times, 11.4 per cent four times, 10 per cent five times, 8.7 per cent six or seven times, and 7.6 per cent eight or more times. The average number of convictions among those arrested during this second check-up period was 3.3 (±.06).[12]

Of the 580 men arrested during the period, 41.2 per cent had new sentences to peno-correctional institutions imposed upon them, while 10.5 per cent were recommitted to institutions by revocation of parole. A fourth of the 580 offenders (26.4 per cent) were placed on straight probation during this period, and 15.9 per cent were given probation under threat of sentence to an institution in case of violation of conditions. Half the youths who were arrested during this second five-year follow-up period (51.9 per cent) were fined,[13] over a third (36.7 per cent) had charges against them filed, 12.2 per

<hr />

[10] Appendix C, 3.   [11] Appendix B, 48.   [12] Appendix B, 47.
[13] This includes a few cases of "restitution" and commitment for non-payment of fine.

cent were released by the probation officer on charges of drunkenness without having to appear in court for trial, 7.6 per cent had cases against them nol-prossed, 7.1 per cent had their cases closed by a finding of "No bill," over a third (36.7 per cent) were found "Not guilty" on various charges.[14]

Considering next the difference in the nature of the dispositions of all the arrests of these young men during the two five-year spans under analysis, we find a decrease, from 30.6 in the first follow-up period to 20.2 in the second, in the percentage of arrests followed by commitment, either on new sentences or by revocation of parole. There was also a great decrease, from 17.4 to 8.7 per cent, in the arrests followed by probation, as well as by probation under suspended sentence, which fell from 9.4 to 5.4 per cent. A slight falling-off occurred also in the proportion of arrests that resulted in filing of cases, from 16.6 per cent in the first five-year follow-up period to 13.9 per cent in the second.

These decreases in the percentages of arrests resulting in commitments, probations, and filing of cases were offset by increases in the percentages resulting in fines (from 13.9 per cent in the first five-year follow-up period to 27.5 per cent in the second), in release by a probation officer without court appearance following arrest for drunkenness (from 1.9 to 4.5 per cent), and in closing of cases by *nolle prosequi* (from .7 to 2 per cent). There was also an increase, from .6 to 1.9 per cent, in the percentage of cases resulting in a finding of "No bill," and a marked increase, from 8.9 to 15.9, in that of arrests that culminated in a finding of "Not guilty."[15]

We will compare next the distribution of offenders by type of disposition of the case in the two periods involved. A slight decrease occurred, from 49.3 per cent in the first period to 41.2 per cent in the second, in the proportion of youths who were newly sentenced to imprisonment. There was a decrease, also, in the ratio of those recommitted to institutions by revocation of parole, from 24.3 to 10.5 per cent. There was a decrease, from 42.5 to 26.4 per cent, in the proportion of offenders placed on probation, and a decrease, from

[14] Appendix B, 50. [15] Appendix C, 9.

25.6 to 15.9 per cent, in the proportion of offenders accorded probation under suspended sentence. In contrast to this, there was a
marked increase in the percentage of offenders who were fined
(from 26.8 in the first five-year period to 51.9 in the second), in
those who were released by a probation officer without court appearance (from 4.5 to 12.2), and in those whose offenses were nol-
prossed (from 2.1 to 7.6). A rise occurred, also, in the percentage
whose arrests (one or more) resulted in a finding of "No bill,"
from 2.0 to 7.1. Finally, there was an increase from 22.4 per cent in
the first five-year period to 36.7 in the second, in offenders found
"Not guilty." However, the proportion of offenders against whom
charges were filed remained about the same in the two periods under comparison—38.1 per cent in the first, 36.7 in the second.[16]

The average number of convictions among those arrested one or
more times remained about stationary—3.1 in the first period, 3.3 in
the second.[17]

The differences between the two follow-up periods may be seen
more clearly in a case-by-case analysis. Of the 196 youths who were
neither arrested nor convicted during the first five-year span, 22.4
per cent were convicted one or more times during the second; while
of the 660 youths who were convicted one or more times during
the first five years, 27.7 per cent either were not arrested or were
arrested but not convicted during the second.

FREQUENCY OF CONVICTIONS

Of 457 youths known to have been arrested more than once during the second follow-up period, the frequency of whose convictions
could be estimated, 12.7 per cent were convicted as often as once in
less than 6 months; 24.7 per cent were convicted once in 6 to 12
months, 18.6 per cent once in 12 to 18 months, 14.5 per cent once in
18 to 24 months, and 29.5 per cent as infrequently as once in 24 or
more months. The average frequency of convictions of those arrested more than once during these second five years was one in
15.43 months ($\pm.25$).[18]

---

[16] Appendix C, 10.   [17] Appendix C, 7.   [18] Appendix B, 49.

Comparison with the frequency of convictions during the first follow-up period shows practically no change.[19] The reader is reminded, however, that a lower proportion of youths were convicted in the second five-year period than in the first, 61.5 per cent as compared with 78.1.[20]

NUMBER, NATURE, AND LENGTH OF PENO-CORRECTIONAL EXPERIENCES

Two-thirds (65.6 per cent) of our youths did not spend any time in peno-correctional institutions during the second five-year span. Of 307 incarcerated for one or more terms in peno-correctional establishments during this period (including not only new sentences but returns by revocation of parole and transfers from one institution to another), 55.7 per cent served one term in an institution, 23.5 per cent served two, 12 per cent three, and 8.8 per cent four or more. The average number of penal experiences among the group who served any sentences in institutions during this period was 2.02 ($\pm$.04).[21]

In what types of peno-correctional institutions were these offenders incarcerated during the second follow-up period? More than one-eighth (14 per cent) of our 307 youths spent some time in correctional schools. It should be remembered that some of them were still under twenty-one years old and therefore subject to return to such institutions until their twenty-first birthday. Almost a third of the youths (31.3 per cent) were incarcerated in reformatories for young adults during this period. Over a half (52.4 per cent) served sentences in jails, houses of correction, and state farms; and a fifth (19.9 per cent) served time in prisons. A few (3.2 per cent) were inmates of institutions for defective delinquents.[22]

As to the length of their confinement, a fourth of the youths (26.5 per cent) spent less than 6 months in peno-correctional institutions of one kind or another during the second five-year period; 17 per cent spent 6 to 12 months in them, 15.4 per cent were incarcerated from 12 to 18 months, 8.8 per cent from 18 to 24 months,

[19] Appendix C, 8.　　　　　[20] Appendix C, 6.
[21] Appendix B, 51.　　　　　[22] Appendix B, 52.

5.8 per cent from 24 to 30 months, 6.2 per cent from 30 to 36 months, 12.1 per cent from 36 to 48 months, 5.9 per cent from 48 to 60 months, and 2.3 per cent for the entire 60-month period. The average number of months spent in penal, reformative, and correctional institutions by the 307 youths was 19.54 ($\pm$.61).[23]

Comparison of the incidence of peno-correctional experiences during the first and second follow-up periods discloses, first, a sharp decrease, from 76.4 in the first five years to 14 per cent in the second, in the proportion of youths who were inmates of correctional schools. This is explained, of course, by the fact that a majority of them were now beyond the age when they could be committed to such institutions. But an increase occurred in the proportion of youths serving sentences in reformatories, from 21.9 per cent in the first five years to 31.3 in the second; in prisons, from 5.2 to 19.9 per cent; and in institutions designed mainly for short-term offenders, such as jails, houses of correction, and state farms, from 21.2 to 52.4 per cent.[24] This latter increase can of course be accounted for by the expanding range in the offenses committed by the group as they grew older, notably of drunkenness and various offenses against the public welfare.

It should be noted that a decreasing proportion of the group as a whole spent any time in peno-correctional institutions—45 per cent in the first five years and 34.4 per cent in the second.[25] However, the average number of penal experiences among those who served time during each period remained the same—2.06 in the first five-year period and 2.02 in the second.[26] A small increase, from 17.9 months to 19.5 months, occurred in the average length of time spent in peno-correctional institutions.[27]

A case-by-case comparison of the number of penal experiences and the time spent by our youths in peno-correctional institutions during the first and second five-year periods reveals more sharply the actual changes that occurred. Of 489 youths who did not spend any time in peno-correctional institutions in the first five-year pe-

[23] Appendix B, 53.   [24] Appendix C, 15.   [25] Appendix C, 11.
[26] Appendix C, 12.   [27] Appendix C, 13.

riod, 82.8 per cent likewise served no time during the second; while of 386 youths who served one or more terms in peno-correctional institutions during the first period, 43.5 per cent were not incarcerated at all during the second.

Considering 128 youths who were imprisoned during both periods, we find that of those who spent less than a year in peno-correctional institutions during the first five-year period, 23.4 per cent served a like amount of time during the second while 21.1 per cent were confined longer, and 55.5 per cent were not incarcerated at all. Of 155 youths who spent one to two years in peno-correctional institutions during the first five years, 14.2 per cent served a like amount of time during the second, 18.7 per cent spent less than a year in incarceration, 22.6 per cent served more than two years, while 44.5 per cent spent no time at all in peno-correctional establishments. Finally, of 103 youths who had previously been incarcerated for two years or more, 42.7 per cent served an equal length of time during the second five-year span, 18.4 per cent spent one to two years in peno-correctional institutions, 11.7 per cent spent less than a year, while 27.2 per cent served no time at all during the second follow-up period.

OFFICIAL AND UNOFFICIAL DELINQUENCY

It will be recalled that 580 youths were arrested during this second follow-up span. They were, therefore, "official" offenders in the sense that their delinquencies were noted by authorities of the law. However, in addition to the 580 who were actually arrested, there were 24 who might be considered official offenders during this period; although not arrested, they were dishonorably discharged or had deserted from the Army or Navy or had spent time in peno-correctional institutions on sentences imposed during the first five-year period. A total of 604 youths could therefore legitimately be designated official delinquents during these second five years.

There were 46 youths who, though not arrested or otherwise officially recognized as delinquents or criminals, were nevertheless offenders, for they pursued a proven course of misconduct for which they might at any time during the second follow-up period have come to the attention of police and courts.

Of a total of 650 delinquents, therefore, the delinquencies of 92.9 per cent must be categorized as official, and of 7.1 per cent as unofficial.[28]

It is to be noted that the proportion of official and unofficial offenders remained about the same during both periods, 93.9 per cent of all the delinquents in the first five-year period having been classified as official, and 6.1 per cent as unofficial.[29]

A case-by-case comparison reveals that of 691 youths who were official delinquents in the first five-year period, 79 per cent were similarly classifiable in the second, 4.9 per cent became unofficial offenders, and 16.1 per cent passed into the category of non-delinquents.

And of 43 youths who were unofficial offenders during the first five years, only 16.3 per cent were such in the second, while 72.1 per cent became officially recognized offenders and 11.6 per cent non-delinquents.

PREDOMINANT OFFENSE

Considering next the predominant delinquencies committed by these 650 offenders during the second five-year period, it is to be noted that two-fifths of the group (39.2 per cent) typically committed property crimes, 22.6 per cent committed offenses against the public welfare, 16.6 per cent were primarily drunkards, 2.6 per cent committed mainly offenses against the family and children (neglect and non-support), 2 per cent offended against chastity, 1.4 per cent committed crimes against the person, while 2 youths (.3 per cent) were primarily drug addicts. Almost a tenth of the group (9.5 per cent) had to be categorized as committing "varied" offenses, their delinquent conduct expressing itself in diverse ways so that no one course of criminality was apparent except this erraticism; while 5.8 per cent committed other offenses not classifiable in any of the above-mentioned categories.[30]

[28] Appendix B, 55.   [29] Appendix C, 16.   [30] Appendix B, 56.

Comparison of the predominant offenses committed by the youths during the first and second follow-up periods reveals a marked decrease, from 65.5 per cent in the first five-year period to 39.2 in the second, in the proportion who were mainly committing property crimes. There was, however, an increase, from 10.7 to 22.6 per cent, in the proportion who were primarily offenders against the public welfare, and an increase, from 4.2 to 16.6 per cent, in the percentage of those who were essentially drunkards. Among those classifiable as offenders against the family and children there was an increase from .5 to 2.6 per cent, largely explained by the fact that more of these youths had family obligations in the second follow-up period.

A negligible increase occurred in offenses against chastity (from 1.5 per cent in the first period to 2 per cent in the second), in drug using (of which there was only one case in the first period and two in the second), and in offenses against the person (from .6 to 1.4 per cent). The percentage of offenders who had to be designated "varied" increased slightly, from 7.6 to 9.5. There was the expected decrease, explainable by advancing years, in the proportion of youths committing such offenses as running away from home or institutions.[31]

Case-by-case comparison of the changes which occurred in the second follow-up period indicates that of 468 youths who primarily committed property crimes during the first five years, 52.4 per cent continued to do so during the second, 15.4 per cent became primarily offenders against the public welfare, and 11.1 per cent primarily drunkards, 4 per cent had to be designated as "varied" offenders, 1.5 per cent as offenders against family and children, 4 youths (.9 per cent) as offenders against the person, 3 (.6 per cent) as sex offenders, one youth (.2 per cent) as a drug addict, while 13.9 per cent were non-delinquents in the second period.

Further light is thrown on the changes which occurred as between the two periods by the fact that of the 79 youths who, in the first five-year span were primarily offenders against the public wel-

[31] Appendix C, 19.

fare, 58.2 per cent continued to be such offenders in the second, 22.8 per cent became non-delinquents, 1.3 per cent became primarily offenders against property, 3.8 per cent became sex offenders, 2.5 per cent became offenders against the family, and 11.4 per cent became drunkards.

Of 34 men who were arrested chiefly for drunkenness during the first follow-up period, 33 continued to be mainly drunkards and one became a non-delinquent.

Finally, of 54 youths whose delinquencies were previously of so erratic a character that they had to be classed as "varied" offenders in the first five-year period, two-thirds (66.6 per cent) continued such a variegated pattern of delinquency during the second follow-up span, 13 per cent became non-delinquents, 3.7 per cent developed clearly into offenders against property, and 7.4 per cent into offenders against the public welfare, a like proportion became typically drunkards, and 1.9 per cent became offenders against the person. One youth who, in the first five-year period, had been a drug addict, and four who had been offenders against the person continued in similar types of misbehavior in the second.

SERIOUS AND MINOR DELINQUENCY

Summarizing in terms of seriousness the conduct of 888 youths whose general behavior during this second span was ascertainable, we find that over a fourth (26.8 per cent) were clearly non-delinquents, 41.4 per cent had to be classified as serious offenders, and 31.8 per cent were minor offenders.[32] Of the 650 youths who committed offenses during the second follow-up period, over half (56.6 per cent) had to be regarded as serious offenders because they committed property crimes, pathological sex crimes, or assaults with intent to rob, rape, or murder.

Comparing the behavior of the youths during the two five-year follow-up periods, we see clearly that an appreciable increase occurred in the proportion of non-delinquents, from 14.6 per cent in the first period to 26.8 in the second. Among those who were delin-

[32] Appendix B, 58.

quents in both spans there was a doubling of the proportion of
minor offenders, from 22.6 per cent in the first period to 43.4 in the
second; and a decrease in the proportion of those who could be
designated as serious offenders, from 77.4 per cent in the first five
years to 56.6 in the second.[33] In this connection it should be recalled
that by the end of the second five-year period these youths were of
an average age of twenty-four years.

The behavior changes which occurred as between the two follow-
up spans are more clearly seen from a case-by-case analysis. Of 135
youths who were non-delinquents in the first five years and whose
behavior during the second could be determined, 88.2 per cent continued to be non-offenders, 8.1 per cent became minor delinquents,
and 3.7 per cent became serious offenders. Of 172 youths who previously were minor delinquents, 66.2 per cent continued as such
during the second five years, 25.1 per cent became non-delinquents,
and 8.7 per cent developed into serious offenders. Finally, of 562
youths who were serious offenders during the first five years, only
60.5 per cent continued to be such in the second five years, 26.5 per
cent became minor offenders, and 13 per cent became non-delinquents.

PRINCIPAL COMPONENT OF MISCONDUCT

The classification as serious offenders of 41.6 per cent of the 650
youths here involved was based on conviction for serious crimes, and
of 4.1 per cent more, on incarceration during part or all of the second period for sentences imposed during the first five-year span.[34]
In 6 per cent of the cases the determination of continued criminality
during the second period was based primarily upon the commission
of serious offenses followed by arrest but not by conviction; these
youths were, however, definitely known to be guilty of serious
crimes. In 4.3 per cent of the cases a judgment of continued criminality was made by reason of the commission of serious offenses for

[33] Appendix C, 20.

[34] In these latter cases there was no delinquency recorded of a more serious character, although some of the men may have committed minor offenses during the time when they
were not in institutions.

which the offenders did not come to official attention. Only 1.2 per
cent of the delinquents were classed as serious offenders primarily
on the basis of dishonorable discharge or desertion from the Army
or Navy.

The remainder of the group were not classifiable as serious offenders since they were neither arrested nor convicted for grave
crimes, did not commit serious offenses for which they might have
been arrested, and were not dishonorably discharged from the
Army or Navy. A third of the group (32.9 per cent) were, however,
categorized as minor offenders by reason of convictions for petty
offenses, an additional 4.1 per cent because of the commission of
misdemeanors for which they were arrested but not convicted, and
5.8 per cent on the basis of the commission of petty offenses for
which they had somehow escaped arrest.[35]

Comparing criminal status in the first and second follow-up periods, we find that a notable decrease occurred, from 67.5 to 41.6 per
cent, in the proportion of youths judged serious offenders because
of actual conviction for grave crimes. There was a slight increase,
from 3.3 to 6.0 per cent, in those classed serious offenders because of
the commission of major offenses for which they were arrested but
not convicted, a slight decrease, from 5.6 to 4.3 per cent, in those
deemed serious offenders because of the commission of grave
crimes for which they were not arrested, and a rise, from .2 to 4.1
per cent, in those judged serious offenders because they were serving terms in penal institutions on sentences imposed in the period
immediately preceding. The proportion judged serious delinquents
primarily because of dishonorable discharge from the Army or
Navy remained about the same. There was, however, a marked increase, from 17.4 per cent in the first period to 32.9 per cent in the
second, in the proportion of those judged minor delinquents because of convictions for minor offenses; an increase, from .9 to 4.1
per cent, in the proportion of those termed delinquents because they
committed petty offenses for which they were arrested but not convicted; and an increase in the proportion of those classed as delin-

[35] Appendix B, 57.

quents, from 4 to 5.8 per cent, by reason of the commission of minor offenses for which they somehow escaped the attention of the police and courts.[36]

MONTHS IN COMMUNITY

Turning now to the length of time these youths spent in the community (that is, were not confined to peno-correctional institutions or mental hospitals, and were not patients in hospitals for the chronically disabled), we must omit from consideration 105 whose whereabouts were either partly or entirely unknown or who died during the period. This leaves 895 young men, of whom 578 (64.6 per cent) lived in the community throughout the second five years. A sixth of this number were in the community from 48 to 60 months, 7.9 per cent from 36 to 48 months, 6.9 per cent from 18 to 36 months, 3.7 per cent for less than 18 months. Thirteen men (1.5 per cent) were not at large in the community at all during this second five-year period. The average length of time spent in the community by those youths who were not "at liberty" during the entire second period was 39.1 months ($\pm$.61).[37]

In comparing the first and second follow-up periods in this regard, we note an increase, from 54.6 to 64.6, in the percentage of those who lived in the community throughout the five years. Despite this rise, there was a slight decrease, from 41.5 months in the first five years to 39.1 in the second,[38] in the average number of months spent in the community by those who were confined for part of each period in institutions of one sort or another.

A case-by-case comparison reveals a sorting out, with the passing of time, of those who tend to reform. Thus of 488 youths who lived in the community throughout the first five-year period, 81.4 per cent also did so in the second. Of 150 who were at large from 4 to 5 years of the first follow-up span, 52.7 per cent also were throughout the second span. Of 137 who were at liberty for 3 to 4 years of the first period, 44.5 per cent lived in the community throughout the second. And of 89 youths who were at large for less than 3 years

[36] Appendix C, 17.   [37] Appendix B, 54.   [38] Appendix C, 14.

of the first five-year span, only 16.9 per cent were allowed to reside in the community throughout the second five years.

*   *   *   *   *

The major finding of this chapter is that by the time our young offenders had arrived at an average age of twenty-four years, over a fourth (26.8 per cent) of the classifiable group had become non-delinquents. This is a marked improvement over the situation at the end of the first follow-up period, when the youths, then of an average age of nineteen, could be credited with non-delinquency in only 15 per cent of the cases. Even among those who continued to recidivate, there was a substantial decrease during the second follow-up period in the proportion committing serious crimes.

Another significant finding is the persistence in the pattern of non-criminal behavior on the part of those who had reformed during the first period—relatively few of them were backsliders during the second five-year span. Unless forces not yet evident should change the trend, it is therefore clear that our original group of juvenile delinquents had by the close of the second five-year follow-up period passed the peak of their criminality. Hence, an analysis of their conduct during a *third* five-year period which has elapsed since their original appearance in the Boston Juvenile Court and their treatment by the Court and its affiliated social agencies ought to be of considerable interest. To such an analysis the next chapter is devoted.

Chapter VI

DELINQUENCY IN THIRD FOLLOW-UP PERIOD

WE have seen that the second five-year period beyond the completion of treatment by the Boston Juvenile Court and associated agencies was marked by an appreciable improvement in the conduct of the youths. Does this continue?

By the end of the third five-year follow-up period death had taken 21 more of the original army of 1,000, in addition to the 39 who had previously passed away.[1] By the end of this third follow-up period the average age of the remaining 940 young men was twenty-nine years ($\pm$.06), the age distribution being: 9 per cent between twenty-one and twenty-five, 62 per cent between twenty-six and thirty, 28.7 per cent between thirty-one and thirty-five, and two men between thirty-six and forty.

In addition to the 60 youths who have died, we must eliminate from further consideration two youths because of incarceration in non-penal institutions during practically all the third five-year span. We are therefore concerned from this point on with the behavior of 938 men.

NUMBER AND NATURE OF ARRESTS

Despite considerable investigation, it is unknown whether 92 of these 938 young men were apprehended during the third five-year follow-up period. Of the 846 whose behavior could be determined, 42.1 per cent were not arrested at all. Of 490 men arrested, 23.7 per cent were apprehended once, 17.3 per cent twice, 12.7 per cent three times, 12.5 per cent four times, 12.7 per cent five or six times, and 21.1 per cent seven or more times. The average number of arrests was 3.78 ($\pm$.07).[2]

These offenders were apprehended 2,195 times, and the reasons for their arrests could be determined in 2,146 instances. Almost a fifth (18.2 per cent) were for property crimes, 22.5 per cent for

---

[1] For causes of death, see Appendix B, 4.　　　　[2] Appendix B, 59.

offenses against the public welfare, 43 per cent for drunkenness, 6.8 per cent for crimes against the person, 3.3 per cent for offenses against the family, 2.6 per cent for sex offenses, and 3 per cent for various other offenses such as escape, "default," and the like; while 12 of the total arrests (.6 per cent) were for drug using or selling.[3]

Of the 490 men arrested during this third period, 42.4 per cent were apprehended on one or more occasions for property crimes, half the group (50.2 per cent) for offenses against the public welfare, and almost half (46.3 per cent) for drunkenness. A fifth of the men (21.2 per cent) were arrested at one time or another during this period for crimes against the person, 9.6 per cent for sex offenses, 8.8 per cent for offenses against the family and children, and 1.6 per cent for drug using or selling.[4]

Considering, now, the changes which occurred between the second and third follow-up periods in the number and nature of arrests, we note first that there was no modification in the average number of arrests among those arrested one or more times during the second and third periods, 3.7 being the average in both spans.[5] However, despite this similarity in the average number of arrests, fewer of the men were apprehended in the third five-year period than in the second (66.1 per cent during the second five years, and 57.9 during the third).[6]

But a change occurred in the nature of the offenses committed by the group. First, there was an appreciable falling off, from 24.6 per cent in the second follow-up period to 18.2 in the third, in the proportion of arrests for property crimes; and a slight decrease, from 7.3 to 6.8 per cent, in offenses against the person (simple assault, and assault and battery), as well as a reduction, from 30.3 to 22.5 per cent, in offenses against the public welfare (vagrancy, disturbing the peace, gaming, violating liquor laws, and the like). These decreases were absorbed by increases in the proportion of total arrests for drunkenness (from 29 per cent in the second period to 43 in the third), for offenses against family and children, such as

---

[3] Appendix B, 60.   [4] Appendix B, 62.
[5] Appendix C, 2.   [6] Appendix C, 2.

neglect and non-support (from 1.6 to 3.3 per cent), and for drug using or selling (from .3 to .6 per cent). The percentage of arrests for sex offenses remained about stationary in the two periods, 2.4 in the second five years and 2.6 in the third.[7]

Comparing now the percentage of men arrested one or more times for each type of offense during the second and third periods, we find a decrease in those arrested for property crimes (from 50.9 per cent in the second five years to 42.4 in the third), for crimes against the public welfare (from 58.8 per cent to 50.2), and for crimes against the person (from 24.3 per cent to 21.2). However, there were increases in the percentages arrested for drunkenness (35.3 per cent to 46.3), for offenses against chastity (from 7.9 to 9.6), and for neglect of family and non-support (from 6.0 to 8.8). This last increase is of course explained by the fact that by the third follow-up period more of the men had assumed marital obligations. The percentage of men arrested for using or selling drugs was about the same in the two periods—1.4 per cent in the second, 1.6 in the third.[8]

Case-by-case comparison of the men arrested in the second and third five-year periods discloses the persistence of conduct patterns already noted in comparing the first and second periods. Thus, of the 525 youths arrested one or more times during the second five-year span, 79.4 per cent were likewise arrested on one or more occasions during the succeeding five years. Of the 285 men not arrested during the second follow-up span, 86.3 per cent were not apprehended during the third; 5.6 per cent were arrested once, 3.5 per cent twice, 2 per cent three times, and 2.6 per cent four or more times.

FREQUENCY OF ARRESTS

Considering now the incidence of arrests of the 367 men apprehended more than once during the third follow-up span, the frequency of whose arrests could be established, we find 24.8 per cent were arrested as often as once in less than 6 months; 14.2 per cent once

---

[7] Appendix C, 4.   [8] Appendix C, 5.

in 6 to 9 months, 10.9 per cent once in 9 to 12 months, 10.1 per cent
once in 12 to 15 months, a like proportion once in 15 to 18 months,
12.7 per cent once in 18 to 24 months, and 17.2 per cent once in 24
or more months. The average frequency of arrests among those
arrested more than once was once in 12.58 months (±.27).[9]

Comparison of frequency of arrests of those arrested more than
once as between the second and third periods indicates a slight increase in the frequency of arrests, from one in 13.2 months to one in
12.5 months.[10]

NUMBER AND NATURE OF DISPOSITIONS BY COURT

How were the 2,195 arrests which were known to have occurred
in the third follow-up span disposed of by the courts? The dispositions of 2,154 of these arrests could be ascertained; of these 20.4
per cent resulted in new sentences to peno-correctional institutions,
1.6 per cent in returns to institutions by reason of revocation of
parole, 6.2 per cent in straight probation, 7 per cent in probation
under suspended sentence. Almost a fifth of all the arrests (19.2
per cent) were followed by fines, 15.9 per cent by a filing of the
charges, 16.3 per cent by a finding of "Not guilty," 9.3 per cent by
release without court appearance, 2 per cent by a nol-prossing of the
indictments, and 1.5 per cent by a finding of "No bill."[11]

Convictions followed 1,527 of the 2,195 arrests. Of 446 men
known to have been convicted one or more times during this third
five-year period, almost a third (31.5 per cent) were convicted once,
18.5 per cent twice, 13.9 per cent three times, 11.6 per cent four
times, 7.3 per cent five times, 7.3 per cent six or seven times, and 9.9
per cent eight or more times. The average number of convictions
among those arrested during the third follow-up span was 3.24
(±.06).[12]

Of the 490 men arrested during this period, 43.7 per cent had new
sentences to peno-correctional institutions imposed upon them,
while 7.1 per cent were recommitted by revocation of parole to in-

---

[9] Appendix B, 61.　　　　　　　[10] Appendix C, 3.
[11] Appendix B, 64.　　　　　　　[12] Appendix B, 63.

stitutions to which they had been sentenced in the previous five years. A fifth of the group (21.2 per cent) were placed on ordinary probation during the third span, and a fifth (20.2 per cent) on probation under threat of commitment to an institution should they violate the conditions of probation. Two-fifths (40.6 per cent) had to pay fines[13] and 39 per cent had charges against them filed. A fifth of all the men arrested (20.8 per cent) were released by probation officers without court appearance, on charges of drunkenness, two-fifths (39.4 per cent) were found "Not guilty," 6.9 per cent had charges against them nol-prossed, and 4.7 per cent had their cases disposed of by "No bill."[14]

Considering, next, the difference in the nature of the dispositions of all the arrests in the third five-year follow-up period as compared with the second, we note that the proportion of arrests followed by new commitments or by revocation of parole increased only negligibly, from 20.2 to 22 per cent. There was a decrease in the proportion of arrests followed by ordinary probation, from 8.7 to 6.2 per cent, and a negligible increase in the use of probation under suspended sentence, from 5.4 to 7 per cent. Fines were resorted to by the courts far less frequently in the third period than in the second—27.5 per cent in the second, 19.8 per cent in the third. No appreciable increase occurred in the filing of cases, in nol-prossing, in the finding of "No bill" or "Not guilty." There was a rise, however, from 4.5 per cent in the second period to 9.3 in the third,[15] in the proportion of arrests resulting in release by the probation officer without court appearance, explained, of course, by the increase in the proportion of arrests for drunkenness.

Comparing, next, the number of men experiencing each type of disposition in the two periods now under review rather than the court disposals of the cases, we find a very slight increase, from 41.2 to 43.7 per cent, in the proportion of men given new commitments in the third period as compared with the second; and there is a de-

---

[13] This includes a few cases of commitment for non-payment of fine and for making of restitution.

[14] Appendix B, 66.   [15] Appendix C, 9.

crease in the ratio returned to institutions by revocation of parole, from 10.5 per cent in the second period to 7.1 per cent in the third. There was a slight decrease, also, from 26.4 to 21.2 per cent, in the proportion of men placed on ordinary probation, and an increase, from 15.9 to 20.2 per cent in the proportion of those given probation under suspended sentence. The third follow-up period also witnessed a decrease, from 51.9 to 40.6 per cent, in the proportion of men whose arrests resulted in fines; a slight increase, from 36.7 per cent in the second period to 39 in the third, in the proportion whose cases were filed; a substantial increase, from 12.2 to 20.8 per cent, in the percentage of men released by the probation officer without court appearance; and also a slight increase, from 36.7 to 39.4 per cent, in the ratio found "Not guilty" at one time or another. The proportion of offenders whose cases were nol-prossed remained about the same in the two periods, 7.6 per cent in the second and 6.9 per cent in the third; but there was a drop, from 7.1 to 4.7 per cent, in the proportion whose arrests resulted in a finding of "No bill."[16]

It will be recalled that despite these changes in the nature of the dispositions of arrests as between the second and third follow-up periods, the average number of convictions among those arrested more than once remained about the same in the two periods.[17]

The changes which took place may be seen more clearly in a case-by-case analysis. Of 325 men who were neither arrested nor convicted in the second follow-up period, only 17.8 per cent were convicted one or more times during the third; while of 486 men convicted one or more times during the second five years, 26.5 per cent either were not arrested during the third or were arrested but not convicted.

FREQUENCY OF CONVICTIONS

Of 350 men known to have been arrested more than once during this third follow-up span, the frequency of whose convictions could be estimated, 18.9 per cent were convicted as often as once in less than 6 months; 17.4 per cent were convicted once in 6 to 12 months,

[16] Appendix C, 10.   [17] Appendix C, 7.

20.2 per cent once in 12 to 18 months, 14.8 per cent once in 18 to 24 months, and 28.7 per cent once in 24 or more months. The average frequency of convictions among those arrested more than once during this third five-year period was once in 15.07 months ($\pm$.29).[18] Comparison with the frequency of convictions in the second follow-up period shows practically no change; for during that time convictions occurred once in 15.4 months on the average.[19]

Although the frequency of convictions among those arrested more than once remains the same, the reader is reminded that in fact a lower proportion of men were convicted in the third five-year period (52.7 per cent) than in the second (61.5 per cent).[20]

NUMBER, NATURE, AND LENGTH OF PENO-CORRECTIONAL EXPERIENCES

The high proportion of 70 per cent of the men spent no time at all in peno-correctional institutions during the third five-year span. Of the 257 who did serve one or more terms in such establishments (including not only new sentences but returns by revocation of parole and transfers from one institution to another), 47.5 per cent spent one term in institutions during this period; 28 per cent spent two terms, 12.1 per cent three, 6.2 per cent four, and 6.2 per cent five or more terms. The average number of penal experiences among the group who served sentences during this period was 2.14 ($\pm$.05).[21]

Almost a fifth (18.3 per cent) of our 257 men were incarcerated in reformatories at one time or another during this third five-year period. Over a third (37.7 per cent) served time in prisons, and almost two-thirds (61.5 per cent) served sentences in jails, houses of correction, or state farms. A few (3.5 per cent) were incarcerated in institutions for defective delinquents; one man was confined in a school for the feebleminded. Naturally, by the third five-year span the men were all too old to be spending time in industrial schools.[22]

A fourth (25.3 per cent) of these 257 men spent less than 6 months in peno-correctional institutions during the third period,

---

[18] Appendix B, 65. [19] Appendix C, 8. [20] Appendix C, 6.
[21] Appendix B, 67. [22] Appendix B, 68.

11.7 per cent were incarcerated for 6 to 12 months, 11.7 per cent for 12 to 18 months, 8.9 per cent for 18 to 24 months, 7.4 per cent for 24 to 30 months, 6.6 per cent for 30 to 36 months, 14.4 per cent for 36 to 48 months, 8.6 per cent for 48 to 60 months, and 5.4 per cent for the entire 60-month period. The average number of months spent in penal establishments by the 257 young men was 23.26 $(\pm.74)$.[23]

Comparing, now, the incidence of peno-correctional experiences in the second and third five-year periods, we note, in addition to the fact that none served time in correctional schools, a marked reduction, from 31.3 to 18.3 per cent, in the proportion incarcerated in reformatories. This phenomenon, like the preceding one, is of course largely attributable to age limitations on the admission of offenders to such institutions. Concomitantly, a sharp increase took place, from 19.9 in the second period to 37.7 in the third, in the percentage of men serving time in prisons, as well as a rise, from 52.4 to 61.5, in the percentage serving sentences in jails and other short-term penal institutions.[24]

It should also be noted that a somewhat smaller percentage of the group spent time in peno-correctional institutions—34.4 per cent in the second follow-up span and 30.0 in the third.[25]

On the other hand, the average number of penal experiences for those actually serving time remained about the same, 2.0 in the second period and 2.1 in the third.[26] But the average length of time spent in penal institutions increased in the third period, from 19.5 months in the second, to 23.2 in the third.[27]

A case-by-case correlation of the number of penal experiences in the second and third follow-up periods, and of the time spent by our men in peno-correctional establishments during these periods, reveals more pointedly the changes which have occurred. Of 236 youths who were compelled to serve one or more terms in peno-correctional institutions in the second follow-up period, 44.5 per cent were not incarcerated at all in the third; while of 557 men

[23] Appendix B, 69. [24] Appendix C, 15. [25] Appendix C, 11.
[26] Appendix C, 12. [27] Appendix C, 13.

who did not serve any time in such institutions in the second five years, 88.3 per cent were not incarcerated in the third.

Of 121 youths who were in peno-correctional institutions for less than a year of the second span, 24.8 per cent served a like amount of time in the third, but 28.1 per cent had a longer period of incarceration. The surprising proportion of almost a half (47.1 per cent) of this group, however, were not incarcerated at all during the third period.

Of 65 men who "served time" for one to two years during the second follow-up period, 15.4 per cent were confined for a like amount of time during the third, a third (33.8 per cent) spent more time than this in penal institutions, a fifth (18.5 per cent) served for less than a year, and a third (32.3 per cent) served no time at all during the third period.

Of 98 men who were incarcerated for two years or longer during the second follow-up span, over a half (55.1 per cent) were likewise incarcerated for two or more years during the third, 14.3 per cent were imprisoned for one to two years, 11.2 per cent for less than a year, while a fifth (19.4 per cent) served no time at all in penal institutions.

Here, again, we see a considerable persistence in conduct patterns, with divergencies becoming more clearly defined as the years pass and the more enduring behavior tendencies of the men becoming crystallized.

OFFICIAL AND UNOFFICIAL DELINQUENCY

The 490 men who were arrested during this period were of course known to the authorities as criminals. There were, in addition, 14 men who, though not arrested in the third period, were nevertheless classed as official offenders. They were so designated either because of dishonorable discharge or desertion from the Army or Navy or because of incarceration on sentences which had been imposed in the previous period. A total of 504 men may thus be considered official offenders during the third follow-up span. There were also 36 men who, though not arrested or in penal institutions during this period, nevertheless committed crime within these five years. This makes a total of 540 offenders, of whom 93.3 per cent were official and 6.7 unofficial delinquents.[28]

It is to be noted that the proportion of official and unofficial delinquents remained about the same in the third follow-up span as it was in the second.[29]

A case-by-case comparison reveals that of 558 youths who were officially recognized criminals in the second five-year period, 80.5 per cent had to be likewise designated in the third, 3.7 per cent entered the category of unofficial offenders, and 15.8 per cent became non-offenders. Of 43 youths who were unofficial offenders in the second follow-up span, 30.2 per cent were so classifiable in the third five years, 55.8 per cent became official offenders, and 14 per cent were non-offenders.

PREDOMINANT OFFENSE

Considering the predominant crimes committed by the 540 who were offenders during the third five-year period, it is to be noted that a third of the group (31.5 per cent) typically committed offenses against property, almost a fourth (23.7 per cent) were primarily drunkards, a fifth (19.9 per cent) were chiefly offenders against the public welfare, 2 per cent were primarily sex offenders, 3.7 per cent were essentially offenders against the family (neglect and non-support), 2 per cent committed crimes against the person, and 4 (.7 per cent) were primarily drug addicts. A tenth of the group (10.9 per cent) had to be designated as "varied" offenders, having committed several different kinds of offenses, no one of which was more typical of their behavior than another.[30]

Comparison of the predominant offenses of the men during the second and third five-year follow-up periods shows a slight decrease, from 39.2 per cent in the second period to 31.5 in the third, in the proportion of men who were mainly offenders against property; there was also a slight decrease, from 22.6 to 19.9 per cent, in the

[28] Appendix B, 71.   [29] Appendix C, 16.   [30] Appendix B, 72.

proportion of those who were primarily offenders against the public welfare. A slight increase occurred, from 2.6 to 3.7 per cent, in the proportion mainly committing crimes involving their domestic relations. There were increases, however, in the proportion of men arrested primarily for drunkenness, from 16.6 to 23.7 per cent; in the ratio of those classifiable as offenders against the person, from 1.4 to 2 per cent; and in the proportion of "varied" offenders, from 9.5 to 10.9 per cent. Four men were now classifiable as drug users or sellers, as compared with two typically committing such offenses during the second five-year period. The proportion of men who were primarily sex offenders was the same in both periods, 2.0 per cent.[31]

A case-by-case comparison of the changes which occurred indicates less persistence in any specific type of crime than would be expected, with the exception of drunkenness. Thus, of 232 men who primarily committed property crimes during the second period, 68.1 per cent continued to commit mainly such offenses in the third, 7.3 per cent became chiefly offenders against the public welfare, 5.2 per cent developed into drunkards, 6.4 per cent became "varied" offenders, 1.7 per cent became essentially offenders against the person, 2 men (.9 per cent) became sex offenders, and 2 (.9 per cent) offenders against the family, one man became a drug addict, and 9.1 per cent improved to the point of classification as nondelinquents.

Of 131 men who were chiefly offenders against the public welfare in the second follow-up span, 58.0 per cent continued as such in the third, 5.3 per cent developed into drunkards, 2 men (1.5 per cent) became offenders against the family, one man turned into a sex offender, one became a drug addict, and one a "varied" offender, while a third (32.8 per cent) of those who were primarily offenders against the public welfare in the second follow-up span became non-offenders in the third.

Further reflecting the changes that have occurred in the predominant offenses of the group is the fact that, of 105 men who were ar-

31 Appendix C, 19.

rested chiefly for drunkenness in the second five-year period, 90.4 per cent continued as drunkards in the third, 2 men became chiefly offenders against the public welfare, one committed mainly property crimes, and 7 (6.6 per cent) became non-delinquents. Of 11 men who were principally sex offenders during the second five-year follow-up period, 6 continued as such in the third, one became mainly an offender against the public welfare, one developed into a "varied" offender, and 3 became non-offenders. Two men who had previously been arrested for drug addiction continued to come into conflict with the law for that reason; and of 7 men who had been mainly offenders against the person, 6 continued as such, and one became a non-delinquent.

Of 35 men who previously had to be classified as varied offenders, two-thirds (67.3 per cent) continued in such erratic anti-social behavior during the third follow-up period, 9.6 per cent developed into drunkards and 5.8 per cent into offenders against the family, one man became a sex offender, another an offender against property, while 13.5 per cent became non-delinquents. Finally, of 226 men who were non-delinquents in the second period, 96 per cent continued as such in the third, 2 men developed into offenders against property, one into a sex offender, 2 into offenders against the public welfare, and 4 into drunkards.

SERIOUS AND MINOR DELINQUENCY

It has already been mentioned that 540 of 852 men whose behavior during the third five-year period could be ascertained were criminalistic. Almost half of the 540 men (47.8 per cent) had to be regarded as serious offenders, because they committed property crimes or pathological sex offenses or assaults with intent to rob, rape, or murder, while 52.2 per cent were minor offenders. The distribution of the whole group of 852 men was as follows: non-delinquents, 36.6 per cent; serious offenders, 30.3; minor offenders, 33.1.[32]

Comparing now the behavior of these men during the second and third follow-up periods, we note, first, an increase, from 26.8

[32] Appendix B, 74.

per cent in the second five-year follow-up period to 36.6 in the third, in the proportion of non-offenders. Furthermore, among those who were criminalistic in each period, there was a decrease in the proportion of serious offenders, from 56.6 to 47.8 per cent; while the proportion of minor offenders increased from 43.4 to 52.2 per cent.[33] In this connection, it should be recalled that by the end of the second follow-up span these men averaged twenty-four years of age, and by the end of the third period, twenty-nine.

The changes which occurred between the two periods are more clearly seen from a case-by-case analysis. Of the 230 men who had been non-offenders in the second follow-up span and whose behavior during the third period could be determined, the high proportion of 94.3 per cent continued to be non-offenders in the third period, 3.1 per cent became minor offenders, and 2.6 per cent became serious criminals. *This indicates a highly desirable persistence of reformation among offenders who have abandoned criminal ways of behavior at a relatively early period in their lives.*

The record of the petty offenders is not as encouraging, though not too bad. Of the 261 men who were minor offenders during the second follow-up span, 72.8 per cent continued to be such in the third five years, 22.6 per cent became non-offenders, while 4.6 per cent developed into serious offenders.

The record of the serious offenders is of course even less encouraging; for of the 341 men who in the second follow-up period were still committing major crimes, 68 per cent continued to be serious offenders in the third, 21.7 per cent became minor offenders, and only 10.3 per cent completely abandoned their careers of crime.

PRINCIPAL COMPONENT OF MISCONDUCT

The classification of a third (34.9 per cent) of our 540 men as serious offenders was based on their convictions for major crimes; in 5.4 per cent on the fact that they were incarcerated in penal institutions in the third period for felonies committed in the second period; in 5.0 per cent on the fact that they were arrested for serious

---

[33] Appendix C, 19.

offenses which, though not followed by conviction, should have resulted so because the men involved were definitely known to be guilty of serious crimes. A few men (2.6 per cent) were judged serious offenders by reason of commission of unofficial major crimes, and so were included in this classification even though they might actually have been convicted of only minor offenses.

Over half the 540 offenders were not classified as serious offenders, for they had not been arrested or convicted for serious crimes, were not in penal institutions for serious offenses, and had not been dishonorably discharged from the Army or Navy; neither had they committed any serious crimes for which they might have been arrested. They were, however, categorized as minor offenders, by reason of convictions for petty crimes in 40.3 per cent of the cases, because of arrests for minor offenses and the commission of unofficial minor offenses in 5.5 per cent, and because of commission of minor offenses for which they were not arrested in 6.3 per cent.[34]

Comparing the various groups that make up the larger groups of serious offenders in the two periods, we find a decrease in the proportion of men judged serious offenders by virtue of conviction for major crimes, from 41.6 per cent in the second period to 34.9 in the third; a slight decrease, from 6 to 5 per cent, in those classed as serious offenders by reason of arrests for felonies not followed by convictions; a slight decrease, from 4.3 to 2.6 per cent, in the proportion of those judged serious offenders on the basis of the commission of serious offenses for which they were not arrested; and a slight increase, from 4.1 to 5.4 per cent, among those judged serious offenders because they were serving time in penal institutions on sentences imposed in the period immediately preceding. The percentage judged delinquent primarily because of dishonorable discharge or desertion from the Army or Navy dropped from 1.2 in the second period to zero in the third. Increases occurred in the percentage of those judged delinquent because of convictions for minor offenses, from 32.9 in the second period to 40.3 in the third; in the percentage judged delinquent on the basis of arrests for minor

[34] Appendix B, 73.

offenses not followed by convictions, from 4.1 to 5.5; and on the basis of the commission of minor offenses not resulting in arrest, from 5.8 to 6.3.[35]

MONTHS IN COMMUNITY

If 139 men are eliminated whose whereabouts during the third five-year span were partly or entirely unknown or who died during that period, it appears that 598 (69.5 per cent) of 861 men lived in the community throughout the third follow-up period. This, it will be recalled, means that they were not incarcerated in peno-correctional institutions, and did not spend any time in mental hospitals or in hospitals for the chronically disabled. Slightly over a tenth of the group (11.5 per cent) resided in the community for 48 to 60 months, 5.8 per cent for 36 to 48 months, 4.6 per cent for 24 to 36 months, 4.3 per cent for 12 to 24 months, 2.2 per cent for less than 12 months, while 2.1 per cent did not live in the community at all during this third period. The average length of free time spent in the community by the men who were in institutions for part of the five-year span was 35.74 ($\pm$.73) months.[36]

A comparison of the length of time spent in the community by the group during the second and third five-year follow-up periods shows a slight increase, from 64.6 per cent in the second period to 69.5 per cent in the third, in the proportion who were able to reside at liberty in the community throughout the five years. Despite this increase there was a slight reduction in the average number of months spent in the community by those who were in institutions of one sort or another for part of each period, from 39.1 months in the second period to 35.7 months in the third.[37]

Case-by-case comparison indicates that of 557 men who lived in the community throughout the second five-year period and whose whereabouts in the third were known, 88.2 per cent continued to do so in the third; while of 126 men who lived outside institutions from 4 to 5 years during the second period, 47.6 per cent spent the entire five years of the third follow-up span "at liberty." Of 66 men

---

[35] Appendix C, 17.   [36] Appendix B, 70.   [37] Appendix C, 14.

who lived in the community for 3 to 4 years of the second period, almost a third (30.3 per cent) were not confined in penal or non-penal institutions throughout the third period. Finally, of 97 men who lived in the community for less than three years of the second follow-up period, only 16.5 per cent were allowed to reside in the community throughout the third five-year period.

*   *   *   *   *

The above analysis discloses a continuing increase in the proportion of non-offenders among our original group of 1,000 juvenile delinquents. *By the end of the third follow-up period, when they had reached an average age of twenty-nine years, more than a third had reformed.* Even the conduct of those who continued to recidivate had improved, showing a still further decline in serious criminality in the third period compared with the second. Whether this improvement will continue or has reached its peak is a matter that can be answered only by pursuing further the careers of these men. This is, however, not within the compass of the present work. When another five or ten years have elapsed we may have at least a partial answer to this question.

Chapter VII

TREND OF CONDUCT

IN the four preceding chapters we have described the behavior of our juvenile delinquents from childhood through three successive five-year periods after their handling by the Boston Juvenile Court and its affiliated community agencies. It will be recalled that these lads were of an average age of nine years and seven months when they showed the first signs of delinquency; we have traced their criminal careers from these early years until their age averaged twenty-nine years.[1] The method of comparing their behavior in each of the three five-year periods with that in the period immediately preceding it has given us some idea of these changes, but we cannot clearly define the *trend* in their conduct until we compare their behavior during the three five-year periods with their conduct before they appeared in the Boston Juvenile Court.

TREND OF ARRESTS

The average age of the group at the time of the arrest for which they were brought before the Boston Juvenile Court was thirteen and a half years. Some two-thirds of the lads (62.5 per cent) had been apprehended one or more times prior to that particular arrest. The proportion arrested reached its peak during the first follow-up span, at which time 79.8 per cent were arrested. At the end of that period our youths were of an average age of nineteen years, almost three-fourths of them (70.8 per cent) being still under twenty-one. In the second follow-up period, there was a drop to 66.1 per cent in the proportion of those arrested, and a still further drop to 57.9 per cent in the third five-year period, by the end of which the men were an average age of twenty-nine years.[2]

The increase in the proportion of youths arrested during the first

---

[1] See Appendix C, 1, for age distribution in each period.

[2] Appendix C, 2. Doubtless the decrease is due partly to increasing facility in avoiding arrest.

follow-up period over those arrested prior to their Court appearance was accompanied by an increase in the average number of arrests among those arrested, from 2.3 arrests in the earlier years to 3.4 during the first follow-up period. Despite the fact that there was a decline in the proportion of youths arrested thereafter, the average number of arrests among those actually apprehended in the successive periods was about the same as in the first follow-up span— 3.7 in both the second and third follow-up periods.[3]

However, these increases in the proportion arrested and in the average number of arrests were not accompanied by any rise in the frequency of arrests among those who were apprehended more than once. The average frequency of arrests in the pre-court period was one in 10.5 months, as compared with one arrest in 14 months during the first follow-up period. After that, however, there was a slight increase in the average frequency of arrests among those apprehended more than once, from one arrest in 14 months in the first five-year period to one in 13 months in the second and one in 12.5 months in the third. This seems to indicate that, although fewer of the men were arrested as they grew older, those who continued to come into conflict with the law were intensifying their antisocial behavior.[4]

The passing of the years has also witnessed a marked change in the nature of the offenses committed by our youths. This is shown in the reasons for their arrests. The most notable change is a decrease in the proportion of arrests for property crimes (larceny, pickpocketing, burglary, and similar offenses), the decline being from 62.9 per cent of all arrests before the Juvenile Court appearance to 48.7 in the first follow-up period, to 24.6 in the second, and down to 18.2 in the third. On the other hand, a marked rise took place in the proportion of arrests for drunkenness. There were none at all in the earlier years, 9.3 per cent during the first follow-up period, 29.0 in the second, and 43.0 in the third. Time has thus clearly defined the chronic alcoholics.

Because of the smallness of numbers involved, other changes in

---

[3] Appendix C, 2.   [4] Appendix C, 3.

the nature of arrests which have occurred with the passing of the years may be regarded as of relatively minor significance. For example, sex crimes increased from .3 per cent in the early years to 2.6 during the third five-year period; offenses against the family (neglect or non-support) rose from none in the early years to 3.3 per cent in the third five-year period; arrests for drug using from none in the early years to .6 per cent in the third follow-up period; crimes against the person (mainly assault and battery) from 2.5 per cent previous to the appearance of the boys in the Boston Juvenile Court to 6.8 during the third follow-up period. The proportion of arrests for crimes against the public welfare, such as violation of license laws, traffic laws, and liquor laws, gaming, and vagrancy, has remained about stationary. Naturally, a marked drop occurred in distinctly juvenile offenses such as truancy, stubbornness, unmanageableness, and malicious mischief.[5]

Turning now from a consideration of the changes in the nature of the offenses for which our youths were arrested to the changes in the proportion of youths arrested for each particular offense, we find a sharp reduction in the proportion apprehended for property crimes. In the early years, 76.6 per cent of the original group of juvenile delinquents were arrested for crimes against property, and almost a like proportion, 74.8 per cent, continued to be arrested for such crimes during the first follow-up period. However, there was a falling off during the second follow-up period to 50.9 per cent, and during the third to but 42.4 per cent.

This decrease is largely offset by the rising proportion arrested for drunkenness, from none in the early years to 13.4 per cent during the first follow-up period, up to 35.3 during the second, and to 46.3 during the third. The decrease in the ratio of property offenders was further offset by a steady rise in the percentage of youths apprehended for the commission of sex offenses of one sort or another— .6 per cent in the early years, 4.7 in the first follow-up period, 7.9 in the second, and 9.6 in the third. These sex offenses ranged from fornication or adultery to rape and pathological sex crimes. There

[5] Appendix C, 4.

also occurred a steady rise in the proportion of men arrested for neglect or non-support of their wives or children, the increase being from none in the early period to .9 per cent in the first five years (when a few of them were old enough for marriage), to 6.0 during the second, and to 8.8 in the third.

From their early years until the end of the second follow-up period, when the group averaged twenty-four years of age, an increasing proportion of those arrested were apprehended for offenses against the public welfare, 32.7 per cent in the early years, 43.7 during the first follow-up period, and 58.8 during the second. However, there was a slight decline during the third five years, when 50.2 per cent of all those arrested were apprehended for crimes against the public welfare. A similar trend is to be seen in the proportion of youths arrested for crimes against the person (mainly assault and battery). In the early years, 4.8 per cent of the young delinquents were apprehended for such offenses, 12.4 per cent during the first follow-up period, and 24.3 per cent during the second, followed by a slight reduction, to 21.2 per cent, during the third five-year period. Considered in the light of the sharp decrease in property crimes, this may be indicative of a general quieting down in the turbulence and aggressiveness of the offenders, probably attributable to temperamental and other changes due to increasing age and to growing experience.[6]

All in all, therefore, it is evident that the peak of arrests in this group of juvenile delinquents was reached roughly during the average age span fourteen to nineteen years. And the commission of property crimes, characteristically begun in their early years, extended with about uniform vigor through an average age of nineteen years, after which there was a sharp decline in this type of offense. This drop has been largely absorbed by a rise in the proportion of those arrested as drunkards, vagrants, and offenders against the person. However, although the drunkards among our group are still on the increase, offenders against the public welfare and

[6] Appendix C, 5.

against the person appear to have reached their peak in the age span nineteen to twenty-four years.

With the passing of the years, a considerable change has occurred in the dispositions made by the courts of the offenses for which our men were arrested. Before the appearance of our 1,000 juvenile delinquents in the Boston Juvenile Court, only 7.6 per cent of all their arrests had resulted in commitments to peno-correctional institutions; but during the first follow-up period 30.6 per cent of all the arrests ended in commitments.[7] Apparently judges were most inclined to send our youths to institutions when the boys were in the average age span of fourteen to nineteen years; for during the second five-year follow-up period, when they averaged nineteen to twenty-four years, the proportion of all the arrests that were followed by commitments to peno-correctional establishments dropped to 20.2 per cent and remained about the same, 22.0, during the third follow-up period.

As was to be expected, when our youths first showed signs of delinquent behavior, judges were inclined to place them on probation rather than to incarcerate them. This is evidenced by the fact that, in the period prior to the appearance of the boys in the Boston Juvenile Court, 44.6 per cent of all their arrests resulted in probation; in the first five-year follow-up period the use of probation declined to 17.4 per cent, during the second follow up period to 8.7, and during the third to 6.2.

In the earlier stages of the delinquent careers of our youths, likewise, judges obviously resorted more frequently to the filing of cases, perhaps on the theory that their early offenses were of an "accidental" character, for which there was, therefore, no need to impose severe punishment; for prior to the appearance of these boys in the Boston Juvenile Court, 27.8 per cent of all their arrests had resulted in the filing of the charges against them without fur-

---

[7] Including commitments to the Department for Defective Delinquents in Massachusetts.

ther action. This proportion dropped to 16.6 per cent of all arrests during the first follow-up period, and remained about the same throughout the later years—13.9 during the second follow-up period and 15.9 during the third.

In earlier years before the contact of the boys with the Boston Juvenile Court, only a very small percentage of arrests (5.2) resulted in the payment of fines. There was an increasing resort with the passing of the years to this mild form of punishment; for during the first follow-up period 13.9 per cent of all the arrests resulted in fines, and during the second, 27.5. However, in the third five-year follow-up period the percentage dropped to 19.8 per cent.

Comparatively, the use of probation under suspended sentence has been limited as a disposition of the arrests of our group of delinquents. In the time preceding their appearance before the Boston Juvenile Court, only 6.3 per cent of all the arrests were thus disposed of; during the first follow-up period 9.4, during the second 5.4, and during the third 7.0. There was also only a very slight recourse to the nol-prossing of cases: .2 per cent in the early years, .7 during the first follow-up period, and 2.0 during both the second and third follow-up periods. There was, likewise, relatively little resort to a finding of "No bill": none in the early years, .6 per cent during the first follow-up period, 1.9 during the second, and 1.5 during the third.

A rise in the proportion of arrests for drunkenness that resulted in the release of the offender by a probation officer without court appearance, from none in the early years to 9.3 per cent in the third period, is of course explainable by the increasing number of arrests for drunkenness with the passing of the years.

Perhaps the growing ratio of arrests resulting in a finding of "Not guilty" was due to more experience on the part of these offenders with court methods and to the greater use of lawyers to defend them; for in the early years and during the first follow-up period slightly over 8 per cent of the arrests among the juvenile delinquents resulted in a finding of "Not guilty" (or not delinquent), while during the second follow-up period, 15.9 per cent of all arrests resulted in acquittals, and in the third five-year period 16.3.

By and large, therefore, it can be said that in the years prior to the contact of these boys with the Boston Juvenile Court, the courts attempted constructive extramural treatment in the form of probation. During the first follow-up period they turned more to incarceration, largely in correctional schools, reformatories, and prisons. Thereafter they tended more toward disposing of arrests by fining or release.[8]

Considering, now, the dispositions of all arrests in the three successive periods, from the point of view of the number of youths undergoing each type of sentence rather than on the basis of the dispositions of individual arrests, we see more clearly the changes that occurred with the passing of the years. During the period prior to the appearance of these youths in the Boston Juvenile Court, 11.2 per cent of the group were committed to peno-correctional institutions (new sentences only). During the first follow-up period the proportion increased markedly, rising to 49.3 per cent. This ratio has been steadily maintained: during the second follow-up period 41.2 per cent of the youths received one or more new sentences to peno-correctional institutions and during the third 43.7 per cent. There was a sharp progressive decline, however, in the proportion of offenders placed on straight probation (without suspended sentence), from 63.0 per cent in the early years to 42.5 during the first follow-up period, to 26.4 during the second, and to 21.2 during the third.

In their early years, somewhat over a tenth of these youths, 11.9 per cent, were placed on probation with suspended sentence of imprisonment. This proportion increased markedly during the first follow-up period, when 25.6 per cent of the youths were given this form of treatment. Far fewer offenders had their arrests disposed of in this way during the second five-year period, however, when only 15.9 per cent of all those arrested were placed on probation under

[8] Appendix C, 9.

suspended sentence. The third follow-up period saw a slight rise, to 20.2 per cent.

Only 9.6 per cent of the young offenders were fined in the early part of their delinquent careers, while during the first follow-up period 26.8 per cent had their cases disposed of in this way. The proportion increased very sharply, to 51.9 per cent, during the second follow-up period, but dropped to 40.6 per cent during the third. The proportion of delinquents whose cases were disposed of by a filing of charges against them remained about the same throughout the years: 32.4 per cent in the period prior to the appearance of the boys before the Juvenile Court, 38.1 during the first follow-up period, 36.7 during the second five years, and 39 during the third.

There was a steady rise over the years in the proportion of delinquents released by the probation officer (without formal court appearance) on charges of drunkenness, and also in the proportion found "Not guilty." In the earlier period of their delinquent careers none of the boys had been released by the probation officer, for the obvious reason that none of them had been arrested for drunkenness at that time. During the first follow-up period, 4.5 per cent of the delinquents were released by a probation officer, and this percentage rose to 12.2 during the second follow-up period, and to 20.8 during the third. "Not guilty" (or not delinquent) was the verdict obtained by 14.9 per cent of the group during the early years. This percentage rose to 22.4 during the first follow-up period, to 36.7 during the second, and to 39.4 during the third.

There was an increase, also, up to the end of the second five-year follow-up period, in the proportion of offenders whose cases were nol-prossed or disposed of by a finding of "No bill," but a slight dropping off in the third period. Less than one per cent had charges against them nol-prossed in the early years of their delinquencies. The percentage rose to 2.1 during the first five-year period and to 7.6 in the second and dropped to 6.9 per cent in the third. Because of the non-criminal procedure in juvenile courts none of the young delinquents had his case disposed of by a finding of "No bill" during the early years; in the first follow-up period 2 per cent of the youths had their cases so disposed of, this proportion rising to 7.1 per cent during the second five-year span, and dropping to 4.7 during the third.

An interesting related finding is the shift which occurred as the years passed in the type of court disposition most often experienced by those who committed crimes. During the early days of their delinquent careers, the largest proportion of offenders, 63 per cent, were placed on probation; while during the first follow-up period the major proportion, 49.3 per cent, received new sentences to peno-correctional institutions, mostly truant and correctional schools. During the second five-year period the highest ratio of offenders, 51.9 per cent, had their cases disposed of by fines; while during the third follow-up span the largest proportion of offenders, 43.7 per cent, were in the group who were given new sentences of imprisonment. It should be remembered in this connection that, with the increasing proportion of drunkards, a rise occurred in short-term jail sentences. This partly accounts for the fact that commitment holds first place among all possible dispositions of arrests in the third follow-up period.[9]

The proportion of convictions following arrests has remained fairly stationary throughout the delinquent careers of our youths. In the years prior to their contact with the Boston Juvenile Court, 93.2 per cent of all their arrests resulted in convictions or findings of delinquency; during the first follow-up period 97.9 per cent resulted in convictions, during the second 92.9 per cent, and during the third 91 per cent.[10]

The average number of convictions among those arrested one or more times rose from 2.2 in the early years to 3.1 during the first follow-up period, and remained about the same during the second follow-up period (3.3), and during the third (3.2).[11] However, the average frequency of convictions among those arrested more than once dropped from one in 11.4 months in the earlier years to one in 15.1 months during the first follow-up span, and has remained about the same throughout the subsequent years, one conviction in

[9] Appendix C, 10.　　　　[10] Appendix C, 6.　　　　[11] Appendix C, 7.

15.4 months occurring in the second follow-up period, and one in 15 months during the third.[12]

Considering next the changes which have occurred with the passing of the years in the incidence and nature of the peno-correctional experiences and in the amount of time spent behind walls, we note first that 7 per cent of our group were in correctional institutions during their early years. This proportion mounted to 45 per cent during the first follow-up period, dropped to 34.4 during the second, and further to 30 during the third.

The average number of peno-correctional experiences among these youths in their early years was 1.7. It rose to 2 during the first five-year period and has remained the same. It should be noted, of course, that while fewer of our youths have been incarcerated with the passing of the years, the average number of peno-correctional experiences among those who were imprisoned has remained constant.[13]

The passing of the years did, however, slightly increase the average number of months spent by the offenders in peno-correctional institutions. In the earlier years and through the first and second follow-up periods, the average was 18 to 19.5 months; during the third follow-up span it rose to 23 months.[14]

There was a marked change over the years in the nature of the peno-correctional experiences of our youths, which is readily explainable on the ground of age. In the early years, for example, when the boys were thirteen and a half years on the average, 95.7 per cent of all their commitments were to truant and correctional schools. During the first follow-up period, this figure dropped to 76.4 per cent. A fifth (21.9 per cent) of all commitments during this period were served in reformatories; 21.2 per cent in jails, houses of correction, or state farms; and 6.9 per cent in prisons. During the second follow-up period a still further change occurred in the nature of the peno-correctional experiences: there was a drop to 14 per cent

---

[12] Appendix C, 8.   [13] Appendix C, 11.   [14] Appendix C, 13.

in truant or correctional school experiences, an increase to 31.3 per cent in terms spent in reformatories, and an increase to 52.4 per cent in commitments to jails, houses of correction, or state farms. A marked increase, to 23.1 per cent, also occurred in the proportion of terms served in prisons. In the third five-year follow-up period, there was a drop to 18.3 per cent in the proportion of reformatory incarcerations; but a continuing increase to 41.2 per cent in terms served in prisons, as well as an increase to 61.5 per cent in those spent in jails. Naturally, in the third five-year period there were no commitments or revocations to truant or correctional schools, because by that time our youths were all too old for such commitments.[15]

Before summarizing the trend in the behavior of our young men, it should be pointed out that in the pre-court period 93.2 per cent of them were not imprisoned and did not spend any time in mental hospitals or in hospitals for the chronically ill. The same may be said of 54.6 per cent of the youths during the first follow-up period, of 64.6 per cent during the second, and of 69.5 per cent during the third. The number of months spent at large (that is, not in prisons or hospitals for the mentally diseased or chronically ill) by those who were not resident in the community throughout each five-year period decreased from an average of 41.5 during the first five-year period, to 39.1 during the second, and to 35.7 during the third.[16]

TREND OF DELINQUENCY AND CRIMINALITY

After this review of the changes that occurred in the arrests, convictions, and peno-correctional experiences of our offenders from their early years to the time when they averaged twenty-nine years of age (at the end of the third five-year follow-up period), it should be helpful to summarize briefly the chief features of the trend in their conduct.

First should be recalled the encouraging finding of *a steady increase in the proportion of those who abandoned their criminalistic activities altogether*. Thus, during the first follow-up period,

[15] Appendix C, 15.   [16] Appendix C, 14.

only 14.6 per cent of the entire group could be classified as non-offenders (which means that they did not commit either official or unofficial offenses); by the second follow-up span this percentage had risen to 26.8, and by the third to 36.6.[17]

Secondly, *even among the men who remained criminalistic throughout the years, there was a notable and on the whole favorable change in the character of their offenses.* It will be recalled that the differentiation made for the purposes of this research between "serious" and "minor" offenders is essentially one between felons and misdemeanants. There was a decrease in the proportion of serious offenders among those who continued to violate the criminal laws throughout the years, from 77.4 per cent of all delinquents during the first follow-up period, to 56.6 during the second, and to 47.8 during the third; and an increase in minor offenders from 22.6 per cent of all the delinquents during the first follow-up span, to 43.4 during the second, and to 52.2 during the third.[18]

The change in the predominant character of the delinquencies of our offenders with the passage of time is significant. Property crimes, for example, were the typical offenses of 71.1 per cent of all our young delinquents before their appearance in the Boston Juvenile Court. During the first follow-up period this proportion dropped to 65.5 per cent; while during the second period only 39.2 per cent of the youths committed offenses mainly against property; and the ratio was still further reduced to 31.5 per cent during the third five-year period. There was also a marked decrease in such offenses as running away from home, truanting, malicious mischief, stubbornness, and like offenses, which are of course distinctly juvenile acts. Sex offenses increased only slightly as typical and characteristic forms of misbehavior. But in the characteristic com-

---

[17] Appendix C, 20.

[18] Appendix C, 18. See also Appendix C, 17. It should be noted that, except for the period prior to the appearance of these boys in the Boston Juvenile Court, when the delinquencies of 63.3 per cent of the group were based on actual arrests or on other "officially" recognized misbehavior (such as dishonorable discharge or escape from institutions), some 93 per cent of the offenders in each of the three five-year follow-up periods were judged delinquent because of the commission of crimes that were given official cognizance by agencies of the law. See Appendix C, 16.

mission of offenses against the public welfare, safety, and policy
(such as vagrancy, being present at gaming, violation of liquor
laws, violation of license laws, and the like), and of drunkenness,
there was a marked increase with the passing of the years. For only
2.2 per cent of our juvenile delinquents had been mainly offenders
against the public welfare during their early years, but the proportion rose to 10.7 per cent during the first follow-up span, and to 22.6
during the second, with but a slight drop, to 19.9, during the third
five-year period. Drunkenness as a predominant offense rose from
no incidence during the early years to being the characteristic offense among 4.2 per cent of all offenders in the first follow-up period, 16.6 in the second, and 23.7 in the third.[19]

In view of the fact that so large a proportion of these youths were
predominantly offenders against property before their appearance
in the Boston Juvenile Court, it is worth noting that 35.2 per cent
of the property offenders had become non-delinquent by the beginning of the third follow-up period, 12.5 per cent had become
predominantly offenders against the public welfare, 15.5 developed
into drunkards, 2.6 evolved into offenders against the family, 1.4
into sex delinquents, 1.4 into offenders against the person, .4 (2
men) into drug addicts, 5.8 into "varied" offenders. Only 25.2 per
cent of the original group of early offenders against property continued to commit such offenses during the third five-year follow-up
period.

Nevertheless, *only 109 of the original group of 1,000 were non-
delinquents throughout the three follow-up spans, while 226 were
serious offenders, and 88 were minor offenders throughout the
fifteen years.* Further, 67 of the entire original group were serious
delinquents during the first and second five-year periods and minor
offenders during the third; 95 were serious offenders during the first
five-year period and minor delinquents during the second and
third; 40 were minor offenders during the first follow-up period
and non-delinquents during the second and third; 23 were minor
offenders during the first and second five-year spans and non-delin-

[19] Appendix C, 19.

quents during the third; 67 were serious criminals during the first follow-up period but non-offenders during the second and third; 36 of the 1,000 youths were serious criminals during the first five-year span, minor offenders during the second, and non-delinquents during the third; and 27 were serious offenders during the first and second periods, and non-offenders during the third. In addition, there are 40 youths whom we have termed "erratic" in their behavior in that they did not progress from more to less serious delinquency, or to non-delinquency.[20]

The above enumeration accounts for the behavior of 818 youths whose delinquencies were known throughout the three five-year follow-up periods. In 155 of the 1,000 cases it was not possible, for one reason or another (unknown, "inapplicable," dead), to describe the behavior of the youths in all the three follow-up periods, although their conduct was ascertainable in one or another of them. In only 27 cases out of the 1,000 was the behavior of our youths entirely unknown throughout the three follow-up periods.[21]

AGE AT WHICH CONDUCT CHANGES OCCURRED

It is important to know at approximately what age the youths changed from the commission of serious to the commission of minor offenses, and likewise at what age delinquent behavior was abandoned entirely. Of 293 youths who were originally serious offenders but became minor delinquents before the end of the fifteen-year span (and it was possible to determine at what age), 34.8 per cent were still under seventeen years old when they began to commit minor offenses, 32.6 per cent were between seventeen and twenty-one, 21.5 per cent were between twenty-one and twenty-five, and 11.3 per cent were twenty-five or older. Their average age

---

[20] Two of this group, for example, were non-delinquents during the first and second five-year periods, but serious offenders in the third; 2 were minor offenders during the first, serious delinquents during the second, and non-delinquents in the third period; 6 were serious offenders in the first five years, minor offenders in the second, and again serious offenders in the third; 4 were minor delinquents during the first and second five years, but serious offenders in the third, and so on.

[21] Appendix B, 75.

at change from the commission of serious to the commission of minor offenses was 18.86 (±.16) years.[22]

There were 312 youths who were definitely non-delinquent by the beginning of the third follow-up period, and 6 more who became non-delinquent after the beginning of the third period. In 6.0 per cent reformation occurred when they were still under twelve years old, in 13.8 per cent between twelve and fifteen, in 23.6 per cent between fifteen and eighteen, in 22.6 per cent between eighteen and twenty-one, in 18.2 per cent between twenty-one and twenty-four, in 12.9 per cent between twenty-four and twenty-seven, and in 2.9 per cent between twenty-seven and thirty. The average age of reformation of these 318 youths was 18.49 (±.17) years.[23]

*   *   *   *   *

The major and most encouraging finding of this chapter is that with the passing of the years there was, among our original group of 1,000 delinquents, *both a decline in criminality and a decrease in the seriousness of the offenses of those who continued to commit crimes.* How account for these changes in behavior? What roles have age and its accompaniments played in influencing improvement in the conduct of these offenders? To this and related questions we shall turn our attention in the next four chapters.

[22] Appendix B, 76.   [23] Appendix B, 77.

Chapter VIII

AGE, MATURATION, AND CHANGES IN CONDUCT

IN the previous chapters we described the changes that occurred in the extent and nature of the delinquency of our 1,000 offenders from the onset of their criminal careers in childhood until they arrived at an average age of twenty-nine years. These changes are in the direction not only of less delinquency in the group as a whole, but of less serious crime among those who have continued their criminal careers.

In this chapter our first question is whether arrival at a particular age-span has any relation to the conduct of delinquents. Our next concern, related to the first, is whether there is in this research any evidence that maturation (regardless of the age when it occurs) plays a major role in behavior changes, as was suggested in *Later Criminal Careers*.[1] In that work, which was a follow-up study of the careers of male Reformatory graduates originally reported on in *500 Criminal Careers*,[2] it was ascertained, from a correlation of 63 factors reflecting every aspect of the lives of these men with the changes in their behavior, that in the factor of maturation through aging lies the most significant explanation of these changes. It was further discovered that mental abnormalities were largely responsible for a blocking or retarding of the natural process of maturation, and hence for persisting misconduct. The interested reader is referred to Chapters IX, X, and XI of *Later Criminal Careers* for a full statement of the findings, which suggest not only that the natural process of maturation mainly accounts for the improvement in respect to criminal conduct, but that a very close relationship exists between such improvement and improvement in respect to other major activities of the offenders, such as industrial adjustment, use of leisure, family life, and the like.

Because, in connection with *One Thousand Juvenile Delinquents,*

[1] Commonwealth Fund, New York, 1937.
[2] Alfred A. Knopf, New York, 1930.

we limited our inquiry to the tracing of their antisocial behavior and omitted from consideration their economic status, family relationships, employment history, use of leisure, and the like, we did not have the data from which, in the present work, directly to determine the reasons for the changes in conduct with the passage of the years.[3] However, there is indirect evidence—some of which will be presented in the latter portion of this chapter and the rest in the three succeeding chapters—that the maturation of the human organism which, in varying degrees, accompanies aging, when aided by certain favorable factors, largely accounts for the improvement which has occurred in the conduct of our offenders.

DELINQUENCY AND CHRONOLOGICAL AGE

Adverting now to the first concern of this chapter—namely, whether arrival at a particular age-span is closely related to the conduct changes of delinquents—we shall examine the behavior of our 1,000 offenders in relation to their ages. But first it will be well to have before us in Table 1 the transformations in the be-

TABLE I. DEGREE OF CRIMINALITY IN FIRST, SECOND, AND THIRD
FOLLOW-UP PERIODS (PERCENTAGES)

	FIRST PERIOD	SECOND PERIOD	THIRD PERIOD
Non-criminals	14.6	26.8	36.6
Minor offenders	19.3	31.8	33.1
Serious offenders	66.1	41.4	30.3

NOTE. Derived from Appendix C, 20.

havior of the group as a whole which have occurred with the passing of the years.

The question which is naturally raised at this point is whether youths who arrived at a specific age-span (say, sixteen to twenty years) during the first follow-up period showed the same propor-

[3] The reasons for the above-mentioned limitation will be found in *One Thousand Juvenile Delinquents*, p. 4, note 3.

tions of criminality and non-criminality as youths who did not reach a like age-span until the second five-year follow-up period.[4] The answer should throw light on whether the behavior changes that occurred are to any significant extent related to the characteristics generally accompanying any particular age-span. Attention is directed to such a comparison in Table 2, from which it is

TABLE 2. COMPARISON OF CRIMINALITY IN AGE-SPAN SIXTEEN TO TWENTY YEARS, IN FIRST AND SECOND FOLLOW-UP PERIODS (PERCENTAGES)

	FIRST PERIOD	SECOND PERIOD
Non-criminals	12.9	31.7
Minor offenders	19.4	26.8
Serious offenders	67.7	41.5

clear that youths who were sixteen to twenty years old during the first five-year period did not resemble in behavior youths who, having begun their delinquencies earlier in life, did not arrive at the age of sixteen to twenty years until the second follow-up period. Moreover, comparison of Table 2 with Table 1 indicates that much the same general improvement occurred with the passage of five years among those who were sixteen to twenty years old in the first and second periods, respectively, as occurred in the entire group, regardless of age. The same phenomenon is noted in Table 3, which

TABLE 3. COMPARISON OF CRIMINALITY IN AGE-SPAN TWENTY-ONE TO TWENTY-FIVE YEARS, IN FIRST, SECOND, AND THIRD FOLLOW-UP PERIODS (PERCENTAGES)

	FIRST PERIOD	SECOND PERIOD	THIRD PERIOD
Non-criminals	18.1	25.4	38.0
Minor offenders	23.4	33.0	31.6
Serious offenders	58.5	41.6	30.4

[4] No comparison could be made with youths of this age during the third five-year follow-up period because, of course, none of our group were still within this low age-span by the time the third follow-up period was reached.

deals with those of our delinquents who became twenty-one to twenty-five years old during each of the three successive follow-up periods. The lack of relationship between arrival at a specific age-span and change in conduct is confirmed in Table 3; for those of the original 1,000 juvenile delinquents who were twenty-one to twenty-five years old in each successive follow-up period did not resemble each other in incidence of criminal conduct. And, again, with the passing of the years, the same changes in behavior occurred within this particular age-span as among the 1,000 offenders as a whole regardless of age.

Still further evidence on this point is presented in Table 4 which

TABLE 4. COMPARISON OF CRIMINALITY IN AGE-SPAN TWENTY-SIX TO
THIRTY YEARS, IN SECOND AND THIRD FOLLOW-UP
PERIODS (PERCENTAGES)

	SECOND PERIOD	THIRD PERIOD
Non-criminals	27.3	36.5
Minor offenders	32.1	32.4
Serious offenders	40.6	31.1

NOTE. Since only two youths were within this age-span during the first five-year follow-up period, they were omitted from consideration.

shows behavior of the youths who were twenty-six to thirty years old during the second follow-up period and those who did not enter this age-span until the third. As in Tables 2 and 3, we note that offenders of like ages (now the twenty-six to thirty-year-olds) did not resemble each other in behavior. With the passing of the years, regardless of their age-span, there occurred the same general upward trend in their conduct as took place in the group of 1,000 offenders as a whole.

All the above evidence tends to establish the point that, at least so far as these particular offenders are concerned, the tendency to settle down or become less aggressive in antisocial behavior is not attributable to arrival at any particular chronological age-span. Not only does the internal evidence of this particular research show this to be true, but it is confirmed by a comparison, in Table 5, of the behavior of our 1,000 juvenile delinquents in the age-span twenty-four to twenty-nine years with another sample of offenders—the

TABLE 5. COMPARISON OF CRIMINALITY OF JUVENILE COURT GROUP AND REFORMATORY GROUP IN AGE-SPAN TWENTY-FOUR TO TWENTY-NINE YEARS (PERCENTAGES)

	JUVENILE COURT GROUP*	REFORMATORY GROUP†
Non-criminals	36.6	21.5
Minor offenders	33.1	31.6
Serious offenders	30.3	46.9

* Derived from Appendix C, 20.

† Derived from *Later Criminal Careers*, Appendix D, Table 54. Actually this group was twenty-five to thirty years old.

500 male criminals reported on in *Later Criminal Careers*—when they were in the *same age-span.* Little resemblance between them in conduct is shown.

If arrival at any particular chronological age were of crucial significance in changing the conduct of offenders, there ought to be greater similarity between these two groups at similar ages. There appears to be no question, therefore, that the characteristics of particular age-spans do not bear a significant or direct relationship to the behavior changes which have occurred in our offenders.

DELINQUENCY AND MATURATION

If the factor of age does not satisfactorily account for the change in behavior with the passage of time, what other factors do? We next turn our attention to evidence in Table 6, which is indirectly confirmative of the finding in *Later Criminal Careers* that, not arrival at any particular age, but rather the *achievement of adequate maturation regardless of the chronological age at which it occurs, is the significant factor in the behavior changes of criminals.*

After discovering that the offenders reported upon here and those described in *Later Criminal Careers* (which groups have been studied with like care and by the same method) did not resemble each other in behavior in similar age-spans, we found that there was, however, a close resemblance between the conduct of the former

TABLE 6. COMPARISON OF CRIMINALITY OF JUVENILE COURT GROUP IN
AGE-SPAN TWENTY-FOUR TO TWENTY-NINE YEARS AND IN
REFORMATORY GROUP IN AGE-SPAN THIRTY TO
THIRTY-FIVE YEARS (PERCENTAGES)

	JUVENILE COURT GROUP*	REFORMATORY GROUP†
Non-criminals	36.6	32.1
Minor offenders	33.1	33.9
Serious offenders	30.3	34.0

* Derived from Appendix B, 74.
† Derived from *Later Criminal Careers*, Appendix C, Table 2–51a.

juvenile delinquents during their average age-span of *twenty-four to twenty-nine years*[5] and the ex-inmates of the Reformatory in their average a ~-span of *thirty to thirty-five years.*[6] This resem-
b̶l̶ ̶̶ ̶s shown . Table 6. Clearly, there was practically the same distribution of no. criminals, minor offenders, and serious offenders within the two groups, though there was a *five-year average age difference between them.* This finding must be interpreted in the light of the facts that the two groups of offenders were drawn from different parts of Massachusetts (the juvenile delinquents originally came entirely from Boston, and the ex-inmates of the Reformatory from cities and towns all over Massachusetts); and that both groups had, since the onset of their criminal careers, scattered to different areas[7] and had been subjected to many differ-

[5] Appendix C, 1. The juvenile delinquents were in this age-span in the third five-year follow-up period.

[6] *Later Criminal Careers*, Appendix C, 2–2; see also page 20. The adult criminals were in this age-span during the second five-year follow-up period.

[7] For whereabouts of juvenile offenders at the end of the third five-year follow-up period, see Chapter XXI, p. 235; and of Reformatory group, see *Later Criminal Careers*, Appendix C, 2–H81b.

ent forms of peno-correctional treatment in different parts of Massachusetts and in other states.

This close resemblance becomes even more significant in the light of the following facts: Not only was there a five-year difference in the average ages of the two groups of offenders at the time of this resemblance in their conduct, but there was a difference of some five years in the average age at which each group *first became delinquent:* the juvenile delinquent group were of an average age of nine years and seven months old when they first showed signs of antisocial behavior,[8] while the ex-inmates of the Reformatory were fourteen years and nine months old at the first manifestations of delinquency.[9] Moreover, there was a difference of about seven years in the average age at which those in each group who reformed actually became non-offenders. The 318 juvenile delinquents who became non-offenders before the end of a third five-year follow-up period did so when they were of an average age of 18.5 years;[10] while the 118 Reformatory graduates who became non-delinquent before the end of a second five-year follow-up period did so when they were of an average age of 25.85 years.[11] It will be seen that the difference in their average ages at the time of reformation is little more than the difference in the actual ages of the two groups at the time when they so closely resembled each other in delinquent conduct.

To summarize, at a point of resemblance in their criminal conduct,

(1) there is a five-year difference in the average ages of the two groups of offenders;

(2) there is a difference of about five years in the average age at which the two groups first showed signs of antisocial behavior;

(3) there is an average difference of seven years in the age at

[8] See *One Thousand Juvenile Delinquents*, Appendix H, 57; and page 95.

[9] See *Later Criminal Careers*, Appendix C, 49. See also *500 Criminal Careers*, page 143. Since the same degree of care and intensity was used in tracing down the earliest delinquencies of the two groups, the difference in the ages at first delinquency is a real one.

[10] Appendix B, 77.   [11] Derived from *Later Criminal Careers*, p. 105.

which those in each group who actually reformed became non-criminal.

In the light of the facts already stated that these two groups of offenders were drawn from different parts of Massachusetts and were subjected to a different variety of peno-correctional treatments over the years, the basic explanation for their resemblance in conduct at different age-spans seems to lie in the fact that both groups have the characteristics of being approximately *the same distance away from the onset of their delinquent behavior and, in the case of those in each group who reformed, of being, at the time of abandonment of their criminalistic conduct, approximately the same distance away from the onset of their antisocial behavior.*

Since the conduct of the two groups of offenders, who were drawn from different places, at different times, at different levels in society's official apparatus for coping with criminality (i.e., juvenile court and young-adult reformatory), and who were studied entirely independently one of the other, was so much alike at a time in their lives when the two groups were found to be approximately the same average distance away from the onset of their criminal careers, we may reasonably conclude that, despite the varying influences to which these two groups must have been subjected, there is some underlying process in the lives of criminals related to their growth or development from the time of onset of their delinquent behavior which seems to play a basic role in the evolution and devolution of their criminal careers. A further check on this finding is the fact that the two groups of offenders resembled each other not only in the age-spans twenty-four to twenty-nine and thirty to thirty-five, respectively, but when five years younger—in the age-spans nineteen to twenty-four and twenty-five to thirty, respectively.[12]

[12] As shown by the following table:

	JUVENILE DELINQUENT GROUP AT 19–24*	REFORMATORY GROUP AT 25–30†
Non-criminals	26.8	21.5
Minor offenders	31.8	31.6
Serious offenders	41.4	46.9

* Derived from Appendix C, Table 20, Period II.
† Derived from *Later Criminal Careers*, Appendix D, 54, Period I.

Our analysis leads to the significant conclusion, therefore, that *not age* per se, *but rather the acquisition of a certain degree of what we have called "maturation" regardless of the age at which this is achieved among different groups of offenders, is significantly related to changes in criminalistic behavior once embarked upon.* Some implications of this finding are discussed in Chapter XXII.

In an effort to glean some clues as to which factors facilitate or hamper this underlying basic one of biologic maturation, we turn our attention in the next three chapters to comparisons, *regardless of age,* between (a) those juvenile offenders who reformed and those who continued to be delinquent, (b) those among the reformed juvenile delinquents who abandoned their criminal conduct when still under twenty-one and those who were older when they became non-criminals, and (c) those who became minor offenders and those who remained serious offenders.

Before turning to the next chapter, however, it will be well to pursue the comparison of the juvenile delinquents and the Reformatory graduates in various aspects of their criminal activities, because it bears out the close resemblance of the two groups at a time equidistant from the onset of their criminal careers. The reader is again reminded that all the following comparisons of the juvenile delinquents and the Reformatory graduates refer to the behavior of the first group when they were of an average age of twenty-four to twenty-nine years, and of the latter when they were thirty to thirty-five years old; and, as just stated, at a stage when the two groups were approximately the same average distance away from the time of the onset of their delinquent careers.

Considering first, in Table 7, the nature of the offenses of both groups as reflected in the reasons for their arrests, we find that the only difference between them that may be of any importance is the proportion of arrests for drunkenness, which was greater in the Reformatory group (51.3 per cent against 43.0 per cent). This is obviously explainable by the fact that this group was older and, therefore, more likely to indulge in drinking because the men had more time to acquire the habit of alcoholism and because they had al-

TABLE 7. NATURE OF ARRESTS OF JUVENILE COURT GROUP IN AGE-SPAN
TWENTY-FOUR TO TWENTY-NINE YEARS, AND OF REFORMATORY
GROUP IN AGE-SPAN THIRTY TO THIRTY-FIVE
YEARS (PERCENTAGES)

	JUVENILE COURT GROUP*	REFORMATORY GROUP†
Offenses against property	18.2	17.3
Offenses against chastity	2.6	1.8
Offenses against family and children	3.3	4.1
Offenses against public peace, morals, welfare, etc.	22.5	17.2
Drunkenness	43.0	51.3
Drug selling	.6	1.2
Offenses against the person	6.8	4.3
Other	3.0	2.8
Number of arrests	2,195	955

* Derived from Appendix B, 60.
† Derived from *Later Criminal Careers*, Appendix C, Table 2–H125.

ready passed the peak of maturation and were therefore drifting into less aggressive and less energetic forms of criminality.

There are further significant similarities between the two groups in average number and frequency of arrests, average number of convictions, dispositions of arrests, and average number of penal experiences among those having such experiences; but there is a marked difference in the nature of their peno-correctional experiences which is clearly due to statutory limitations on the commitment of offenders of certain chronological ages to certain institutions.

During the respective periods in their lives that are under comparison, a like proportion of the juvenile delinquents and Reformatory graduates (57.9 per cent of the former and 55.1 per cent of the latter) were arrested.[13] We note this striking resemblance not only between the proportion of offenders in each group who were arrested, but also in the average number of their arrests. Our 1,000

[13] Derived from Appendix B, 59; *Later Criminal Careers*, Appendix C, 2–58.

juvenile delinquents were apprehended an average of 3.78 (±.07) times[14] in the age-span twenty-four to twenty-nine; while our Reformatory graduates were arrested an average of 3.71 (±.12) times in the age-span thirty to thirty-five. There is a further striking resemblance between the two groups of offenders in the average frequency of arrests among those who were arrested more than once during the periods in question. Our juvenile delinquents were arrested an average of once every 12.58 months (±.27),[15] while our Reformatory graduates were arrested once in 12.5 months (±.45).

Turning to a comparison of the frequency of convictions among juvenile offenders in the twenty-four to twenty-nine-year span and the Reformatory graduates in the thirty to thirty-five-year span, we find a further striking resemblance between the two groups. Although this, and the next factor of dispositions (convictions and sentences), reflects not the offenders' conduct but the action of courts toward such conduct, the close resemblance in the handling of their cases is significant in that it further confirms the recognition of a strong similarity in the behavior of the two groups at the respective periods in their lives which are under comparison.

First, among the juvenile delinquents who were arrested more than once, the average frequency of convictions was once in 15.07 (±.29) months; while among the Reformatory graduates one conviction occurred every 15.65 (±.48) months.[16] Second, as Table 8 shows, there is a strong resemblance between the two groups in the dispositions, by courts, of the arrests of the Juvenile Court group in the age-span twenty-four to twenty-nine and of the ex-inmates of the Reformatory in the age-span thirty to thirty-five, when, as already emphasized, both groups of offenders were the same average distance away from the onset of their antisocial behavior. This resemblance is doubly significant because, as already stressed, the juvenile group were originally drawn from Boston while the Reformatory graduates came from various parts of the

---

14 Appendix C, 2; *Later Criminal Careers*, p. 62.
15 Appendix C, 3; *Later Criminal Careers*, p. 64.
16 Appendix C, 8; *Later Criminal Careers*, p. 66.

TABLE 8. DISPOSITIONS OF ARRESTS OF JUVENILE COURT GROUP IN AGE-
SPAN TWENTY-FOUR TO TWENTY-NINE YEARS, AND OF RE-
FORMATORY GROUP IN AGE-SPAN THIRTY TO
THIRTY-FIVE YEARS (PERCENTAGES)

	JUVENILE COURT GROUP*	REFORMATORY GROUP†
Imprisonment (including recommitment on revocation of parole)	22.0	30.7
Probation (including probation under suspended sentence)	13.2	13.6
Fine (including commitment for non-payment of fine and restitution)	19.8	20.7
File	15.9	14.8
Release by probation officer following arrest for drunkenness	9.3	5.4
Nol-pros	2.0	1.2
No bill	1.5	.7
Not guilty or released	16.3	12.9
Number of known dispositions	*2,154*	920

* Derived from Appendix B, 64.
† Derived from *Later Criminal Careers*, Appendix C, Table 2–H126.

state of Massachusetts; the court's recognition of this resemblance
is confirmed by the similarity of the sentences imposed on the two
groups. The only difference of any significance is the higher proportion of institutional commitments in the older group of offenders. The differences in the chronological ages (as opposed to what
might be called "maturation ages") of the two groups probably
accounts for this, for proportionately more of the older group were
committed to institutions on short-term sentences following drunkenness and proportionately fewer were released by the probation
officer.

Comparison of the peno-correctional experiences of our juvenile
delinquents in the age-span twenty-four to twenty-nine years with
the Reformatory graduates in the age-span thirty to thirty-five years
indicates a further close resemblance between them: 30 per cent of
the juvenile delinquents and 36.8 per cent of the Reformatory

graduates were in peno-correctional institutions during the period in question.[17] The slightly higher proportion in the Reformatory group is obviously accounted for by the difference in the chronological age of the two groups. The older offenders experienced more jail sentences, as is seen from Table 9, owing to the fact that they were to a greater extent drunkards and vagrants.

There is a difference, but only a small one, between the groups in the average number of penal experiences—2.14 ($\pm$.05) among the juvenile delinquents and 2.72 ($\pm$.12) among the Reformatory graduates[18]—and in regard to the average number of months spent in penal institutions: the juvenile delinquents were incarcerated for an average of 23.26 ($\pm$.74) months, and the Reformatory graduates for an average of 24.26 ($\pm$1.05) months.[19]

Coming now to a comparison of the institutional experiences of the two groups of offenders as shown in Table 9, we note a marked

TABLE 9. INSTITUTIONAL EXPERIENCES OF JUVENILE COURT GROUP IN AGE-SPAN TWENTY-FOUR TO TWENTY-NINE YEARS, AND OF REFORMATORY GROUP IN AGE-SPAN THIRTY TO THIRTY-FIVE YEARS (PERCENTAGES)

	JUVENILE COURT GROUP*	REFORMATORY GROUP†
Schools for feebleminded and institutions for defective delinquents	3.2	7.4
Reformatories	15.1	1.7
Prisons	31.1	23.3
Jails	50.6	67.6
Number of penal experiences	*312*	*421*

* Derived from Appendix B, 68.
† Derived from *Later Criminal Careers*, Appendix C, Table 2–H139.

difference in the nature of the institutional treatment of the two groups, obviously due in large measure to the difference in their

[17] Derived from Appendix B, 67; *Later Criminal Careers*, Appendix D, 46.
[18] Appendix C, 12; *Later Criminal Careers*, Appendix D, 46.
[19] Appendix C, 13; *Later Criminal Careers*, Appendix D, 49.

chronological ages. This is due partly to a belated diagnosis of mental defect in the older group and is also related to age limitations in commitment laws. The large proportion of commitments to institutions for mental defectives among the older group and in commitments to reformatories in the younger group are clearly attributable to the two influences mentioned above. On the other hand, the high percentage of jail commitments among the older men, with a corresponding decrease in prison commitments, is partially attributable to the "settling down" or deteriorative effect of aging beyond the peak of maturation, which all persons sooner or later experience.

* * * * *

In the foregoing analysis we have answered, at least partially, the query whether it is primarily arrival at a particular age-span or achievement of a requisite degree of maturation, regardless of the specific age-level at which this occurs, that explains the significant improvement in the conduct of offenders with the passing of the years.[20]

Apparently abandonment of criminal conduct does not occur at any specific chronologic age-level, but rather after the passage of a certain length of time from the point of first expression of definite delinquent trends. On the whole, if the acts of delinquency begin very early in life, they are apparently abandoned at a relatively early stage of manhood, provided various mental abnormalities do not counteract the natural tendency to maturation that brings with it greater powers of reflection, inhibition, postponement of immediate desires for more legitimate later ones, the power to learn from experience, and like constituents of a mature personality. If, on the other hand, the acts of delinquency begin in adolescence, the delinquent tendency seems to run its course into a later stage of adulthood, again provided the natural maturation process is not inter-

---

[20] Not all factors significant in original propensity to delinquency are necessarily significant in determining at what stage criminality will be abandoned. This distinction has been alluded to in our previous works.

fered with. In both instances, distribution of the delinquents into comparable proportions of persistent offenders and non-offenders occurs not at any particular age-level but rather during a quite definite period beyond the age when delinquent impulses first express themselves in antisocial acts. In both instances, it appears that if the offenders are to reform at all before the wasting effects of age have intervened, their improvement in conduct occurs after they have "gotten delinquency out of their systems," as it were, that is, after the antisocial impulses have run their course; and this process seems to take about the same length of time regardless of whether delinquent conduct first occurs in childhood or during adolescence.

Obviously, many questions are raised by these findings, answers to which the materials obtainable for this research cannot give. Why is it, for example, that one group of offenders begin their criminal careers later than others? Do differences in ethnic origins, in intelligence, in temperament account for this?[21] Or may the explanation be found in other differences? Much exploration would be necessary to arrive at the answers. But it seems evident from even the brief sampling reflected in footnote 21 that there are significant differences between the two groups. It may well be that such differences in make-up account for the variation in average age at which these two groups first embarked upon delinquent careers. The important points are, however, that with these differences in the characteristics of the two groups, their behavior, once they

[21] A comparison of the nativity of the parents of the two groups indicated that twice the proportion of parents of the Reformatory group as of the Juvenile Court group were native born (27.2 per cent and 13.2 per cent). (Derived from *500 Criminal Careers*, p. 118, and *One Thousand Juvenile Delinquents*, p. 303, Table 2.)

Further, a comparison of the intelligence of the two groups shows a higher proportion of persons of normal intelligence among the Juvenile Court group (41.6 per cent against 33 per cent) and a lower proportion of definitely feebleminded (13.1 per cent against 20.6 per cent). (Derived from *One Thousand Juvenile Delinquents*, p. 102, and *500 Criminal Careers*, p. 156.)

A comparison of the mental condition of the two groups as ascertained in their early years shows the presence of mental disease or personality distortions of one sort or another among a lower proportion of the Juvenile Court group than among the Reformatory graduates (55.7 per cent and 72.7 per cent). (Derived from *One Thousand Juvenile Delinquents*, p. 310, Table 37, and *Later Criminal Careers*, p. 276, Table 70.)

have embarked on delinquency, follows a pattern largely determined by the underlying process of maturation,[22] and that this pattern is uniform, being somehow related to the span of time inter-
vening between the average age of offenders at the origin of their
delinquency and the passage of a certain number of years thereafter. Two series of offenders, quite different in make-up and background and significantly different in the fact that one began to be
delinquent (on the average) five years before the other, have been
shown to resemble each other strikingly in conduct, *not at similar
ages, but rather at a similar distance removed from the time they
began to be delinquent.* This would seem to indicate that what
may be called, after Quételet,[23] "the propensity to criminality" has
a more or less definite life span regardless of the age at which delinquent behavior actually begins. Of course, it may be that as the
two groups approach old age they will tend more and more to resemble each other in behavior, not at the same distance from the delinquent starting point, but rather at the same chronological age-
levels. But certainly in the segment of the life cycle so far analyzed,
it seems clear that it is not arrival at a certain age that determines
the nature of delinquency, but rather arrival at a certain distance
from the age at which delinquency began.

Under such a theory, the age (on the average) at which delinquency begins is significant as fixing the point at which the symp-

[22] To avoid clumsiness of phraseology, we have not used the expressions "maturation-
disintegration" or "maturation-settling down." Such expressions, however, more accurately
express the processes involved; for it is not only the achievement of a certain degree of
physical-intellectual-emotional maturity and integration that leads to abandonment of
criminality or change to less aggressive and less serious forms of misbehavior on the part of
former offenders, but the gradual loss of such qualities as initiative, recklessness, daring,
and physical health. This matter is discussed in Chapter XXII.

[23] M. A. Quételet, *A Treatise on Man and the Development of His Faculties,* translated
from the French, 1842, p. 82. "Supposing men to be placed in similar circumstances, I call
the greater or less probability of committing crime, the propensity to crime. . . . I have
said that the circumstances in which men are placed ought to be similar, that is to say,
equally favourable, both in the existence of objects likely to excite the propensity and in the
facility of committing the crime. It is not enough that a man may merely have the intention
to do evil, he must also have the opportunity and the means. Thus the propensity to crime
may be the same in France as in England, without, on that account, the *morality* of the
nations being the same."

toms of abnormal functioning of the maturation process first manifest themselves in the form of delinquent conduct of a kind serious and consistent enough to be called to the attention of the authorities. Given a sufficient period of time, plus an equipment not unfavorable, it may be expected that a significant proportion of such offenders will abandon their criminality either because they have achieved sufficient integration to seek more legitimate goals for their desires or to inhibit or sublimate their antisocial impulses or because they have passed the stage in which they had the energy and daring to commit crimes. Some who never achieve a sufficient degree of maturation until they have finally lapsed into those forms of antisocial behavior which require less and less energy, planfulness, and daring, such as drunkenness and vagrancy, will not abandon a life of crime. But those who do reform will do so after an adequate maturation time has elapsed since the first signs of delinquency, and this regardless of whether they were first delinquent at around nine years of age (on the average) or around fifteen.[24] We shall discuss this concept further in Chapter XXII.

[24] The special class of offenders who do not really commit their first crimes until they are men of twenty-five or more are unrepresented in the two series under discussion; and they probably represent quite a different type of person and different problems of criminogenesis and reform.

Chapter IX

COMPARISON OF REFORMED AND UNREFORMED
OFFENDERS

IN the previous chapter it was inferentially determined that the biological process of maturation is the chief factor in the behavior changes of criminals. Whether, with the passage of time, certain factors—personal and social—in the early lives of our former juvenile delinquents inhibited or accelerated the natural process of maturation and the growing differentiation between the two groups may be at least partially determined from a series of three comparisons dealing with the characteristics of the delinquents at the time of, or prior to, their appearance in the Boston Juvenile Court. From comparisons between (1) those who reformed and those who continued to recidivate; (2) those who reformed when they were under twenty-one and those who did not reform until they were older; and (3) those who remained serious delinquents and those who became minor offenders, there should at least emerge suggestive clues to the factors which tend to aid or hamper the biological process of maturation.

The first comparison is the subject of the present chapter.[1] The other two will be dealt with in the succeeding chapters.

[1] In comparing those juvenile delinquents who reformed during the fifteen-year span with those who did not, we are omitting from consideration 40 youths whom we had to designate as "erratic" offenders during the fifteen-year span because they did not definitely progress from more to less serious delinquency or to non-delinquency. Two of the 40 were non-delinquents during the first and second five-year follow-up periods and serious offenders in the third; 2 were minor offenders during the first five-year span, serious offenders during the second, and non-delinquents during the third; 5 were non-delinquents during the first five years but serious or minor offenders during the second and third. Six were serious offenders during the first five-year span, minor in the second, and again serious in the third; 4 were minor offenders during the first and second five years and serious offenders in the third; 5 were minor offenders during the first five-year span and serious offenders during the second and third; 4 were non-delinquents during the first and second follow-up spans and minor in the third; one was a minor offender during the first five-year period, non-delinquent during the second, and minor during the third; 4 were serious delinquents during the first five-year period, non-delinquents during the second, and again serious

RESEMBLANCES

The factors in which the reformed and unreformed resemble each other must be considered neutral factors; they cannot hold the explanation of the differences in the ultimate conduct of the young delinquents who are under scrutiny. It is well to review these resemblances, however, because, in a negative sense, they are as important as the differences.

The two groups of boys are in similar proportions white and Negro. They resemble each other in the average age of the younger of their living parents, in the average difference between the ages of their parents, and in the average age of the younger of their parents at time of marriage. The same proportion of those delinquents who ultimately reformed as of those who continued to recidivate had in childhood enjoyed the affectionate regard of their mothers. In both groups, also, the proportion of mothers who had to work to supplement the family income was the same. The two groups further resemble each other in being to an equal extent the products of homes which had been broken by the desertion, separation, divorce, or death of their parents before the appearance of the boys in the Boston Juvenile Court.[2] The two groups were to a uniform extent reared in homes and neighborhoods in which the conditions of life were poor and difficult. The families from which the reformed and unreformed sprang were of equal size, and the same percentage of each were compelled to seek the aid of social welfare agencies during the childhood of the boys.

offenders during the third; one was a non-delinquent during the first follow-up period, a minor offender during the second, and again a non-delinquent during the third; one was a serious offender during the first five-year span, a non-delinquent in the second, and a minor offender during the third; and 5 were non-delinquents during the first five years, serious delinquents during the second, and minor during the third.

A comparison of the characteristics of this group of 40 youths with the characteristics of those who reformed during the fifteen-year span, and in turn with those who continued to be serious or minor offenders, indicates that the "erratic" offenders have certain characteristics of each one of these three groups. It seemed best, therefore, to omit them from consideration to insure the purity of the comparison.

[2] At that time, it will be recalled, they were of an average age of thirteen and a half years.

Those who reformed and those who continued to recidivate were also alike in respect to health, as determined at the time of their examination in the Judge Baker Foundation Clinic. The two groups had in equal proportion belonged to gangs in childhood or had spent considerable time loafing in the streets with other boys. And, finally, both groups began to work at the same average age and were in equal proportion engaged in street trades during the earliest years of their industrial activity.

SLIGHT DIFFERENCES

There is a series of very slight differences in the characteristics of those juvenile delinquents who reformed during the fifteen-year follow-up span and those who did not, to which it is well to give separate consideration. In these respects, the differences in incidence of a particular characteristic between the two groups are between 4 per cent and 10 per cent, and although these small individual differences may of themselves be of little account, they are of a kind which, cumulatively, foreshadow a trend of significant difference between the two groups.

The delinquents who eventually reformed and those who did not differed thus slightly as follows: A higher proportion of those who reformed than of the unreformed were of foreign birth; the parents of the former had not been in the United States for quite as long a time as the latter. The parents of the reformed group had slightly less formal schooling than the parents of the youths who continued to recidivate—a finding explained by the slightly higher proportion of foreign-born parents among those offenders who eventually reformed.

Continuing the comparison of slight differences between those who reformed during the fifteen-year follow-up span and those who continued to recidivate, it is found that the former had, in somewhat higher proportion than the latter, been reared by parents whose conjugal relations were good, and that a slightly higher proportion of the fathers of the former had borne a real affection for their sons. A higher percentage of the youths who reformed than of the persistent offenders came from homes of relatively comfortable economic status.[3]

More of the reformed than of the unreformed were reared in homes in which the ideals were wholesome and in which there was no delinquency among either their parents or their brothers and sisters; and the proportion of families in which there was a history of mental disease or defect was somewhat lower in the former group than among the persistent offenders.

A slightly higher proportion of the juvenile delinquents who eventually reformed than of those who continued to recidivate were first-born children. A slightly lower proportion of the former than of the latter suffered abnormal environmental experiences, such as being separated from their homes because of conditions sufficiently serious, unusual, or marked to create a breach in their family or community ties.

As regards intelligence, it is found that a somewhat higher proportion of those who reformed were of normal or superior intelligence; and there was a slightly lower proportion of school retardates in the reformed group.

Those who eventually reformed had bad habits in childhood to a slightly lesser extent than those who did not; and slightly more of the former had in childhood belonged to clubs and other supervised groups for the use of leisure time.

In regard to the age at first arrest of those who reformed and those who did not, the former were somewhat older at the time of their first arrest than were the recidivists; and in the reformed group, also, slightly less time had elapsed between their first misbehavior and first arrest. One more factor of small difference is found in the lower proportion of lone offenders[4] among those who eventually reformed; among the reformed there were slightly

---

[3] In that there were sufficient resources in the family to maintain them for at least four months if their income ceased; most of these "comfortable" homes were only a little over the poverty line, however. See Appendix A for definition of *Economic Status*.

[4] As reflected in the particular offense which brought them before the Boston Juvenile Court.

more who had committed their offenses in the company of other boys.

MARKED DIFFERENCES

We now come to a series of factors in which the differences between those who reformed during the fifteen-year span and those who continued to be delinquent are quite marked. Because these differences reveal much of significance, it is well to present them in detailed tabular form.

First, there are three factors which appear to reflect a difference in the ethnic origin and associated background cultures of the reformed group and the recidivists.

In Table 10 is a comparison of the birthplace of the parents of

TABLE 10. REFORMED AND UNREFORMED: BIRTHPLACE OF PARENTS
(PERCENTAGES)

	REFORMED		UNREFORMED	
	Fathers	*Mothers*	*Fathers*	*Mothers*
United States	15.5	17.3	19.5	19.5
Italy	35.7	34.6	31.8	30.6
Russia, Poland, Lithuania	24.1	25.3	14.6	14.7
Ireland	6.9	10.7	18.2	19.3
Other	17.8	12.1	15.9	15.9
Total number of known cases	*291*	*289*	*446*	*441*

the juvenile delinquents who reformed and those who did not, from which it is evident that the reformed group were in significantly excessive proportion sons of fathers born in Slavic lands, while the recidivists were in greater degree sons of fathers born in Ireland. The same trend is seen in regard to the birthplace of the mothers of these boys, although not in quite as marked degree.

That these differences may have some explanation in variations in ethnic stock and associated cultures is further reflected in Table 11, in which the religion of the parents of the two groups is compared. In this connection, it must be borne in mind that parents of

TABLE 11. REFORMED AND UNREFORMED: RELIGION OF PARENTS
(PERCENTAGES)

	REFORMED	UNREFORMED
Both Catholic	66.4	81.4
Both Protestant	9.9	7.7
Both Hebrew	21.6	8.8
Mixed	2.1	2.1
Total number of known cases	*283*	*430*

Irish birth were mainly Catholics (96.6 per cent) while those of Russian, Polish, or Lithuanian birth were mostly Hebrews (60.9 per cent). From this table it will be seen that a higher proportion of youths of Catholic parents continued to recidivate than reformed during the fifteen-year follow-up span; while an appreciably higher proportion of youths of Hebrew parentage reformed than continued to be delinquent.

The facts derived from Tables 10 and 11 must be very carefully interpreted in relation to the factors which are about to be presented. From Table 12, for example, it will be noted that a signifi-

TABLE 12. REFORMED AND UNREFORMED: DISCIPLINE BY PARENTS
(PERCENTAGES)

	REFORMED		UNREFORMED	
	Fathers	*Mothers*	*Fathers*	*Mothers*
Good	8.6	5.0	1.3	.3
Fair	29.7	31.0	25.3	25.5
Poor	61.7	64.0	73.4	74.2
Total number of known cases	*185*	*239*	*297*	*385*

cantly higher proportion of those who reformed during the fifteen-year follow-up span than of the youths who continued to recidivate were sons of fathers and mothers who had been satisfactory disciplinarians. Whether or not the better disciplinary practices of some parents than of others bear any relationship to their ethnic, religious, or cultural background remains at present a matter of conjecture. But one is tempted to raise the question at this point whether those parents who were good disciplinarians did not make a real contribution to the straightening out of the boys, as reflected in the significantly higher proportion of reformed youths in the group whose parents were firm, fair, and consistent disciplinarians than among the others.

Another significant difference between the young men who reformed during the fifteen-year follow-up span and those who continued to commit crimes appears in Table 13, in the difference

TABLE 13. REFORMED AND UNREFORMED: MENTAL CONDITION
(PERCENTAGES)

	REFORMED	UNREFORMED
No mental disease, distortion, marked liabilities of personality, or marked adolescent instability	51.2	39.5
Mental disease or distortion	9.6	17.3
Marked personality liabilities or marked adolescent instability	39.2	43.2
Total number of known cases	*303*	*474*

in their mental condition as determined at the time of their examination at the Judge Baker Foundation Clinic. From this table it is clear that a significantly higher proportion of the youths who eventually reformed were without the burden of abnormal mental conditions or personality deviations of one sort or another; while a markedly higher percentage of the recidivists than of the reformed group were tainted with some mental disease or distortion, or burdened with marked personality liabilities.[5]

[5] Incidentally, the findings indicate that, however vague certain psychiatric diagnoses may be, the sharp eye of the experienced clinician can detect deviations of personality and temperament early in childhood. There has been considerable criticism of psychiatric diagnosis on the ground of its often roughly defined categorization; but as Table 13 indicates, the diagnoses made during the childhood of offenders turn out to have an appreciably high association with their conduct many years after the diagnoses were made.

TABLE 14. REFORMED AND UNREFORMED: SCHOOL CONDUCT
(PERCENTAGES)

	REFORMED	UNREFORMED
No school misconduct	25.2	12.2
Truancy	65.2	77.2
No truancy, but other misbehavior	9.6	10.6
Total number of known cases	250	386

As Table 14 shows, there was a higher proportion of school truants or boys who otherwise misbehaved in school among those
who continued to be delinquent than among those who reformed.
This would seem to indicate that impulses to misconduct that are
likely to persist manifest themselves early in antisocial or otherwise abnormal reactions to school life.

Closely bound up with this finding is one in Table 15 concern-

TABLE 15. REFORMED AND UNREFORMED: AGE AT FIRST KNOWN
MISBEHAVIOR (PERCENTAGES)

	REFORMED	UNREFORMED
Under 9 years	33.8	37.4
9 to 12 years	43.5	49.8
13 to 16 years	22.7	12.8
Average age	*12.0 years*	*10.5 years*
Total number of known cases	207	305

ing the age at first known misbehavior of those delinquents who
continued to commit crimes and those who did not. It is note-
worthy that almost twice the proportion of youths who reformed
as of the persistent offenders did not begin their delinquencies
until reaching the higher age groups. This would seem to indicate
that where the maladjustment known as "delinquency" begins
early in life it is rooted more deeply, is of a tougher fibre, and
more probably is related to the hereditary, biologic make-up of
the individual than in cases where it does not begin to manifest it-

self until the adolescent years, when it may merely reflect a temporary or accidental deviation from an otherwise normal personality.

*   *   *   *   *

These are the most striking points of difference between the reformed and the unreformed. It is evident, even in the slight differences and assuredly in the more marked differences, that those who abandoned their criminalistic behavior were more favorably endowed and circumstanced than were those who continued to recidivate. As a group, they were in better mental health, they had been markedly better disciplined in boyhood, they did not begin to show signs of delinquent conduct as early in their development as did the men who continued to recidivate, and they had not misbehaved as much in school. And the slight differences between the groups tend to substantiate the facts that the former were reared in more wholesome early surroundings and that they had an appreciably better biological endowment than the recidivists, as suggested by less history of mental disease or defect in the members of their families and as reflected in their own higher intelligence.

Assuming the importance of the process of maturation in counteracting and in many cases finally stopping or diverting an original tendency toward delinquent behavior, the foregoing findings would seem to indicate that there are certain superior qualities of Nature, as well as of Nurture, which distinguish the offenders who reformed within a fifteen-year span following their control by the Juvenile Court from those who continued to commit crimes. In the former, the natural maturation process was facilitated, or at least not blocked, with the passing of the years; in the latter, aging did not bring with it that development and integration of forces which are translated into social adaptability and law-abiding conduct. Whether further aging will in a substantial number of cases result in adequate maturation and abandonment of criminalistic expression can only be determined by further follow-up investigations.

Chapter X

COMPARISON OF YOUNGER AND OLDER
REFORMED OFFENDERS

IN the preceding chapter we compared the juvenile delinquents who reformed during the fifteen-year span following contact with the Boston Juvenile Court and the Clinic of the Judge Baker Foundation and those who continued to recidivate. The analysis indicated that the differences between the two groups lie chiefly in the more favorable hereditary and environmental background of those who reformed. In this chapter we are concerned only with those of our juvenile delinquents who reformed, in order to determine if possible why some were younger than others when so marked a change in behavior occurred.

It should be recalled that of the 318 youths who reformed before the end of the fifteen-year span, 19 were under twelve years of age at reformation, 44 were between twelve and fifteen years old, 75 were between fifteen and eighteen, 72 were between eighteen and twenty-one, 58 were between twenty-one and twenty-four, 41 were between twenty-four and twenty-seven years old, and 9 were between twenty-seven and thirty years of age.[1] Their average age at reformation was eighteen and one-half years. A comparison of the characteristics of these youths in the various age-spans indicates that the sharpest differences are between those who reformed when they were under twenty-one and those who reformed when they were older; we therefore take this age as the dividing line. Such a comparison may furnish some clues to the factors which facilitated the earlier reformation of some of the delinquents.

RESEMBLANCES

Clearly, no clues to the reason for earlier or later reformation are to be looked for in the resemblances between the two groups of

---

[1] Appendix B, 77.

reformed delinquents. But by determining the points of resemblance those factors which could not possibly hold the explanation for the difference in age at reformation will at least be ruled out of consideration.

The two groups come from families of equal size, and the birth rank of the offender among his brothers and sisters is the same in both; the younger of their parents were of like age at the time of the examination of the boys by the Judge Baker Foundation Clinic; a like proportion of the parents regarded them with affection; they were reared in homes of equal economic status; their mothers were to the same extent gainfully employed; the childhood homes of the two groups had been equally lacking in physical comforts.

The two groups further resembled each other in that a like proportion came from families in which there was a history of mental disease or defect, and from homes broken by death, separation, desertion, or divorce. And, finally, those who reformed when they were under twenty-one were of the same average age at the onset of their delinquent careers as were those who did not abandon their delinquent behavior until later.

SLIGHT DIFFERENCES

We next consider a series of factors in which slight differences are evident in the background and characteristics of those who reformed at an early age and those whose rehabilitation did not occur until later. Although each of these differences may of itself be quite insignificant (because there is only a 4 per cent to 10 per cent variation in the incidence of certain sub-categories of the factors involved) they may, in combination, at least suggest clues as to why some of the youths reformed earlier than others, despite their like average age at the onset of delinquent conduct.

Those who reformed when they were under twenty-one were, in slightly greater proportion than the others, sons of foreign-born parents; and they were to a lesser degree sons of parents of mixed nationality (one parent native born, one foreign). One reason for their earlier reformation may be that although the delinquency of children of foreign-born parents is to a certain extent engendered by the situation of culture conflict in which they find themselves, such delinquency is not always deep-seated and, therefore, not of such long duration. A comparison made elsewhere between those of the 1,000 juvenile delinquents who were native sons of native parents and those who were native sons of foreign-born parents revealed that such differences as there were between them sprang mainly from the situation of culture conflict in which the native-born sons of foreign-born parents had been placed.[2]

It is noted that those whose reform came early in life were in slightly greater proportion than the others the sons of Catholic and Protestant families. Their mothers were younger at marriage than the mothers of the group that reformed later, and the difference in age between the parents was greater. These facts are probably associated with the greater proportion of foreign-born mothers among the earlier reformed men. (Foreign-born women marry early and they are likely to marry men who are considerably older than themselves; such marriages are customary in foreign countries.) Also associated with the higher proportion of foreign-born parents of the younger than of the older-reformed group is the more limited schooling of the parents of the former, who could not have had the opportunities in foreign countries for even a common school education.

The youths who reformed when they were under twenty-one are, to a greater extent than those whose change for the better occurred later, the sons of parents whose conjugal relations were good. The early-reformed group were likewise, to a slightly greater degree than the others, the offspring of families in which delinquency among the parents or brothers and sisters was not common. They were also members of families who caused less concern to social agencies than did the families of the youths who did not reform until they were over twenty-one, and this despite the fact that both

[2] Glueck, Eleanor T., Culture Conflict and Juvenile Delinquency, *Mental Hygiene,* 21: 46, January 1937.

groups came of families of equally poor economic status. Apparently these families were better able to manage their own problems than were the families of youths who reformed when they were older. This fact becomes even more significant when we consider that during their boyhood the families of the younger-reformed group lived in even poorer neighborhoods than did the families of the others.

As for the youths themselves, those who were under twenty-one when they reformed were in slightly better health at the time of their examination in the Judge Baker Foundation Clinic than were those who were over that age. They were slightly younger when they began to work, but had fewer early abnormal environmental experiences (i.e., they were to a slightly less extent than the older-reformed group separated from their parental homes because the homes were broken or otherwise inadequate for the rearing of children).

The younger-reformed group did not idle about in the streets as much with other boys as did the older, although they had in boyhood been to a like extent members of gangs. The boys who reformed earlier in life were not the victims of bad habits to so great an extent as were the later-reformed. A slightly lower proportion of the former group had been lone offenders—a fact reflected in the manner in which they had committed the particular offenses which brought them before the Boston Juvenile Court. This would appear to indicate that they were perhaps more suggestible than the others and hence fundamentally less inclined to antisocial behavior. The youths who reformed when they were under twenty-one had behaved better in school and were school truants to a lesser extent than the others.

Keeping in mind these slight differences between the boys who reformed at an early age and those whose abandonment of delinquent ways was postponed to later years, let us next consider the more marked differences in the background and characteristics of the two groups. For in these differences we should find some explanation of why certain offenders reformed earlier than others, despite the fact that the average age at onset of delinquent conduct was the same in both groups.

MARKED DIFFERENCES

It is first of all significant that those who reformed when under twenty-one were on the average a half year younger at the time of first arrest. As both groups were of the same average age when first delinquent, it is evident that the early-reformed came to the official attention of legal authorities sooner after the onset of their misbehavior manifestations than did those who did not reform until they were twenty-one or older. This is seen from Table 16. It is reasonable

TABLE 16. OFFENDERS WHO REFORMED BEFORE AND AFTER AGE TWENTY-ONE: TIME BETWEEN FIRST DELINQUENCY AND FIRST ARREST (PERCENTAGES)

	REFORMED BEFORE 21	REFORMED AFTER 21
None (first offense)	15.2	6.0
One year or less	39.4	31.3
Over one year	45.4	62.7
Total number of known cases	*132*	67

to assume that prompt arrest after delinquency began had a salutary influence upon certain offenders, causing them to modify their antisocial ways sooner. That this is not the only reason, however, for their readier abandonment of delinquent behavior is reflected in the following comparisons, which to a large extent indicate that those who reformed when they were young were more advantaged than those whose favorable change of behavior did not occur until later in life.

First, a comparison in Table 17 of the moral standards of the families of the two groups reveals a significant difference in favor of those who reformed while still under twenty-one. It is clear that the early-reformed group were reared in homes of better moral standards than the later-reformed group.

TABLE 17. OFFENDERS WHO REFORMED BEFORE AND AFTER AGE TWENTY-
ONE: FAMILY MORAL STANDARDS (PERCENTAGES)

	REFORMED BEFORE 21	REFORMED AFTER 21
Good	15.5	12.9
Fair	20.6	11.8
Poor	63.9	75.3
Total number of known cases	*194*	*93*

A comparison, in Table 18, of the disciplinary practices of the parents of the two groups of offenders further reveals the more favored background of those who abandoned their life of crime when they were still under twenty-one years of age. Obviously the disciplinary measures of the fathers of the youths who reformed earlier were distinctly better than of the fathers of those who did not abandon delinquent conduct until they were older. This is likewise true of the disciplinary practices of the mothers.

TABLE 18. OFFENDERS WHO REFORMED BEFORE AND AFTER AGE TWENTY-
ONE: DISCIPLINE BY PARENTS (PERCENTAGES)

	REFORMED BEFORE 21		REFORMED AFTER 21	
	Fathers	*Mothers*	*Fathers*	*Mothers*
Good	11.0	7.2	3.1	2.6
Fair	34.6	32.9	18.5	21.8
Poor	54.4	59.9	78.4	75.6
Total number of known cases	*127*	*167*	*65*	*78*

That sounder discipline by their parents may have had something to do with the earlier reformation of the one group of offenders appears to be the case. However, in the light of further information about these two groups of youths we are led to the conclusion that it is not alone better disciplinary practices which bring about early reformation but also the fact that certain kinds of children respond more effectively to discipline than others. In this connection, a comparison in Table 19 of the intelligence of the two groups of boys

TABLE 19. OFFENDERS WHO REFORMED BEFORE AND AFTER AGE TWENTY-ONE: INTELLIGENCE (PERCENTAGES)

	REFORMED BEFORE 21	REFORMED AFTER 21
Superior	9.9	3.7
Normal	42.4	32.7
Dull	25.1	35.5
Borderline	13.8	15.9
Defective	8.8	12.2
Total number of known cases	*203*	*107*

makes it evident that those youths who abandoned their delinquent acts when they were still under twenty-one were of higher intelligence than those whose reform was delayed. Furthermore, those who reformed earlier were not as much retarded in their school work (that is, behind grade for their age) as the others. This is shown in Table 20.

TABLE 20. OFFENDERS WHO REFORMED BEFORE AND AFTER AGE TWENTY-ONE: SCHOOL RETARDATION (PERCENTAGES)

	REFORMED BEFORE 21	REFORMED AFTER 21
Not retarded	24.9	10.1
Retarded one year	26.4	24.2
Retarded two or more years	48.7	65.7
Total number of known cases	*193*	*99*

The greater school retardation of those whose reformation was delayed was not due, of course, entirely to their lower intelligence. In comparing the psychiatric condition of the two groups at the time of their appearance before the Boston Juvenile Court at an average age of thirteen and a half years, we find a further significant differentiation between them (Table 21) which throws light on the reasons for less school retardation in the group that abandoned delinquent conduct comparatively early in life. Obviously

TABLE 21. OFFENDERS WHO REFORMED BEFORE AND AFTER AGE TWENTY-ONE: MENTAL CONDITION (PERCENTAGES)

	REFORMED BEFORE 21	REFORMED AFTER 21
No mental disease, distortion, marked personality liabilities, or marked adolescent instability	56.5	38.9
Mental disease or distortion	8.1	13.0
Marked personality liabilities or marked adolescent instability	35.4	48.1
Total number of known cases	209	108

those who reformed when they were under twenty-one were far less burdened with mental disease, distortion, or marked liabilities of personality than were those whose reform was delayed until later in life.

The next two factors do not, like the others, favor the group whose reformation occurred early in life, but in both instances the

TABLE 22. OFFENDERS WHO REFORMED BEFORE AND AFTER AGE TWENTY-ONE: MEMBERSHIP IN SUPERVISED RECREATIONAL GROUPS (PERCENTAGES)

	REFORMED BEFORE 21	REFORMED AFTER 21
No	75.9	61.0
Yes	24.1	39.0
Total number of known cases	199	105

differences may be legitimately explained by the difference in the age of the two groups. In connection with these two factors, it should be mentioned that at the time of their appearance before the Boston Juvenile Court, the youths who reformed earlier in life were of an average age of twelve years and nine months; while the group whose reformation occurred later were of an average age of fourteen years. It is not surprising, therefore, to find (Table 22) that up to the time of this particular appearance in the Boston

Juvenile Court, a significantly lower proportion of the former than of the latter had never been members of well-supervised recreational groups; being younger they had had less opportunity to join recreational groups.

In regard to the nature of their early employment—that is, the jobs they were in at the time of or just prior to their appearance in the Boston Juvenile Court—there is also a significant difference, shown in Table 23, between the two groups of offenders. The

TABLE 23. OFFENDERS WHO REFORMED BEFORE AND AFTER AGE TWENTY-ONE: NATURE OF EARLY EMPLOYMENT (PERCENTAGES)

	REFORMED BEFORE 21	REFORMED AFTER 21
Street trades or night work	62.0	52.5
Other	38.0	47.5
Total number of known cases	*142*	80

greater proportion in street trades among the boys who abandoned delinquent behavior earlier is clearly attributable to their ages at the time of appearance in the Boston Juvenile Court. The younger children just out of school, or doing part-time work during their school years, naturally tended to enter the street trades, moving into other types of employment as they grew older.

*   *   *   *   *

Great caution is, of course, necessary in drawing any positive conclusions from one sample of cases about the reasons why certain of our juvenile delinquents reformed earlier than others. We wish first to record the fact itself as one worthy of study; and then to venture the suggestion that the earlier reformation of some offenders may be accounted for by their better innate equipment, early environment, more intelligent discipline by parents, and the apparently helpful effect of earlier arrest and contact with the juvenile court. On the whole, it is safe to say that the natural process of maturation that accompanies aging was facilitated by more favorable characteristics and circumstances among those who reformed when they were still under twenty-one. This is of great significance in the light of the fact that the two groups of boys under study were of the same average age at the time of the onset of their delinquent behavior.

Chapter XI

COMPARISON OF SERIOUS AND MINOR OFFENDERS

IN the two previous chapters we were concerned with comparisons of the offenders who reformed and those who continued to recidivate, and the offenders who reformed when they were under twenty-one and those who did not abandon delinquent behavior until they were twenty-one or over.

We now turn our attention to a comparison of those of the continuing offenders who remained serious criminals throughout the fifteen-year follow-up period and those who became minor offenders before the end of that time, to see if we can derive any clues to this differentiation in behavior which has occurred with the passing of time.

RESEMBLANCES

A comparison of those of our juvenile delinquents who persisted in serious delinquency throughout the fifteen-year span and those who became minor offenders shows a number of resemblances between the two.

First of all, it should be mentioned that the average age of the younger of their parents was the same at the time of marriage, and that the difference in age between the younger and older of their parents was the same. Both sets of parents, also, had the same limited schooling. Furthermore, like proportions of the serious and minor offenders were reared in homes in which the moral standards were poor and in which other members of their immediate families (brothers, sisters, or parents) were delinquents. They came from families of equal size, and the offender's rank among his brothers and sisters was the same in both groups.

It is also significant that the youths who continued to be serious delinquents and those who became minor offenders sprang from families in which there was a like incidence of mental disease or defect. Further, both serious and minor delinquents were reared in homes in which the living conditions were poor. And social agencies were, during the boyhood of the serious and minor offenders, to an equal extent actively concerned in the welfare of their families.

The serious and minor delinquents were of the same average age at the time of their first arrest. They were, further, of the same age when they began to work. They entered the same kind of early employment, and to a like extent they never belonged to well-supervised recreational clubs. And, finally, at the time of their examination at the Judge Baker Foundation Clinic (when both groups were of an average age of thirteen and a half years), they were found to be in the same state of health.

Apparently, therefore, none of the above factors of resemblance between the two groups of offenders can have played any noticeable part in their eventual differentiation into serious and minor delinquents.

SLIGHT DIFFERENCES

Turning now to the slight differences between those who continued to be serious offenders and those who became minor delinquents in the fifteen-year follow-up span, we find a number of them in their background and environmental circumstances. These differences do not amount to more than 4 to 10 per cent in the incidence of certain categories of the factors involved.

First, it should be noted that there is a slightly higher proportion of Negroes among those of our juvenile delinquents who continued to be serious offenders during the fifteen-year follow-up span than among those who became petty offenders, and also a slightly higher proportion of men of native birth. Further, although a like proportion of the serious and minor offenders were the sons of Catholic parents, a slightly higher percentage of the serious criminals than of the minor were of Protestant parentage, and a far lower proportion of the serious offenders than of the minor were of Hebrew parents.

A comparison of the average age of the younger of their parents reveals that the parents of the youths who continued to be serious offenders were a little younger than were the parents of those who became minor offenders during the fifteen-year follow-up span. Further, it is evident that the economic circumstances of the parents of the continuously serious offenders were poorer than of those who eventually became minor delinquents. A somewhat higher proportion of the serious offenders than of the minor offenders were reared in homes broken by the death, separation, desertion, or divorce of the parents. Those of our juvenile delinquents who persisted in serious crime had been subjected, to a greater extent than the others, to abnormal environmental experiences of one sort or another during their childhood—i.e., they had left or were removed from their parental homes before they reached an average age of thirteen and a half years, this being partly due to the unsuitability of the homes for the rearing of children. A higher proportion of the mothers of the youths who continued to be serious criminals than of the petty offenders had been gainfully employed outside the home.

It is evident, also, that the serious criminals were, to a greater extent than the petty offenders, reared in homes in which the conjugal relations of the parents were poor. As a group, the continued serious criminals had less affection from their parents than the youths who ultimately became petty delinquents, and the disciplinary practices of their mothers were poorer.

Although it may seem paradoxical, it should be noted that the early neighborhood influences surrounding the homes of our juvenile delinquents were slightly better in the case of the youths who continued to be serious offenders than of those who eventually became minor offenders. This is not the place to enter into any discussion of the effect of neighborhood conditions on delinquency, but there appears to be some evidence here that, although bad neighborhood conditions may play some role in the etiology of crime, they do not necessarily determine its future character.

So much for the background of our youths. As to the offenders themselves, it should be mentioned that a greater proportion of those who persisted in serious delinquencies than of those who eventually became minor offenders had vicious habits in their childhood; and that the former had been street habitués and members of gangs to a greater extent than the latter. As regards mental status and intellectual attainment, it is evident that those youths who persisted in serious crimes were of a somewhat lower level of intelligence, and had among their numbers more school retardates, than the youths who became minor offenders.

Since the differences thus far described between the two groups are slight, it may be that each item in itself is of little significance. It is a fact, however, that, with the exception of the slightly better neighborhood influences surrounding the homes in which the persistently serious offenders were reared, these slight differences taken together weigh in favor of those who became petty offenders. The significance of these minor differences can only be determined, however, in the light of the more marked differences between the two groups of offenders.

MARKED DIFFERENCES

We are now ready to examine a group of factors in the background and early lives of our juvenile delinquents which reveal more marked differences between those who persisted in serious criminality during the fifteen-year follow-up span and those who became minor offenders.

First, a difference is to be noted in the nativity of the parents of serious and minor offenders. Table 24 discloses that the youths who

TABLE 24. SERIOUS AND MINOR OFFENDERS: NATIVITY OF PARENTS (PERCENTAGES)

	SERIOUS OFFENDERS	MINOR OFFENDERS
Parents native born	17.5	9.1
Parents foreign born	67.5	81.8
One parent native born, one foreign born	15.6	9.1
Total number of known cases	206	230

persisted in serious crime were, in markedly greater proportion than the others, the sons of parents one or both of whom was native born; and that those who became minor offenders were to a greater extent sons of foreign-born parents. This suggests that the prior serious offenses of those who eventually became minor offenders were due partly to certain unfavorable circumstances in their early lives growing out of the conflicting cultures of foreign parents and American children.[1]

TABLE 25. SERIOUS AND MINOR OFFENDERS: DISCIPLINE BY MOTHERS
(PERCENTAGES)

	SERIOUS OFFENDERS	MINOR OFFENDERS
Good	–	.5
Fair	17.9	32.0
Poor	82.1	67.5
Total number of known cases	179	206

Another significant difference that we find between those who persisted in serious crimes and those who became minor offenders is in the disciplinary practices of their mothers. It will be noted (Table 25) that the mothers of the persistently serious offenders were substantially worse disciplinarians than the mothers of the delinquents who eventually became minor offenders.

We now arrive at a series of comparisons which concern the offenders themselves.

First of all it is to be noted, in Table 26, that there was a substantial difference in the school conduct of the serious and minor offenders. Obviously those youths who persisted in serious delinquency misbehaved in school, especially as truants, to a markedly greater extent than did the youths who became minor offenders.

[1] Three other comparisons, one dealing with length of time parents were in the United States, another with birthplace of fathers, and the third with birthplace of mothers, have been omitted because they only serve to detail a little the comparison already made in Table 24.

TABLE 26. SERIOUS AND MINOR OFFENDERS: SCHOOL CONDUCT
(PERCENTAGES)

	SERIOUS OFFENDERS	MINOR OFFENDERS
No school misconduct	2.5	22.7
Truancy	92.0	61.1
No truancy, but other misbehavior	5.5	16.2
Total number of known cases	*201*	*185*

We find also substantial differences between those who persisted in serious crime during the fifteen-year follow-up span and those who became minor offenders. From Table 27 we see that a higher proportion of the persistently serious offenders had some mental disease or distortion or some marked personality liability or were

TABLE 27. SERIOUS AND MINOR OFFENDERS: MENTAL CONDITION
(PERCENTAGES)

	SERIOUS OFFENDERS	MINOR OFFENDERS
No mental disease, distortion, marked personality liabilities, or marked adolescent instability	34.1	44.4
Mental disease or distortion	20.4	14.5
Marked personality liabilities or marked adolescent instability	45.5	41.1
Total number of known cases	*226*	*248*

unstable early adolescents (as determined in the Clinic of the Judge Baker Foundation, when they were of an average age of thirteen and a half years) than were the youths who eventually became petty offenders.

We note, also, a substantial difference in the age of first misbehavior in the two groups of offenders (Table 28). It is evident that the continuing serious delinquents were, as a class, younger when they first showed signs of antisocial behavior than were those who became minor offenders.

TABLE 28. SERIOUS AND MINOR OFFENDERS: AGE AT FIRST KNOWN
MISBEHAVIOR (PERCENTAGES)

	SERIOUS OFFENDERS	MINOR OFFENDERS
Under 9 years	42.9	31.6
9 to 12 years	47.4	52.3
13 to 16 years	9.7	16.1
Average age	*9.1 years*	*9.9 years*
Total number of known cases	*156*	*149*

There is one more factor of substantial difference between the
two groups of offenders, which possibly reflects participation in
crime by some offenders through the influence of delinquent companions. The comparison made in Table 29 shows whether or not

TABLE 29. SERIOUS AND MINOR OFFENDERS: ACCOMPLICES IN OFFENSE
FOR WHICH THEY WERE BROUGHT BEFORE BOSTON JUVENILE
COURT (PERCENTAGES)

	SERIOUS OFFENDERS	MINOR OFFENDERS
Offense committed alone	35.3	20.3
Offense committed with one other	24.2	27.7
Offense committed with two or more others	40.5	52.0
Total number of known cases	*190*	*202*

the particular offenses which originally brought the two groups to
the attention of the Boston Juvenile Court were committed alone
or with one or more companions. From this comparison it is evident that a substantially greater proportion of those juvenile delinquents who persisted in serious crime had committed the particular offense which brought them to the Boston Juvenile Court
without the aid of others. In other words, they were apparently to
a less extent of the type who are drawn into criminalistic behavior
through the influence of companions than were those who be-

came minor delinquents. Their criminality was more deep-seated and less subject to the influence of others.

* * * * *

From this series of comparisons of the characteristics of those former juvenile delinquents who continued to be serious offenders during the fifteen-year follow-up span and those who became minor offenders, it is evident that the differences which exist between them are in favor of the minor offenders. The continuing serious delinquents had a worse innate equipment and were reared in less favorable circumstances and conditions than those who eventually became minor offenders. They were to a greater extent characterized by mental disease or distortion or personality liabilities. Their mothers were worse disciplinarians. They had a worse record of school misbehavior, they were younger when their antisocial behavior first manifested itself, and they were to a greater extent of the type who commit their offenses alone. It seems clear that, in the lives of the continued offenders, partially inherited and partially acquired handicaps helped to mold their adulthood and in time differentiated them into persisting serious criminals and petty offenders. Once again, therefore, it is reasonable to conclude that the maturation of the organism which normally may be expected to proceed at a certain pace has been delayed or inhibited by factors in the hereditary and early-conditioned make-up of the offenders, so that it is difficult for some to substitute less aggressive, petty criminality for the serious crimes which they had previously committed, and difficult for all to abandon criminalistic behavior altogether.

This exploration into the Nature and Nurture of our juvenile delinquents has, it seems to us, indicated that the presence of a more favorable hereditary and early social equipment tends to release the forces in the human organism which make for an effective degree of integration of the human personality; and that, because of it, a natural process of maturation with aging can proceed at a normal rate. Where the offender's hereditary and early social equipment is less favorable, however, the process of maturation is hampered and slowed up if not blocked altogether. To what extent the original and early-acquired equipment of the individual offender can be controlled and modified in order to facilitate the normal process of maturation is a fundamental question which requires further study.

Chapter XII

PREDICTING BEHAVIOR DURING A
FIFTEEN-YEAR SPAN

WE have now compared the backgrounds and characteristics
of offenders who reformed before the end of the fifteen-year
span and those who continued to recidivate; of offenders who were
under twenty-one when they abandoned delinquent conduct and
those who were twenty-one or older at reformation; and of offenders who continued to commit serious crimes throughout the fifteen-
year follow-up period and those who became minor offenders before the end of the span. From this series of comparisons have
emerged certain differences between the reformed and unreformed,
on the one hand, and between the serious and minor offenders, on
the other. These differences made it clear that those who reformed,
those who reformed when still under twenty-one, and those who became minor offenders were more advantaged in certain aspects of
their Nature and Nurture than were the others. Although the differences were not necessarily always sharp, they indicated that the
scales were weighted in favor of those who behaved better in each
of the three groups compared. That differences exist between them
shows us the possibility of predicting with reasonable accuracy the
future behavior of offenders appearing in a juvenile tribunal.

It would undoubtedly be helpful to a judge to have answers to
questions such as these: What is the likelihood of reformation of
a particular offender? If an offender's chances of reformation are
high, when is he likely to become non-delinquent? If his chances
of reform are low, what is the likelihood that he will at least become a minor offender? A prediction table which would answer
these queries for judges would obviously be of invaluable aid in
the formulation of a treatment plan in an individual case, based as
it would be upon organized experience with hundreds of similar

cases. We shall therefore turn our attention to the preparation of such a prognostic instrument.

With one exception, all the prediction tables which we have heretofore constructed have been confined to the probable behavior of offenders over a five-year span following a particular form of treatment. The interested reader is referred to Chapter XVIII of *500 Criminal Careers,* in which a prediction table is presented covering the probable behavior of male criminals during a five-year period following the expiration of their sentences to a reformatory; to Chapter XVII of *Five Hundred Delinquent Women* in which the predictive table covers the probable behavior of female offenders during a five-year period following expiration of sentence to a reformatory; and to Chapter XI of *One Thousand Juvenile Delinquents* in which is presented a table showing the probable behavior of boy delinquents during a five-year span following the end of treatment by a juvenile court. In only one of our researches did we attempt the preparation of a prediction table covering the behavior of offenders over a ten-year span; the reader is referred to Chapter XII of *Later Criminal Careers,* in which the behavior of former inmates of the Massachusetts Reformatory, originally reported upon in *500 Criminal Careers,* was carried through a second five-year follow-up span, enabling us to construct a prediction table of the probable behavior of reformatory inmates during the ten years following the expiration of their sentence to the reformatory.

The advantages of a predictive device covering fifteen years rather than five are patent. With such a table, a juvenile court judge would be able more easily to relate his immediate treatment plan for the individual delinquent to a larger segment of the offender's life-cycle. He would thus more readily be able to decide whether an offender appearing before him needed a long or short commitment for the sake of both the protection of society and the offender's own interests; or whether he might just as well be treated extramurally, but for a long rather than a short period of probation. There is an added advantage in the long-term prediction table of giving the judge some idea of the age at which a particular offender is likely to reform, or to change from the commission of more socially aggressive and dangerous behavior to less harmful conduct. While, as has been suggested in Chapter VIII, it is not *per se* arrival at any particular age-span, but rather arrival at an adequate degree of biologic maturity, that accounts for reformation, the ages at which persons of varying backgrounds and traits are likely to become sufficiently mature to abandon their criminalism is ascertainable by the prediction method.

METHOD OF CONSTRUCTING PREDICTION TABLES

Perhaps the reader is not familiar with the method of constructing prediction tables that we have developed in our prior researches, based upon the selection of those factors in the lives of offenders precedent to a particular form of peno-correctional treatment which bear a significant relationship to their conduct following the end of treatment. Once the relationship of all the factors has been established, either the five which are most highly related to behavior during a particular time span or any five of a group of factors significantly associated with the outcome are selected for inclusion in the predictive device. Experience shows that for the purposes of prediction it is not necessary to utilize the five factors bearing the highest relationship to later behavior (as determined either by inspection or, in doubtful cases, through a coefficient of mean square contingency). All that is necessary is that the group of factors selected bear a sufficiently high relationship to later behavior to assure a workable prognostic instrument. The interested reader is referred to the chapters mentioned above for detailed accounts of the selection of the predictive factors in each instance.

Once the factors to be utilized in a particular prediction table have been determined upon, the next step is to set down the percentage of recidivism (total failure) of offenders who are classifiable within each particular sub-category of a factor. For example, in *One Thousand Juvenile Delinquents* it was determined that of those offenders *who had not seriously misbehaved in school* (a sub-category of the factor "School Misconduct"), 72.4 per cent continued to be delinquent during the five-year span following the end of treatment by the Boston Juvenile Court; while of those *who had misbehaved in school*, 91.3 per cent committed crimes during the follow-up span.[1] A similar analysis is applied to all the factors which have high predictive value. These percentages are, then, the likely "failure scores" of offenders who might be classified within any particular sub-category of a factor.

After the percentage of recidivism of offenders falling within each sub-category of the factors to be utilized in the prediction table has been noted, the lowest percentages of recidivism within each of the five factors are summated and then the highest, giving the two possible extremes of a "total failure score" within which zone all the offenders must fall. This zone is divided into score-classes. A tabulation of all offenders is then made which indicates the score-class in which a particular offender belongs, on the one hand, and his actual conduct (criminality or non-criminality) during a particular follow-up span, on the other. From the resulting correlation table it is possible to forecast the probable behavior of other offenders with similar characteristics.

A description of the construction of the particular prediction table which forms the basis of this chapter should clarify the details of the method.

FACTORS FOR PREDICTING BEHAVIOR OVER A FIFTEEN-YEAR SPAN

A correlation of some 60 factors in the lives of our juvenile delinquents with the boys' behavior during the fifteen-year span following the end of oversight by the Boston Juvenile Court revealed that seven factors, *Birthplace of father*, *Birthplace of mother*, *Time parents were in United States*, *Religion of parents*, *Affection of mother for offender*, *Age of offender at first misbehavior*, and *Time between onset of misbehavior manifestations and examination at the Clinic of the Judge Baker Foundation*, were all sufficiently related to the behavior of the delinquents during the fifteen years to be utilized in a prediction table. As experience has

---

[1] See page 187 of that book.

TABLE 30. FACTORS PREDICTIVE OF BEHAVIOR DURING FIFTEEN-YEAR SPAN FOLLOWING TREATMENT BY JUVENILE COURT

PREDICTION FACTORS AND SUB-CATEGORIES*	COEFFICIENT OF MEAN SQUARE CONTINGENCY	PERCENTAGE INCIDENCE OF SERIOUS CRIMINALITY
Birthplace of father	.26	
Russia, Poland, Lithuania		19.0
Italy, Ireland		25.2
Other foreign countries		30.2
United States		45.0
Birthplace of mother	.22	
Russia, Poland, Lithuania		16.0
Italy, Ireland		25.8
United States or foreign countries (except Italy, Ireland, Russia, Poland, Lithuania)		36.1
Time parents were in United States†	.20	
Not for life		22.9
For life		36.8
Religion of parents	.20	
Both Hebrew		11.5
Both Catholic or Protestant		30.0
Mixed		37.5
Age of offender at first misbehavior	.22	
Thirteen to sixteen years		16.1
Nine to twelve years		28.9
Under nine years		35.3

* Whatever contractions have been made of the original more detailed sub-categories of the factors are based on an examination of the raw tables, from which it could readily be determined which sub-categories to combine.

† Refers to length of time in United States of whichever parent had been in this country longer, at time of offender's appearance before the Boston Juvenile Court.

shown it to be unnecessary to use more than five factors in a prediction table, two were eliminated—*Affection of mother for offender* (because information on this point could not be gathered as readily by a court as could factors of a more objective nature); and *Time between onset of misbehavior and examination at the Clinic of the Judge Baker Foundation* (in order not to narrow the usefulness of this prediction table only to cases that happen to be referred by a juvenile court to a clinic for examination and treatment recommendations). This elimination left five factors of adequate predictive capacity, all of which are for practical purposes easily gathered by the court officers (Table 30).

After setting down the factors to be included in the prediction table, their sub-categories, and the percentage of serious criminality (failure-score), the next step was to determine the lowest and the highest possible "failure-score," and finally to score and then classify each case. It should be pointed out that naturally only those cases could be utilized in constructing the prediction table about which all five factors as well as the conduct of the men over the fifteen-year span were known.

The individual scoring of cases was accomplished by a summation of the failure-scores of the sub-categories of the five predictive factors.

The following scoring was done for each case.

Case A: Became a non-criminal before the end of the fifteen-year follow-up span.

Birthplace of father: United States	Failure-score: 45.0 per cent
Birthplace of mother: United States	Failure-score: 36.1 per cent
Time parents were in United States: Life	Failure-score: 36.8 per cent
Religion of parents: Catholic	Failure-score: 30.0 per cent
Age of offender at first misbehavior:	
9–12 years	Failure-score: 28.9 per cent
Total failure-score	176.8 per cent

PREDICTION TABLE

The next step in the procedure was to set out score classes in units of 10.[2] Then each case was put into its particular score group and into its behavior classification during the fifteen-year follow-up span. Behavior was, for the purposes of the present research, divided into (a) non-criminal [that is, became non-delinquent before the end of the fifteen-year follow-up span], (b) serious offender [that

---

[2] The more detailed classification indicated to us which broader classifications are really significant. See Tables 31 and 32 below.

is, was a serious offender throughout the fifteen-year span], (c) minor offender [that is, became a minor offender before the end of the fifteen-year span], and (d) erratic offender.[3]

The summation of the lowest failure-scores of sub-categories within each factor at one end of the scale and the highest at the other established the score classes as ranging between 84.4 and 190.7. In the first tabulation of the cases made in Table 31 a more detailed

TABLE 31. SERIOUS CRIMINALITY SCORE RELATED TO BEHAVIOR IN FIFTEEN-YEAR SPAN (UNCONTRACTED)

SERIOUS CRIMINALITY SCORE	NON-CRIMINALS		SERIOUS OFFENDERS		MINOR OFFENDERS		ERRATIC OFFENDERS		TOTAL
	Number	Per cent	Number	Per cent	Number	Per cent	Number	Per cent	Number
Under 100	25	61.0	7	17.0	7	17.1	2	4.9	41
100 to 110	8	42.1	4	21.1	6	31.5	1	5.3	19
110 to 120	5	35.7	3	21.5	5	35.7	1	7.1	14
120 to 130	15	39.6	7	18.4	13	34.2	3	7.8	38
130 to 140	54	34.5	39	24.8	58	36.9	6	3.8	157
140 to 150	10	40.0	10	40.0	4	16.0	1	4.0	25
150 to 160	5	41.7	4	33.3	3	25.0	–	–	12
160 to 170	14	35.9	14	35.9	9	23.1	2	5.1	39
170 to 180	13	32.5	17	42.5	8	20.0	2	5.0	40
180 and over	11	36.7	17	56.6	2	6.7	–	–	30
Total	160		122		115		18		415

score classification was utilized to ascertain which contractions would be the most useful.

Examination of this preliminary table indicated that it would be well to establish the final score classes as follows: under 100, 100–140, 140–180, 180 and over. This contraction resulted in Table 32, covering the probable behavior of juvenile offenders during a fifteen-year span following handling by a juvenile court.

[3] The men in this latter group of offenders were perhaps non-delinquent and then became delinquent, or were minor offenders and then became serious offenders for a period of time and again minor offenders or non-delinquent and so on; that is, they did not progress consistently from more serious to less serious delinquency or to non-delinquency.

From this prediction table it is seen that if a boy appearing in juvenile court scores less than 100 on the five predictive factors, he has six chances in 10 of reforming at some time during the fifteen-year span following the end of supervision by or through the court; one and a half chances in 10 of being a serious offender; a like probability of becoming a minor offender; and only

TABLE 32. SERIOUS CRIMINALITY SCORE RELATED TO BEHAVIOR IN
FIFTEEN-YEAR SPAN (CONTRACTED)

SERIOUS CRIMINALITY SCORE	NON-CRIMINALS		SERIOUS OFFENDERS		MINOR OFFENDERS		ERRATIC OFFENDERS		TOTAL
	Num-ber	Per cent	Num-ber	Per cent	Num-ber	Per cent	Num-ber	Per cent	Num-ber
Under 100	25	61.0	7	17.0	7	17.1	2	4.9	41
100 to 140	82	36.0	53	23.2	82	36.0	11	4.8	228
140 to 180	42	36.2	45	38.8	24	20.7	5	4.3	116
180 and over	11	36.7	17	56.6	2	6.7	–	–	30
Total	*160*		*122*		*115*		*18*		*415*

$$C = .28$$

half a chance in 10 of developing into an erratic offender. If he scores 100–140 he has three and a half chances in 10 of reforming at some time during the fifteen-year period after the end of control by the court, two chances in 10 of becoming a serious offender, three and a half chances in 10 of becoming a minor offender, and only half a chance in 10 of being an erratic offender. If he scores 140–180 he has a chance similar to the youth scoring 100–140 of reforming during the fifteen-year span, but four rather than two chances in 10 of remaining a serious offender, two rather than three and a half chances in 10 of becoming a minor offender, and half a chance in 10 of turning out to be an erratic offender. If he scores 180 or more he has as much chance of becoming a non-delinquent (three and a half out of 10) as the youth who scores 100–140 or 140–180; but five and a half chances out of 10 of remaining a serious offender throughout the fifteen years, and less than one chance in ten of becoming a minor offender; while the likelihood of his becoming an erratic offender is nil.

PREDICTING AGE AT CHANGE FROM SERIOUS TO MINOR DELINQUENCY

It has already been mentioned that this is the first prediction table we have been able to prepare covering a fifteen-year span. We have attempted to increase the table's usefulness by making it possible to determine approximately the age at which a juvenile offender who has some chance of becoming a minor delinquent is

TABLE 33. SERIOUS CRIMINALITY SCORE RELATED TO AGE AT CHANGE FROM SERIOUS TO MINOR DELINQUENCY DURING FIFTEEN-YEAR SPAN

SERIOUS CRIMINALITY SCORE	UNDER 15 Per cent	15 TO 21 Per cent	21 AND OVER Per cent	TOTAL Number
Under 100	28.6	42.8	28.6	7
100 to 140	20.7	47.6	31.7	82
140 to 180	29.2	33.3	37.5	24
180 and over	–	–	100.0	2

likely to change from the commission of serious to the commission of minor offenses; and also the age at which those youths who have some chance of reformation are likely to become nondelinquents. Such a refinement of the prediction table, possible only where behavior over long segments of time is determinable, greatly enhances its usefulness.

In order to sharpen the predictive instrument, therefore, the offenders who became minor delinquents during the fifteen-year span were next distributed into the various age-spans in which they had actually changed from serious offenders to minor delinquents. The results of this tabulation are presented in Table 33.

A juvenile court judge utilizing this information in connection with Table 32 would be able to determine, for example, that a youth with a serious delinquency score of 100–140, and therefore having (according to Table 32) about three and a half chances in 10 of becoming a minor offender, would have almost three chances in 10 of becoming such when he was under fifteen years old, four and a half chances in 10 when he was between fifteen and twenty-one, and three chances in 10 of becoming a minor offender when he was twenty-one or older. Such information would naturally serve as a useful guide to a juvenile court judge in determining in a general way whether to give a boy a longer or shorter sentence in a peno-correctional institution, or a longer or shorter period of probation. From the point of view of social protection, it is important for the judge to know that a boy has seven chances in 10 of becoming a minor delinquent when still under twenty-one years old, which is the limit of the period during which a juvenile court would usually have jurisdiction over a juvenile offender. In such a case a judge would be likely, for the sake of the public protection, to arrange to keep a boy under close supervision until he was twenty-one, but to curtail supervision if the delinquent actually became a minor offender earlier, as Table 33 shows that he has some chance of doing.

Another illustration of the use of the prediction table and age chart may be clarifying. A twelve-year-old boy scoring 140–180 on the five predictive factors has, according to Table 32, two chances in 10 of becoming a minor offender during the fifteen-year span. Consultation of the age chart (Table 33) discloses that he has six chances in 10 of becoming a minor delinquent before he is twenty-one. This information would probably cause the judge to provide for a considerable period of close supervision for the youth until he actually did become a minor offender. Supervision might then be relaxed entirely or continued until it was felt that he is no longer a severe menace to himself or the public.

PREDICTING AGE AT REFORMATION

A further refinement of Table 32 has been made possible by the preparation of Table 34, in which is presented the age at which offenders having specific criminality scores actually did reform during the fifteen-year span. From objectified experience with this particular group of cases, a juvenile court judge would know within what age-range offenders in a certain score class on the five predictive factors are likely to reform. For example, a boy appearing in a juvenile court who scores less than 100 on the five predictive factors, and therefore has six chances in 10 of becoming non-delinquent during the fifteen-year span following treatment by the court (Table 32), has less than two chances in 10 of becoming completely non-criminal while under fifteen, almost five chances in 10 of reforming between fifteen and twenty-one years of age, and three and a half in 10 of reforming when he is twenty-one or older. Such information would, then, guide the judge in the length of

TABLE 34. SERIOUS CRIMINALITY SCORE RELATED TO AGE AT REFORMA-
TION DURING FIFTEEN-YEAR SPAN

SERIOUS CRIMINALITY SCORE	UNDER 15 *Per cent*	15 TO 21 *Per cent*	21 AND OVER *Per cent*	TOTAL *Number*
Under 100	16.0	48.0	36.0	25
100 to 140	24.4	45.1	30.5	82
140 to 180	21.4	45.2	33.4	42
180 and over	10.2	54.5	27.3	11

probation or other supervision which would be necessary in order to insure to such an offender and to the public the widest protection.

Or, if a youth appearing before a juvenile court scores 140–180, the general prediction table (Table 32) indicates that he has about three and a half chances in 10 of ultimately abandoning his criminal conduct; and Table 34 shows that such a youth has but two chances in 10 of becoming non-criminal while under fifteen, four and a half chances in 10 of reformation when he is between fifteen and twenty-one, and only about three chances in 10 when he is twenty-one or older. On the basis of such information the judge can determine the probable length of supervision necessary for such an offender.

* * * * *

The usefulness of a prediction table indicating behavior over a fifteen-year span following handling in a juvenile court, with the added refinement of a determination of the approximate age-span during which an offender is likely to change from the commission of serious to minor offenses, or to reform entirely, would naturally be enhanced by a series of tables which would indicate the likelihood of good behavior *during periods of peno-correctional supervision.* Such tables are presented in Chapter XIX.

We can now turn our attention to the behavior of our group of offenders during the various types of peno-correctional treatments to which they were subjected from the onset of their delinquent careers until the end of the third five-year follow-up span.

Chapter XIII

BEHAVIOR DURING VARIOUS FORMS OF PENO-
CORRECTIONAL TREATMENT

THUS far we have given no particular attention to the conduct
of our juvenile offenders *during* the various peno-correctional
treatments which they experienced. Nor have we in our previous
researches particularly studied the behavior of criminals during
treatment. We know, however, that some offenders react differently during some forms of peno-correctional treatment than during others. In *500 Criminal Careers,* for example, we noted that,
although 30 per cent of the ex-inmates of the Massachusetts Reformatory were non-criminal during parole supervision, a lower
proportion, 21.1 per cent, were non-criminal during a five-year
period following the end of parole.[1] We also noted in that work
that 17.5 per cent of the group did not violate any of the institution's rules and were in other ways "model prisoners"; but the remainder, 82.5 per cent, were in varying degrees not amenable to the
institutional regime. Some 86 per cent of those who misbehaved
committed serious offenses in the institution, such as rebellion
against authority, violence against the person, offenses against property, and sex offenses; while about 13 per cent could be designated
minor offenders.[2] We further noted in our more intensive studies
of individual delinquents that particular offenders, although behaving very well in a reformatory, misbehaved during periods of
probation or parole; and that other offenders did not respond well
either in institutions or during periods of extramural treatment.

We observed that some offenders who underwent frequent periods of institutionalization responded very poorly in their earlier
years but later grew more amenable to institutional regimes. We
also noted in previous researches, as well as the present one, that

[1] *500 Criminal Careers,* table 16, page 190.
[2] *500 Criminal Careers,* pages 158–159, 163.

some offenders who misbehaved during probation or parole proved most amenable to life in the Army or Navy; and that others who behaved well under probation or parole came into conflict with legal authorities very shortly after such supervision ceased. We noted, in addition, that some offenders, though not behaving satisfactorily in reformatories and prisons where the regimes are strict, got along acceptably in the laxer atmosphere of jails; and that some offenders always behaved well during probation or parole, while others behaved acceptably under these forms of treatment only when the supervision was very strict.

From these observations of variation in behavior during different forms of peno-correctional treatment, we were impelled in the present study to ascertain the differences in the characteristics of offenders who respond variously to extramural and intramural supervision, and to construct prediction tables for behavior during each form of peno-correctional treatment. It will be recalled in this latter connection that in our other follow-up studies we have ascertained those factors in the life histories of groups of offenders that would be predictive of the behavior of similar groups of offenders in the years *following* a particular form of peno-correctional treatment. In *500 Criminal Careers* and *Later Criminal Careers* these predictions dealt with conduct after expiration of sentence to a men's reformatory; in *Five Hundred Delinquent Women* with the behavior of female offenders in the years following expiration of sentence to a women's reformatory; and in *One Thousand Juvenile Delinquents* with conduct following the completion of supervision by a juvenile court as recommended by a child guidance clinic.

We have come to see the importance of determining probable behavior not only following treatment but *during* treatment. In order to provide the foundations for a study of the characteristics of what might be called "treatment types," and for the construction of prediction tables covering behavior during each of several forms of peno-correctional treatment, we determined, in connection with the present check-up on the boys originally described in *One Thousand Juvenile Delinquents,* to record in chronological order all forms of peno-correctional treatment to which each boy had been subjected from the earliest onset of delinquency through the Juvenile Court "treatment period" and the three five-year follow-up periods, and to secure information from recorded sources concerning the behavior of these offenders during their various "treatments." These treatments consisted of ordinary probation, probation under suspended sentence, incarceration in correctional or truant schools, reformatories, prisons, or jails, and parole. In some cases, of course, an offender had only one or two forms of peno-correctional treatment during this span of twenty to twenty-five years (covering, as already indicated, not only the years prior to appearance in the Boston Juvenile Court but also the original "treatment period" and the fifteen years thereafter). A very large proportion, however, had been subjected to many periods of probation, parole, or imprisonment.

Coming to this task so many years after the treatment experiences had occurred, it was not possible for us to obtain at first hand information regarding the details and nuances of the conduct of the offenders during treatment, nor could we hope to find such information in the records of probation or parole departments or institutions. It may well be, for example, that an occasional offender whom we have classified as a failure during a particular period of probation behaved very poorly in the early part of his probation but improved markedly toward the latter part. It may likewise be that a youth who misbehaved during the early part of a stay in a correctional school later adjusted himself well to its routine.[3] Not only could we not secure such detailed information with any degree of uniformity, but it was not possible by this method of filling in data so many years after the event, and from official records so unevenly kept and by so many persons, to determine the deep-lying reasons why a particular offender behaved well during some periods

---

[3] We do not wish at this stage to enter into the important question of whether an inmate's docile adherence to a prison's rules is always a true indication of his reform or is, in the long run, socially desirable. From the standpoint of the prison administrator, however, an inmate who does not violate institutional rules and goes about his duties without causing trouble is deemed a "success."

of treatment and poorly during other similar periods. All we can do is to infer that he was more closely or less closely supervised during one period of probation or commitment than during another, or that he liked or disliked a particular probation officer or institutional official, or that the content and quality of probation in one court was quite different from that in another, and so on.

Where the raw data were so sketchy, it would only have been misleading to venture upon the reasons for the varying responses to what is presumably the same form of "treatment." It was necessary, therefore, to define "success" and "failure" under the various forms of peno-correctional treatment by an objective standard that could not be seriously questioned, and to eliminate from consideration any treatment about which the basic information could not be readily determined.

We have not made any guesses about an offender's behavior during various forms of peno-correctional treatment, nor have we depended upon the memory or opinion of the offender or of peno-correctional officials. Cases in which conduct data had not actually been recorded contemporaneously or in which the criminal records, gathered by us from many sources,[4] did not clearly indicate that misbehavior had or had not occurred during a particular period of treatment, were classified as "unknown." In view of the fact, however, that a very large proportion of the offenders underwent more than one period of extramural treatment (probation, parole) and likewise more than one period in institutions, it was actually possible to secure information about some, if not all, of the treatment experiences of 962 youths.[5]

The preliminary procedure employed in gathering these data was to enter on a card in chronological order the various peno-correctional treatments. The next step was to fill in the responses to treatment as indicated by the criminal record itself, and then to search for recorded information on the remaining treatment experiences. The following is an illustration of this procedure:

[4] See Chapter XXI, Method of This Research.
[5] Appendix B, T–80.

Chronological List of John G's Treatment Experiences

TREATMENT	DATES	BEHAVIOR
X Truant School	July 1912—December 18, 1913	Success
Parole from X Truant School	December 18, 1913—March 22, 1918	Failure: arrested March 22, 1918, for larceny
X Truant School	March 22, 1918—January 21, 1919	Success
Parole from X Truant School	January 21, 1919—April 1, 1922	Failure: arrested May 18, 1921, for forgery; June 16, 1921, for larceny
Probation for larceny	June 16, 1921—October 24, 1922	Failure: arrested September 1, 1922, for larceny
Probation for larceny	September 1, 1922—February 28, 1923	Failure: defaulted
Y House of Correction	June 13, 1923—July 12, 1923	Period too short to be judged
Y House of Correction	October 29, 1925—April 22, 1926	Success
Z Reformatory	April 22, 1926—April 23, 1927	Failure: attempted theft
Parole from Z Reformatory	April 23, 1927—January 17, 1928	Failure: parole revoked; defaulted
Probation under suspended sentence for larceny	September 19, 1929—March 19, 1930	Failure: defaulted
Probation under suspended sentence for non-support	May 31, 1932—June 1, 1934	Failure: arrested June 22, 1932, for fornication; June 24, 1932, for violation of liquor laws
Probation under suspended sentence for violation of liquor laws	July 8, 1932—July 18, 1932	Failure: July 9, 1932, defaulted
Probation for bastardy	July 9, 1932—July 5, 1933	Failure: arrested August 1, 1932, for no license; September 8, 1932, for larceny
Probation under suspended sentence for larceny	September 18, 1932—October 5, 1932	Success: held only until restitution paid
Y House of Correction	January 31, 1933—December 20, 1933	Success

From this record it is clear that John G could be regarded as a failure during his first parole period from December 18, 1913, to March 22, 1918, when he was at liberty from the X Truant School, because his criminal conduct as discovered through the Massachusetts Board of Probation revealed that this parole was terminated by an arrest for larceny. Likewise, he was clearly a failure during the second parole period, January 21, 1919, to April 1, 1922, because his official criminal record indicated that on May 18, 1921, he was arrested for forgery and on June 16, 1921, for larceny. John could also be judged a failure in his first probation period, June 16, 1921, to October 24, 1922, because his criminal record revealed that on September 1, 1922, he was arrested for larceny.

The interested reader can see clearly that the behavior of John G during many of his probation and parole periods could readily be determined merely from an examination of his court record. It was not possible, however, to secure all the information necessary in John's case merely from his criminal record. For example, the records of the X Truant School had to be examined to determine John's behavior in that institution from July 1912 to December 1913 and also from March 1918 to January 1919; we had to examine the court records for John's conduct during the probation period of September 1922 to February 1923; and it was necessary to communicate with the institutional authorities for information about John's incarceration in the Y House of Correction for the periods June to July 1923, October 1925 to April 1926, and January to December 1933, and with the officials of the Z Reformatory for information about his behavior during his incarceration from April 1926 to April 1927. Further, the court's record of John's probation under suspended sentence for the period from September 1929 to March 1930 had to be personally examined, as well as the record of his probation under suspended sentence of September to October 1932.

This procedure was followed in each of the 962 cases.

DEFINITIONS OF "SUCCESS" AND "FAILURE" DURING TREATMENT

After gathering the available data on the behavior of our offenders during peno-correctional treatment, it was necessary to differentiate successful conduct during treatment from misconduct. The distinction between "success" and "failure" during treatment is essentially that between criminality and non-criminality as applied to the behavior of our group of delinquents in the successive five-year periods following their treatment by a juvenile court and clinic, except that no attempt was made to separate failures into minor and serious. It would hardly have been possible to do this in any large number of cases because, as already indicated, the sketchy materials available for this aspect of the study did not furnish a safe basis for such a fine differentiation.

The categorization of *failure during a period of extramural treatment* (probation, probation under suspended sentence, parole, and placement in a foster home ordered by the court) was, in cases of probation or parole, based on actual arrests during the period of such treatment; or on more than occasional violations of probation or parole; or on surrender to an institution for violating probation under suspended sentence or parole; or by the known or recorded commission of offenses for which an offender might well have been arrested (such as stealing, sex offenses, drinking, and so on). An occasional minor infringement of the rules of probation or parole (such as neglect to report on time or changing jobs without permission or arrest for traffic violations) was not regarded as failure. In the case of foster home placement, a boy was classified as a failure if he ran away from the foster home, was arrested during the period of placement, or committed any offenses (except minor traffic violations) for which he might have been arrested.

The question may justly be asked at this point whether all cases in which evidence of failure was not recorded were then considered to have succeeded during a particular treatment. It should be emphasized that if there was insufficient data on which to make a judgment of conduct, the case was classed as "unknown." The following examples will show the method.

A boy was known to have been on probation from August 6, 1920, to June 28, 1921, for larceny. During this period he was not arrested. The judge committed him temporarily to the care of the Department of Public Welfare for placement in a foster home, but since the boy's brother and father objected to this, the judge agreed to give him a trial on active probation under the close supervision of his brother. The court record indicates that supervision of the boy was left largely to the brother, whom the probation officer saw only occasionally, his reports indicating that the brother was beginning to lose interest in supervising the boy. The notation appears in the court record that "although the home slack and there is not very intelligent control of the boy, case was filed." As all this occurred some seventeen years ago it was not possible for us to secure any further information. There was no proof in the record that the boy did not misbehave during this probation period, and as the probation officer's reports were infrequent and sketchy, the boy's behavior during this particular probation period had to be classified as "unknown."

In another instance the offender was on probation for six months in 1934 for assault and battery on his wife. The man was to live with his brother during the probation period, and the wife with her parents. Shortly after the beginning of probation, the probationer called on his probation officer seeking work, which fact was entered in the record. There is a notation four months later that he again called to report that he was estranged from his wife. The probation officer, apparently wishing to bring the husband and wife together, notified them both to come to his office on a particular day. Neither of them appeared, however, and on recommendation of the supervising probation officer the case was "dismissed." Here, as in the previous illustration, the supervision given by the probation officer was lax, or the reports were extremely sketchy, and there was not sufficiently clear evidence that the man in question had behaved well throughout the probation period, even though he was not arrested during that time. Therefore his behavior during this particular period of probation had to be classified as "unknown."

In a case like the following, however, it was clearly possible to categorize the offender as successfully completing a period of extramural supervision.

This youth was on parole from a correctional school from 1925 to 1929, during which time he lived with his parents and worked steadily, earning $25 a week. According to the record, the boy was seen personally by the parole officer every six months, and it was clear that the officer checked each time on the youth's employment and conduct. The boy continued to live at the same address with his parents throughout these years. He worked steadily, holding three different positions. The father, mother, and brother, whenever visited by the parole officer, were full of praise for him, and his brother commented that "he better do good or he will go back." From this particular case report, sketchy as it may be for certain purposes, we nevertheless had sufficient information to determine that this youth behaved satisfactorily during his period of parole.

One more illustration is given of how proof of good behavior as well as of poor was required before we made a judgment of success or failure during treatment.

A youth was on probation under suspended sentence in a juvenile court from June 1918 to October 1920 for breaking and entering a building with other boys. Placement in a foster home was determined upon and was accomplished two months after the beginning of probation. Although from this point on the boy was under supervision of a children's society, the probation officer made frequent inquiries from the agency about him. The society kept close watch over the boy and visited him frequently. The record indicates that he was steadily promoted in school and that he was thoroughly happy in his foster home. Although the boy's mother wished to have him at home, the court decided that he should remain with his foster parents. The agent of the child-placing society was frequently asked for reports concerning the boy's progress, and these are contained in the court record. In view of his excellent conduct in the foster home, the boy was finally permitted by the court to return to his own home, but with the understanding that he be supervised by the society. After three months of such supervision, the court was satisfied that the case could be filed. Here, as in the preceding case, there was sufficient evidence of the boy's good behavior to designate him a success on probation.

According to our definition, *failure during a period of intramural treatment* (correctional school, reformatory, prison, jail, institution for defective delinquents) was determined from the conduct reports kept by institutional officials. If such records revealed that an inmate was a constant disciplinary problem, frequently running away from the institution or stealing or inciting others to misbehavior or instructing others in the commission of sex offenses or otherwise generally disturbing the routine of the institution, he was rated a failure. Sometimes no such detailed information was given in the record, but it was indicated that a youth had been punished by being placed in solitary confinement. This was sufficient evidence that he did not get along satisfactorily.

It may be, as we have already indicated, that a youth behaved well for part of a stay in an institution. For obvious reasons, we could not, however, make such subtle distinctions in connection with this particular research. An offender who was reported as being entirely or usually amenable to the institution routine, and only very occasionally violating the rules, was categorized a *success during a particular period of intramural treatment*.

We must not leave these definitions of success and failure without saying a word about responses to treatment under Army or Navy discipline. Although this is not a peno-correctional treatment, we gathered information on the behavior of our group during periods in the Army or Navy, because, as pointed out at the beginning of this chapter, we occasionally noted that some men got along very well in the Army or Navy but did not behave well under various forms of peno-correctional treatment. The routine and discipline of military life require a certain degree of adaptability not wholly unlike that required in institutional life. *Failure in the Army or Navy* was determined entirely from the official reports of Army or Navy authorities; dishonorable discharge or desertion, or imprisonment by the military or naval authorities, was the test of failure. *Success in the Army or Navy* was, for our purposes, determined by honorable discharge.

GENERAL SUMMARY OF BEHAVIOR DURING EXTRAMURAL AND INTRA-MURAL TREATMENT

Before proceeding to a detailed description of the responses of our delinquents to specific forms of intramural and extramural treatment which they experienced during their antisocial careers, it would be well to make a general summary of their responses to both types of treatment.

We were able to secure some, though not always complete, information about the behavior of 962 of our original 1,000 offenders from the onset of their delinquent careers through the fifteen-year follow-up span. Of these, 562 (58.4 per cent) experienced both extramural and intramural treatment of one sort or another; 393

(40.8 per cent) had extramural treatment only (including a few who possibly did have intramural treatment about which we could not secure information), and 7 had intramural treatment only.[6]

In all, 955 offenders had extramural correctional experiences. Of these, 160 (16.8 per cent) always succeeded during these periods of oversight (mainly probation and parole), 428 (44.8 per cent) consistently failed, while 367 (38.4 per cent) sometimes did well and sometimes did not.

Of the 569 youths who had intramural treatments at one time or another during their delinquent careers, 236 (41.5 per cent) always behaved acceptably in institutions, 142 (25 per cent) always failed in institutions, while 191 (33.5 per cent) sometimes responded well during periods of intramural treatment and at other times did not.[7]

We find that the 562 youths who experienced both extramural and intramural treatment and whose behavior during both forms of treatment was classifiable can be divided into four general types, as follows:

1. Those who succeeded during some though not necessarily all intramural and extramural treatments
2. Those who failed during all intramural and extramural treatments
3. Those who succeeded during intramural treatments but failed during extramural treatments
4. Those who failed during intramural treatments but succeeded during extramural treatments

On this basis we found that 209 (37.2 per cent) behaved satisfactorily during some if not all their treatments, which indicates that they had an immediate or latent capacity to succeed in both forms of treatment; 91 (16.2 per cent) failed during all the treatments to which they were subjected; 214 (38.1 per cent) though failing in all extramural supervision, succeeded in some or all the intramural treatments to which they were subjected; and 48 (8.5

---

[6] Calculated from Appendix B, T–80. Thirty-eight of the 1,000 boys are omitted from consideration either because they had no treatment experiences or because no record of their experiences could be found.

[7] Calculated from Appendix B, T–80.

per cent), though failing in all the intramural treatments, behaved well during some or all extramural treatments.

In the following chapters we shall make comparisons of the characteristics of the youths who succeeded in extramural treatments with those who failed, those who succeeded in intramural treatments with those who failed, those who succeeded in both types with those who failed, and those who succeeded in both types of treatment with those who failed in one type or the other. Such comparisons furnish a basis for determining the probable responses of other groups of offenders to extramural and intramural treatment and therefore carry us a step further in the building up of prediction tables which we hope will be useful in guiding judges, parole boards, and other peno-correctional officials in handling offenders.

BEHAVIOR DURING SPECIFIC TYPES OF EXTRAMURAL TREATMENT

After this general analysis of the behavior of the 962 youths whose conduct under official supervision was known, we can turn to a more specific description of their responses to probation, parole, and various forms of incarceration without, however, at the moment taking account of these responses in relation to the average age of the youths when under a particular form of treatment.

Of 806 youths who were on *straight probation* (unaccompanied by a suspended sentence or incarceration), at one time or another during their delinquent careers, and about whose behavior on probation sufficient information could be secured to determine success or failure, 164 (20.3 per cent) always behaved well, 467 (57.9 per cent) always failed, and 175 (21.8 per cent) sometimes failed and sometimes succeeded under this form of treatment.[8]

As for *probation under suspended sentence,* of the 500 youths who were placed under this form of supervision, 100 (20 per cent) behaved well, 348 (69.6 per cent) always failed, while 52 (10.4 per cent) sometimes did well and at others did not.[9]

In regard to *parole* (including parole not only from reformatories and prisons but also from juvenile institutions), of 472 youths who

[8] Appendix B, T-79.   [9] Appendix B, T-79.

were on parole at one time or another during their delinquent careers, and about whom information could be gathered, 66 (14.0 per cent) always behaved satisfactorily, 334 (70.8 per cent) always misbehaved sufficiently to be considered failures, while 72 (15.2 per cent) sometimes did well under parole oversight and at other times did not.[10]

Of the 72 youths who were placed in *foster homes during periods of probation or parole,* 22 (30.5 per cent) behaved well in their foster homes, 47 (65.2 per cent) did not get along satisfactorily, while 3 (4.3 per cent) sometimes behaved acceptably and at other times did not.[11]

For reasons already explained, we made a study of the behavior of our youths under *Army or Navy discipline.* This is not included in the summary of behavior during various forms of intramural and extramural peno-correctional treatment, but there is significance in the fact that of 121 youths who were in the Army or Navy at one time or another and about whom information could be secured, 50 (41.3 per cent) conducted themselves well while in the Service, 56 (46.3 per cent) did not get along satisfactorily, and 15 (12.4 per cent) behaved well during some enlistments but not during others.[12]

BEHAVIOR DURING SPECIFIC TYPES OF INTRAMURAL TREATMENT

Since our youths began their delinquent careers very early in life, a considerable proportion of them had been committed to *industrial and truant schools.* Of 420 boys who were at one time or another sent to such institutions and about whose conduct it was possible to secure information, 171 (40.7 per cent) behaved well under the regime of such schools, 180 (42.9 per cent) did not, while 69 (16.4 per cent) at times did well and at times did not.[13]

A very small group of boys were committed by judges to *schools for the feebleminded* and, of the 31 boys about whom information

---

[10] Appendix B, T–79.

[11] These figures have been derived from Appendix B, T–79.

[12] Appendix B, T–79.   [13] Appendix B, T–79.

could be secured, 10 (32.3 per cent) got along well in such schools, 17 (54.8 per cent) had to be regarded as failures, while 4 (12.9 per cent) succeeded during some periods of treatment in schools for the feebleminded but not in others.[14]

Of 162 youths who served sentences in *reformatories for young adults* and about whose conduct under such treatment it was possible to secure sufficient information to make a judgment of their success or failure, 72 (44.4 per cent) behaved acceptably, 69 (42.6 per cent) did not conduct themselves satisfactorily, and 21 (13 per cent) succeeded during some reformatory commitments but failed during others.[15]

Of 111 youths who were committed to *prison* at one time or another during their criminal careers and about whose behavior it was possible to secure information, 69 (62.2 per cent) were always amenable to prison life, 27 (24.3 per cent) never were, and 15 (13.5 per cent) behaved acceptably during some commitments and poorly during others.[16]

There were only 15 offenders who were committed to *institutions for defective delinquents* about whose behavior information could be secured. Of these, 8 behaved well in such institutions, 5 did not, while 2 failed during some commitments and succeeded during others.[17]

In regard to sentences served in *jails, houses of correction, state farms,* and similar establishments for short-term commitments, we have information on the behavior of 185 of our youths. Of these, 121 (65.4 per cent) always got along satisfactorily during such incarcerations, 33 (17.8 per cent) always failed, and 31 (16.8 per cent) did well during some commitments and poorly during others.[18]

PROPORTIONAL INCIDENCE OF SUCCESS AND FAILURE DURING SPECIFIC
  TYPES OF TREATMENT

The reader has undoubtedly already noted the fact that there is considerable variation in the proportion of success and failure un-

[14] Appendix B, T-79.   [15] Appendix B, T-79.   [16] Appendix B, T-79.
[17] Appendix B, T-79.   [18] Appendix B, T-79.

der the different forms of peno-correctional treatment, and that there are more failures during periods of extramural supervision than during intramural treatment. It will be helpful at this point to present, in Table 35, the responses of our youths to the various forms of peno-correctional treatment which they experienced at one time or another.

From Table 35 it is evident that the highest proportion of failure

TABLE 35. BEHAVIOR DURING VARIOUS FORMS OF PENO-CORRECTIONAL TREATMENT AND IN ARMY AND NAVY (PERCENTAGES)

	ALWAYS FAILED	ALWAYS SUCCEEDED	SOMETIMES SUCCEEDED	TOTAL CASES IN WHICH BEHAVIOR WAS KNOWN
Probation	57.9	20.3	21.8	806
Probation under suspended sentence	69.6	20.0	10.4	500
Parole	70.8	14.0	15.2	472
Foster home placement (during probation or parole)	65.2	30.5	4.3	72
Industrial and truant schools	42.9	40.7	16.4	420
Schools for feebleminded	54.8	32.3	12.9	31
Reformatories	42.6	44.4	13.0	162
Prisons	24.3	62.2	13.5	111
Jails	17.8	65.4	16.8	185
Army and Navy	46.3	41.3	12.4	121

during treatment occurred under parole. It must be remembered, of course, that a large part of the parole supervision refers to parole from juvenile institutions and that, as will be seen later in this chapter, there is a higher failure rate on parole during the early than during the late years. The proportion of failure during probation under suspended sentence is about the same as the proportion of failure under parole supervision. In a sense these two forms of extramural oversight are the same, because in both cases failure to behave in accordance with the rules is likely to result in commitment or recommitment to an institution.

The proportion of failures during placement in foster homes is only slightly higher than the proportion of failures during periods of straight probation, but is slightly lower than during periods of parole or during probation under suspended sentence.[19]

It should be noted that there was a lower failure rate under Army and Navy discipline than under straight probation or any of the other forms of extramural correctional treatment. Apparently the rigid discipline of the Army, voluntarily sought, had a salutary effect in certain cases.

During institutional commitments our youths obviously behaved more satisfactorily than they did under extramural supervision. As shown in Table 35, the highest institutional failure rate occurred in schools for the feebleminded, a finding possibly explained by the fact that borderline defective delinquents are not as likely to get along as well in institutions as those with higher mental powers. The explanation may also lie partly in the fact that younger rather than older offenders are sent to schools for the feebleminded, and that the success rate in institutions as a whole appears to be lower among younger than among older inmates (see Table 36).

CHANGES IN BEHAVIOR DURING SPECIFIC TYPES OF TREATMENT

We are now ready to consider the changes that occurred with the passing of the years in the proportion of offenders responding satisfactorily to various forms of intramural and extramural peno-correctional treatment, omitting, because of smallness of numbers, foster home supervision, schools for the feebleminded, and institutions for defective delinquents.

First considering *probation,* we find that, during the years prior to the appearance of our youths before the Boston Juvenile Court, 22.9 per cent of the 323 boys who were on probation at one time or

---

[19] Incidentally, it should be mentioned that we made the differentiation in this study between probation under suspended sentence and "straight probation" in order to ascertain whether the threat of commitment would result in a better showing on probation. It has obviously not done so, and the reason probably lies in the fact that judges select more recalcitrant offenders for probation under suspended sentence than they are likely to place on ordinary probation.

TABLE 36. BEHAVIOR IN EACH PERIOD DURING VARIOUS FORMS OF PENO-
CORRECTIONAL TREATMENT AND IN ARMY AND NAVY
(PERCENTAGE OF SUCCESS)

	PRIOR PERIOD	FIRST FOLLOW-UP PERIOD	SECOND FOLLOW-UP PERIOD	THIRD FOLLOW-UP PERIOD
Probation	22.9	33.0	26.6	39.4
Probation under suspended sentence	17.8	24.0	21.7	23.0
Parole	2.5	14.5	25.4	34.4
Correctional schools	49.1	52.5	53.1	–
Reformatories	–	38.8	53.4	78.0
Prisons	–	–	63.4	70.8
Jails	–	66.7	75.8	78.5
Army and Navy	–	51.0	60.4	63.6
Average age	*Under 13½ years*	*14 to 19 years*	*19 to 24 years*	*24 to 29 years*

another, and whose behavior could be determined, behaved satisfactorily under such oversight (see Table 36). This means that they
violated the rules of probation only occasionally and then in minor
fashion, were not arrested, and did not commit any offenses for
which they might have come to the attention of the authorities.
During the first five-year follow-up period, there was some improvement in adjustment to probation supervision, for 33.0 per cent
of 303 youths could by that time be considered successful. Although
during the second five-year period there was a slight drop—to 26.6
per cent—in the proportion of youths behaving well under probation, an increase to 39.4 per cent occurred in the third follow-up period. Thus, although there has not been an altogether uniform trend
in the proportion of offenders behaving well under probation, the
direction has been toward increasing adjustment to probation—
from 22.9 per cent in the early years when the juvenile delinquents
were, on the average, less than thirteen and a half years old, to 39.4
per cent during the years when the youths had reached an average
age of twenty-four to twenty-nine years.[20]

[20] Appendix C, 21.

As for response to *probation under a suspended sentence,* which involves the threat of commitment if the conditions of probation are violated, there was practically no increase with the passing of the years in the proportion of those offenders who responded well to this form of peno-correctional treatment. In the early years, 17.8 per cent of the offenders who were placed under such extramural supervision made a successful adjustment during the probation period; during the first five-year follow-up period the percentage increased only slightly, to 24.0; and it remained about the same in the third five-year period.[21] It would appear, therefore, that the effectiveness of the threat of return to an institution does not increase with the passing of the years. This is probably related to the fact that offenders subjected to this particular form of extramural treatment are, on the whole, more serious criminals than those selected by judges for straight probation.

Coming now to changes in behavior during *parole,* it is of especial significance that of the youths who were on parole before they reached an average age of thirteen and a half (which of course means that they were on parole from juvenile training schools), only 2.5 per cent made a successful adjustment under such oversight. But the percentage who comported themselves satisfactorily under this form of extramural supervision rose to 14.5 during the first five-year follow-up period, when the youths ranged from fourteen to nineteen years on the average, to 25.4 during the second follow-up period, and to 34.4 during the third. Thus we see a marked and consistent improvement with the passing of the years in the adjustment made by offenders while on parole.[22]

It has already been noted that a considerably higher percentage of offenders did well in the *Army or Navy* than under probation or parole. Our youths were of course too young to have had any service in the Army or Navy in the years prior to their appearance before the Boston Juvenile Court. But during the first five-year follow-up period, 51 of the 100 youths who served enlistments either in the

---

.[21] Appendix C, 22.   [22] Appendix C, 23.

Army or Navy made a successful adjustment—a fact established by their honorable discharge; during the second period the percentage of those responding well rose to 60.4, and in the third follow-up span to 63.6.[23]

Turning now to the conduct of our group in *correctional schools,* we find that during their early years, 49.1 per cent of the 55 boys who had been committed to correctional or truant schools, and whose behavior there was known, made an acceptable adjustment to this form of intramural treatment. This means that they were readily amenable to the institutional routine and only occasionally, if at all, committed minor offenses. Practically no change occurred in the responses of our offenders to this form of treatment as they grew older, for during the first five-year follow-up period 52.5 per cent of the 326 youths whose behavior in correctional or truant schools was determinable conducted themselves satisfactorily in such institutions, and during the second follow-up period 53.1 per cent of 32 youths made an adequate adjustment to the routine of correctional schools. By the beginning of the third five-year span the men were too old to serve terms in juvenile training institutions.

In considering the fact that no change occurred in the response of our youths to treatment in correctional and truant schools, it should be remembered that they could not be given new commitments to such schools after they were seventeen years old, and that they could be returned to such institutions by revocation of their parole permits only up to the statutory age of twenty-one.[24]

Coming now to behavior in *reformatories,* we note a considerable improvement with the passing of the years. It should be kept in mind that in Massachusetts offenders may be committed to reformatories at seventeen, but that the average age at commitment to such institutions is higher. During the first five-year follow-up period, when our youths averaged fourteen to nineteen years of age, 38.8 per cent of those "serving time" in reformatories made satisfactory adjustments to the regime; during the second period, when they

[23] Appendix C, 24.   [24] Appendix C, 25.

averaged nineteen to twenty-four years, 53.4 per cent behaved acceptably; and during the third, when they averaged twenty-four to twenty-nine years, 78.0 per cent of the youths serving reformatory sentences made successful adjustments to reformatory life.[25] It is evident, therefore, that there was marked improvement in the behavior of our offenders in reformatories with the passing of the years. The extent to which this is to be attributed to "learning the ropes" of frictionless institutional life as the inmates gained experience in imprisonment cannot of course be determined. But it is reasonable to assume, as we shall see from the discussion on pages 267–270, that part of the increase in satisfactory adjustment to the demands of an institutional regime may be credited to the integrative and "settling down" processes that come with advancing years.

As very few of our youths were old enough for prison sentences until the beginning of the second five-year follow-up period, no consideration need be given to their adjustment to prison life before that time. During the second five-year span, 63.4 per cent of the 52 youths who were committed to prison and whose behavior was ascertainable were good prisoners; and this proportion increased to 70.8 per cent during the third follow-up period, when they ranged in age from 24 to 29 years on the average. Obviously there is greater adjustment to life in institutions for adults than in institutions for juveniles. This may be partly due to a difference in the nature of the regimes and partly to a growing experience in outward adherence to prison regulations, but it appears to be far more readily explainable by age differences at the time of commitment to such institutions.[26]

As for changes in behavior in jails with the passing of the years, we find that during the first five-year follow-up period, when the offenders ranged in age from fourteen to nineteen years, 66.7 per cent of those committed to jails, houses of correction, or state farms behaved acceptably in such institutions; during the second follow-up span, when they were between nineteen and twenty-four years

[25] Appendix C, 26.   [26] Appendix C, 27.

old, the proportion of those making satisfactory adjustments increased to 75.8 per cent; and during the third, to 78.5 per cent.[27] This somewhat better adjustment to life in jails than in prisons is probably explained by the fact that the incarceration is not of such long duration and the regulations are less stringent.

In order to visualize more clearly the changes that have taken place over the years in the behavior of our juvenile delinquents under various extramural and intramural peno-correctional treatments, we have set down in Table 36 the proportion of offenders who behaved acceptably during each form of peno-correctional treatment prior to their appearance in the Boston Juvenile Court, and in each of the three successive five-year follow-up periods. From this table it is clear that, although there is improvement with the passing of the years in the behavior of offenders during extramural treatment (straight probation, probation under suspended sentence, and parole), the improvement in conduct during intramural treatment is more marked. It is clear, also, that during every period in the delinquent careers of these youths, they behaved better in institutions than they did under extramural supervision. It should be pointed out, however, that some conducted themselves very much better in the Army or Navy than they did while under probation or parole, and almost as well as they did during confinement.

* * * * *

Many questions are raised by the analysis of the behavior of our group of offenders during various forms of peno-correctional treatment, to which we cannot give definite answers from the materials available. Why is it, for example, that although there was increasing improvement during all forms of treatment, there was more improvement under certain forms of treatment than others? What differences are there in the actual quality of the various treatments? How does maturation actually play its part in progressively increasing good behavior during any specific form of treatment?

[27] Appendix C, 28.

Answers to these and other questions about the conduct of offenders during treatment would require a much more detailed and intimate knowledge of the various treatment and rehabilitative processes than we have been able to assemble within the scope of this investigation. In a research now beginning we will study at close range the behavior of a large group of offenders under every form of peno-correctional treatment to which the law happens to subject them, so that we may know more about the subtleties of conduct during treatment, as well as about the quality of the treatment and the role which the interaction of the personalities of officers and offenders plays in the treatment process.[28] But within the confines of the present research, in which the various forms of peno-correctional treatment have been described on the basis of a lowest common denominator, we can still extract much of value; and we have broken the ground for more intensive studies of behavior during treatment. We have a basis, crude though it be, for constructing prediction tables for the probable responses of offenders to different forms of peno-correctional treatment.

[28] That there is a very real difference in the quality of both extramural and intramural peno-correctional treatment in different places is evident in the fact that during the period when a group of our boys were on probation to the Boston Juvenile Court by recommendation of the Judge Baker Foundation, at which time they were of an average age of thirteen and a half years, they behaved better than they had during any previous period of probation or during any period until they arrived at an average age of twenty-four to twenty-nine years. Thus, in the years prior to the appearance of these boys before the Boston Juvenile Court, when they had been subjected to probation in many different courts, only 22.9 per cent of them could be considered successes on probation, while during the particular probation in the Boston Juvenile Court just mentioned, 37.6 per cent of the youths behaved satisfactorily. During the five years following this particular probation period, 33 per cent of the youths subjected to probation supervision by various courts succeeded under probation, during the second five-year span 26.6 per cent, and during the third 39.4 per cent.

Chapter XIV

OFFENDERS WHO SUCCEEDED DURING EXTRAMURAL TREATMENT AND THOSE WHO FAILED

AS the first in our series of analyses of conduct types, a comparison is made between the former juvenile delinquents who succeeded during extramural supervision and those who failed thereunder, to see whether and how they may be differentiated. In order to sharpen this comparison, we are omitting a group of offenders who did not always behave satisfactorily during extramural treatment, and are confining our attention strictly to those who succeeded during all the extramural treatments to which they were subjected (160 offenders) and those who failed during all such experiences (428 offenders).[1] In making prediction tables for response to different forms of peno-correctional treatment we shall, of course, take this third group into account.[2] An examination of their characteristics indicates that they more nearly resembled those who always succeeded; they apparently had the capacity to succeed during extramural treatment but did not always do so, perhaps because of the nature of some specific treatment or because, as we have noted in a previous chapter, their adjustment was delayed to later years.

RESEMBLANCES

It is evident that the factors of resemblance between the offenders who always succeeded and those who always failed during periods of extramural treatment, since they are neutral factors, cannot be the ones that contributed to their varying responses. But it is well

---

[1] In this chapter as well as in any others in which comparisons are made between two series of cases of unequal numbers, the significance of the differences was estimated by relating the size of the differences to their probable errors. The difference was considered significant if it was three or more times the probable error.

[2] See Chapter XIX.

to consider these resemblances before proceeding to a description of the differences in the characteristics of the two groups.

First, the extramural successes and failures were alike in the percentage incidence of their countries of birth. They were also alike in the average age of the younger of their parents at the time the boys appeared before the Boston Juvenile Court, and in the average difference in age between the younger and older of their parents. Their mothers were to the same extent gainfully employed to help supplement meagre family incomes. Both groups were reared in neighborhoods in which the surrounding influences were poor. They came from families of equal size, and they were of the same birth rank among their brothers and sisters. They were alike in the extent to which they had not belonged in childhood to well-supervised boys' clubs, and also in the extent to which they were members of gangs or ran about the streets with crowds of boys. And, finally, they resembled each other in the average age at which they began to work, and in the nature of their early employment.

Since none of these factors of resemblance could have any part in differentiating these youths into those who succeeded during extramural treatment and those who failed, we are justified in laying them aside in our search for the reasons for the differences in their behavior while under supervision outside institutions.

SLIGHT DIFFERENCES

We next come to a group of factors in which small differences are found to exist between the two groups we are now considering. These differences do not amount to more than 4 to 10 per cent in the incidence of any particular characteristic. Although none can be given much significance in itself, taken together they at least tend to show the trend of difference in the characteristics of those who succeeded and those who failed during extramural treatment.

For example, a slightly higher proportion of white boys than of Negroes behaved well during extramural treatment. Further, there was a higher proportion of youths of Hebrew parentage than of Catholic or Protestant among those who always succeeded, and there were also more sons of parents who had been in the United States for a brief period of time and who had had no schooling. The last is obviously due to the fact that those who succeeded during extramural treatment are to a greater extent than the failures the sons of foreign-born parents. This will be more clearly seen in the next section of this chapter.

It should be noted particularly that offenders who always behaved well during extramural treatment were reared in homes in which

TABLE 37. EXTRAMURAL SUCCESSES AND FAILURES: NATIVITY OF PARENTS (PERCENTAGES)

	SUCCESSES	FAILURES
Parents native born	10.7	15.5
Parents foreign born	82.0	68.5
One parent native born, one foreign born	7.3	16.0
Total number of known cases	*150*	*381*

the basic physical conditions of life were even worse than in the all too poor homes of those who did not respond well. Obviously, whatever influence they may exert on the origins of delinquency, the childhood physical surroundings of an offender do not have much, if anything, to do with his response to periods of officially supervised freedom under legal control. It is to be noted, however, that there was slightly less need for intervention by social agencies in the families of offenders who conducted themselves well under extramural treatment than among the families of those who did not.

MARKED DIFFERENCES

We come now to a series of factors in which there are greater differences between those offenders who always succeeded during extramural oversight and those who always failed.

Table 37 indicates that a greater proportion of those who behaved well than of those who did not were the sons of foreign-born parents. Table 38 shows the countries of birth of the parents; the percentage of Irish parents and of those born in the United States was much lower among the successes than among the failures, that of Italian parents was somewhat higher, and that of Russian, Polish, and Lithuanian parents was much higher.

TABLE 38. EXTRAMURAL SUCCESSES AND FAILURES: BIRTHPLACE OF PARENTS (PERCENTAGES)

	SUCCESSES		FAILURES	
	Fathers	*Mothers*	*Fathers*	*Mothers*
United States	15.4	14.6	24.2	23.9
Italy	34.6	33.8	29.3	27.8
Russia, Poland, Lithuania	28.2	29.8	14.3	14.9
Ireland	8.3	8.6	15.6	18.0
Other	13.5	13.2	16.6	15.4
Total number of known cases	*156*	*151*	*392*	*389*

Considering now a series of factors that reflect the social and psychological differences in the early background of the offenders, we find that among those who behaved well under supervised freedom the proportion who were reared in homes in which the economic conditions were good was greater than among the failures (Table 39) and that the moral standards of their families were on the whole more satisfactory (Table 40). Proportionately more of the successes came from families in which the conjugal relations of the parents were good (Table 41), they were to a greater extent held in affection by their parents (Table 42), and the disciplinary methods of a

TABLE 39. EXTRAMURAL SUCCESSES AND FAILURES: ECONOMIC STATUS OF PARENTS (PERCENTAGES)

	SUCCESSES	FAILURES
Comfortable	32.2	20.2
Marginal	60.4	70.4
Dependent	7.4	9.4
Total number of known cases	*149*	*392*

TABLE 40. EXTRAMURAL SUCCESSES AND FAILURES: FAMILY MORAL
STANDARDS (PERCENTAGES)

	SUCCESSES	FAILURES
Good	18.2	8.9
Fair	19.6	15.8
Poor	62.2	75.3
Total number of known cases	*148*	*380*

TABLE 41. EXTRAMURAL SUCCESSES AND FAILURES: CONJUGAL RELATIONS
OF PARENTS (PERCENTAGES)

	SUCCESSES	FAILURES
Good	69.6	55.6
Fair	14.8	17.4
Poor	15.6	27.0
Total number of known cases	*135*	*333*

TABLE 42. EXTRAMURAL SUCCESSES AND FAILURES: AFFECTION OF
PARENTS FOR OFFENDERS (PERCENTAGES)

	SUCCESSES		FAILURES	
	Fathers	*Mothers*	*Fathers*	*Mothers*
Good	81.4	92.4	61.0	77.6
Fair	11.8	6.1	25.5	15.2
Poor	6.8	1.5	13.5	7.2
Total number of known cases	*102*	*131*	*251*	*348*

TABLE 43. EXTRAMURAL SUCCESSES AND FAILURES: DISCIPLINE BY
PARENTS (PERCENTAGES)

	SUCCESSES		FAILURES	
	Fathers	*Mothers*	*Fathers*	*Mothers*
Good or fair	53.9	50.8	20.0	20.8
Poor	46.1	49.2	80.0	79.2
Total number of known cases	*102*	*128*	*250*	*342*

TABLE 44. EXTRAMURAL SUCCESSES AND FAILURES: BROKEN HOMES
(PERCENTAGES)

	SUCCESSES	FAILURES
Home not broken	60.9	48.9
Home broken	39.1	51.1
Total number of known cases	*156*	*409*

larger proportion of the parents were at least fair (Table 43). Table 44 shows that the successes were to a significantly less extent than the failures the products of broken homes, and Table 45 shows that they were not in childhood to so great an extent removed from the parental roof because of the death, separation, desertion, or divorce of their parents or because their homes, although not broken, were unsuitable for the rearing of children.

TABLE 45. EXTRAMURAL SUCCESSES AND FAILURES: EARLY ABNORMAL
ENVIRONMENTAL EXPERIENCES (PERCENTAGES)

	SUCCESSES	FAILURES
No abnormal environmental experience	67.8	41.8
Abnormal environmental experiences	32.2	58.2
Total number of known cases	*152*	*400*

Turning now to certain early characteristics of the youths themselves, we find, first and foremost, that those who succeeded while on probation or parole were an average age of 10.3 years when they began to misbehave, while those who consistently failed were a year younger. However, the time between onset of antisocial behavior and first arrest was shorter for those who always succeeded than for those who failed (Table 46).

Table 47 shows that proportionately fewer of the successes than of the failures were "lone offenders," as reflected in the offense for which they appeared before the Boston Juvenile Court. Fewer of the successes had vicious habits (Table 48), there were fewer school truants among them (Table 49), they were not as much retarded in school (Table 50), and, as shown in Table 51, they were to a far less extent than the failures characterized by mental disorder, distortion, marked personality liabilities, or serious adolescent instability (as determined at the time they were examined by the Judge Baker Foundation Clinic).

TABLE 46. EXTRAMURAL SUCCESSES AND FAILURES: TIME BETWEEN FIRST DELINQUENCY AND FIRST ARREST (PERCENTAGES)

	SUCCESSES	FAILURES
None (first offense)	18.2	5.6
One year or less	43.4	40.4
Over one year	38.4	54.0
Total number of known cases	99	*285*

From all these marked differences in the ethnic background, in the socio-psychological configurations of their family life, and in their personal capacities and characteristics, it is evident that those of our offenders who always succeeded during extramural treatment were much more favorably equipped and circumstanced than were those who always failed during such treatment. Clearly, therefore, factors of the kind herein enumerated should be given great attention by sentencing judges and correctional administrators in determining which offenders are likely to respond satisfactorily to extramural supervision and which need to be incarcerated for their own sake and for that of society.

TABLE 47. EXTRAMURAL SUCCESSES AND FAILURES: ACCOMPLICES IN OFFENSE FOR WHICH THEY WERE BROUGHT BEFORE THE BOSTON JUVENILE COURT (PERCENTAGES)

	SUCCESSES	FAILURES
Offense committed alone	21.0	32.6
Offense committed with one other	29.7	25.4
Offense committed with two or more others	49.3	42.0
Total number of known cases	*138*	*347*

TABLE 48. EXTRAMURAL SUCCESSES AND FAILURES: HABITS OF OFFENDERS (PERCENTAGES)

	SUCCESSES	FAILURES
No bad habits	34.6	22.0
Bad habits	65.4	78.0
Total number of known cases	*159*	*427*

TABLE 49. EXTRAMURAL SUCCESSES AND FAILURES: SCHOOL CONDUCT (PERCENTAGES)

	SUCCESSES	FAILURES
No school misconduct	33.3	10.3
Truancy or other school misconduct	66.7	89.7
Total number of known cases	*126*	*367*

TABLE 50. EXTRAMURAL SUCCESSES AND FAILURES: SCHOOL RETARDATION (PERCENTAGES)

	SUCCESSES	FAILURES
Not retarded	24.0	12.6
Retarded one year	26.0	23.9
Retarded two or more years	50.0	63.5
Total number of known cases	*146*	*398*

TABLE 51. EXTRAMURAL SUCCESSES AND FAILURES: MENTAL CONDITION (PERCENTAGES)

	SUCCESSES	FAILURES
No mental disease, distortion, marked liabilities of personality, or marked adolescent instability	57.9	35.1
Mental disease or distortion	8.8	17.6
Marked personality liabilities or marked adolescent instability	33.3	47.3
Total number of known cases	*159*	*427*

Chapter XV

OFFENDERS WHO SUCCEEDED DURING INTRAMURAL TREATMENT AND THOSE WHO FAILED

FROM the comparison in the preceding chapter it is evident that the former juvenile delinquents who responded satisfactorily to extramural treatment had more favorable backgrounds and characteristics than those who did not. In this chapter we are concerned with a similar comparison of the men who always behaved satisfactorily during periods of intramural treatment and those who always failed.

It will be recalled from Chapter XIII that an inmate of a peno-correctional institution who was a constant disciplinary problem, frequently ran away from the institution, committed crimes therein, incited others to misbehavior, or otherwise generally disturbed the smooth conduct of the institution was considered a *failure;* while an inmate who was entirely or usually amenable to the institution's routine, only occasionally violating institution rules, was deemed to be a *success.* On the basis of such a differentiation, 236 youths were known to have succeeded throughout intramural treatment and 142 to have failed.[1] For the sake of the sharpness of the comparison, we have omitted from consideration 191 youths who sometimes behaved acceptably in peno-correctional institutions. We shall, however, include them later in the prediction tables dealing with behavior during specific intramural treatments.[2]

RESEMBLANCES

Considering first the resemblances between the intramural successes and failures, we find a great many factors in which the two groups are alike. In these factors of resemblance there cannot, of

---

[1] See Chapter XIII, p. 157; see also footnote 1 on page 169 regarding the probable error of the difference in the two series of cases.

[2] See Chapter XIX.

course, be any clues to the difference in their responses to treatment in peno-correctional institutions.

To begin with, both groups of boys had the same average number of brothers and sisters, and they held the same birth rank in their respective families. Those who behaved well in institutions and those who did not were in similar proportions white and Negro boys. They were of like nativity and were the sons of parents of like nativity. Those of their parents who were foreigners migrated from the same countries and had been in the United States for equal periods at the time the boys were brought before the Juvenile Court. Further, the two groups derived in like proportion from the same religious background. The average age of the younger of their parents at the time of marriage was the same in both groups.

The offenders who behaved acceptably in peno-correctional establishments and those who did not had in many ways the same kind of up-bringing. For instance, the disciplinary practices of their parents were to a   poor. The two groups were sons of parents with similar educational limitations and of like economic status; and an equal proportion of the families were aided in one way or another by social agencies during the boyhood of the offenders. The resemblance in economic condition is further indicated by the fact that the mothers of the two groups were to a like extent compelled to be gainfully employed during the childhood of the offenders.

There is further resemblance between those offenders who behaved well in institutions and those who did not in that they were to a like extent subjected to early abnormal environmental experiences, which means that they left their parental homes or were removed from them because of the death, desertion, divorce, separation, illness, or imprisonment of their parents, or because social agencies felt that their homes were not conducive to the healthy rearing of children.

Those who adjusted to institutional life and those who did not resembled each other in the extent to which they were truants from school or otherwise seriously misbehaved, and in the degree of their school retardation. They also resembled each other in the age at which they began to work, in the extent to which they belonged to gangs in boyhood or ran about the streets with crowds of boys, and the extent to which they failed to join well-supervised boys' clubs for wholesome use of leisure time. The health of these two groups of boys, as revealed at the time of their examination by the Judge Baker Foundation Clinic, was the same. And finally, the same amount of time elapsed between the onset of their first misbehavior manifestations and their first arrest.

SLIGHT DIFFERENCES

In the factors in which those offenders who consistently succeeded during intramural treatment and those who always failed differed from each other only slightly (a 4 to 10 per cent difference), we may find some clues to the reasons for the difference in their behavior.

First, it is to be noted that the younger of the parents of those offenders who behaved well were on the average a little older than the younger of the parents of the youths who did not get along well in institutions. Also, there was a slightly greater difference in age between the parents of those offenders who always behaved acceptably in institutions than between the parents of those who always failed.

The youths who always responded favorably to life in peno-correctional institutions were reared in somewhat better neighborhoods than the others and in homes in which the living conditions were slightly more satisfactory, the conjugal relations of their parents were better; also the boys were somewhat older at the onset of their misbehavior manifestations than were those who always failed.

We now come to a few factors which suggest that those offenders who responded well to life in peno-correctional establishments may have found in such institutions a welcome refuge from the poor conditions surrounding them; for these youths were in somewhat greater proportion than the others, members of families in which parents and/or brothers and sisters were also delinquents, there was a somewhat greater incidence of mental disease or defect in their families, and they were to a slightly greater extent than the institutional failures the sons of parents who had little affection for them.

It should be added, however, that the youths who behaved well in institutions were of slightly higher intelligence than those who failed, that on the whole they had somewhat better habits, and that they suffered less than the others from mental disorders, distortions, or marked liabilities of personality (as determined at the time of their examination in the Clinic).

It will be recalled that among the boys who experienced extramural treatment those who succeeded had a better background on the whole than those who failed. This does not hold true of the boys who had intramural treatment; an erraticism is evident in the differences between the two groups, the successes being more favorably characterized in some respects and less so in others than the failures. It is clear, therefore, that for explanations of the difference in their behavior behind walls we must look to other factors of difference than those already described.

MARKED DIFFERENCES

In only two factors is there a marked difference between the intramural successes and failures. One is the age at first arrest; those who behaved acceptably in institutions were a year younger on the average on the occasion of their first arrest than were those who did not adjust themselves to institutional life. It would appear, therefore, that the youths who behaved acceptably in institutions had a shorter period of unrecognized delinquency than those who always failed. Their habits of delinquency were less deeply ingrained and, perhaps for this reason, they more easily adjusted themselves to institutional life.

The other factor of marked difference between those who behaved satisfactorily during intramural treatment and those who did not is to be found in Table 52, in the extent to which they committed offenses in the company of other boys, as reflected in the offense which brought them before the Boston Juvenile Court. The offend-

TABLE 52. INTRAMURAL SUCCESSES AND FAILURES: ACCOMPLICES IN
OFFENSE FOR WHICH THEY WERE BROUGHT REFORE BOSTON
JUVENILE COURT (PERCENTAGES)

	SUCCESSES	FAILURES
Offense committed alone	27.5	38.7
Offense committed with one other	32.8	20.2
Offense committed with two or more others	39.7	41.1
Total number of known cases	*189*	*119*

ers who succeeded in intramural treatment were, to a significantly less extent than the others, youths who committed their offenses alone. This would indicate that the boys who got along satisfactorily in institutions were to a greater extent than the failures influenced in their behavior by others; they were evidently of the companionable, suggestible type, capable of being influenced by their associates. Apparently, therefore, offenders who are easily influenced can adapt emselves more readily to the group life of institutions than can the "lone wolves" whose misbehavior is apparently not dependent on the influence of companions.

Even these two differences between the successes and failures in intramural treatment are not very marked; certainly these two groups do not differ nearly as much as do those who succeeded and those who failed during periods of extramural treatment. The reason for this can probably be traced to the fact that supervision in institutions is much closer than under probation or parole and the chances of misbehavior therefore are fewer.

On the basis of this evidence it seems reasonable to conclude that less habituation in delinquency and greater adaptability to group life afford at least a partial explanation of the better adjustment of certain offenders to institutional life.

Chapter XVI

OFFENDERS WHO SUCCEEDED DURING BOTH EXTRA-MURAL AND INTRAMURAL TREATMENT AND THOSE WHO FAILED

IN the two preceding chapters certain gross differences were shown to exist between the characteristics and background of offenders who responded successfully to extramural oversight and offenders who did not, and between those of offenders who responded successfully to intramural treatment and offenders who did not. In this comparison we found some clues to the reasons why offenders respond in different ways to extramural and intramural treatment. In the present chapter we make another grouping of our "conduct types"—those who behaved successfully during at least some, though not necessarily all, treatments, both extramural and intramural (es) and those who always failed during both   treatment (91 cases).

RESEMBLANCES

There are a number of factors of resemblance between the offenders who behaved well during both extramural and intramural treatment and those who did not. Both groups had the same proportion of white and Negro youths among them; they were of like nativity; the average difference in age between the younger and the older of their parents was the same; the families of the two groups were of equal size; to a like extent other members of the families were also delinquents; and a similar proportion of the mothers had wholesome affection for their sons.

They further resemble each other in the extent to which the families were aided by social agencies during the boyhood of the offenders. An equal proportion of the boys in the two groups had health handicaps, as determined at the time they were examined in the clinic of the Judge Baker Foundation. Those offenders who succeeded during some or all extramural and intramural treatments were of the same intelligence level as those who failed, they were equally retarded in school, and in like degree had misconducted themselves in school. Like proportions of both groups of offenders did not, in boyhood, belong to well-supervised recreational clubs, preferring gangs or running about with crowds of boys. And finally, the offenders who behaved satisfactorily during at least some of their peno-correctional experiences resembled those who persistently failed in age at onset of misbehavior, age at first arrest, and amount of time that elapsed between onset of misbehavior and first arrest.

These resemblances certainly do not explain the reasons for the difference in response to peno-correctional treatment.

SLIGHT DIFFERENCES

We will now consider the slight differences between the two groups of offenders. First of all, the offenders who succeeded in at least some extramural and intramural treatments were, in slightly greater proportion than the failures, the sons of foreign-born parents. Second, in a considerable series of factors they were slightly less underprivileged than those who failed, for a somewhat smaller percentage of the former group were the products of broken homes and a larger proportion of them had the affection of their fathers and were better disciplined by their fathers and mothers than were the youths who did not react well to treatment. Further, a lower proportion of the offenders who responded satisfactorily were reared by mothers who had to be frequently absent from home because of outside employment. More of them grew up in homes in which the living conditions were better, and their homes were in somewhat better neighborhoods. The offenders who behaved acceptably during some or all peno-correctional treatments came from families in which there was less mental disease or defect than did the offenders who misbehaved during both intramural and extramural supervision. Slightly fewer of the successes were first-born children.

A slightly higher proportion of the youths who behaved well during at least some treatments committed the offense for which they were brought into the Boston Juvenile Court in company with other boys, which indicates that their commission of delinquent acts was determined at least partially by the influence of others, and that they were not such confirmed offenders as were the youths who committed their offenses alone.

Perhaps none of these slight differences is of great significance, but taken together they serve to indicate that, by and large, the offenders who behaved acceptably during at least some periods of both extramural and intramural treatment were less disadvantaged than those who did not respond satisfactorily to treatment either in the community or behind walls.

MARKED DIFFERENCES

Turning now to a series of factors in which there are greater differences between those who responded satisfactorily to at least some extramural and intramural treatments and those who did not, we find at least some clues to the reasons for the variation in their response.

First of all, as seen in Table 53, the youths who behaved well during both types of treatment were, to a greater extent than the failures, the sons of parents who did not have the advantage of formal schooling. This finding has only indirect significance, being explainable by the fact that a higher proportion of the parents of the successes than of the failures were foreign born and came from countries in which there was often a lack of educational opportunity. Table 54 shows that more of the youths who succeeded under treatment than of the failures were reared in homes of adequate economic status. Table 55 shows that those who succeeded during both forms of peno-correctional treatment were in still another way more privileged than those who failed, in that they were to a greater extent the sons of parents whose conjugal relationships were satisfactory; and Table 56 indicates that as children they were not so often subjected to abnormal environmental experiences.

From Table 57 it is evident that those who succeeded during both forms of treatment were to a less extent than the failures the victims of vicious habits in their boyhood. Table 58 reveals another significant difference between the successes and failures, namely, that a lower proportion of the former than of the latter had any mental or personality distortions or disorders, as determined at the time of their examination at the Judge Baker Foundation Clinic.

From these more marked differences between the youths who behaved well during at least some extramural and intramural penocorrectional treatments and those who did not respond satisfactorily to either, it is evident that the former group were in many respects more privileged in their background and characteristics than were those who failed. It would seem reasonable to infer, therefore, that the traits and background of the offenders themselves were of great significance in determining their divergent reactions to treatment, whether this consisted of incarceration or supervision in the community.

TABLE 53. OFFENDERS WHO SUCCEEDED IN BOTH TYPES OF TREATMENT
AND THOSE WHO FAILED: EDUCATION OF PARENTS
(PERCENTAGES)

	SUCCESSES	FAILURES
No formal schooling	61.9	44.7
One or both attended common school	34.2	46.1
One or both entered high school	3.9	9.2
Total number of known cases	257	76

TABLE 54. OFFENDERS WHO SUCCEEDED IN BOTH TYPES OF TREATMENT
AND THOSE WHO FAILED: ECONOMIC STATUS OF PARENTS
(PERCENTAGES)

	SUCCESSES	FAILURES
Comfortable	24.6	14.6
Marginal	70.4	76.4
Dependent	4.9	9.0
Total number of known cases	203	89

TABLE 55. OFFENDERS WHO SUCCEEDED IN BOTH TYPES OF TREATMENT AND THOSE WHO FAILED: CONJUGAL RELATIONS OF PARENTS (PERCENTAGES)

	SUCCESSES	FAILURES
Good	66.1	52.1
Fair	12.9	11.3
Poor	21.0	36.6
Total number of known cases	*171*	*71*

TABLE 56. OFFENDERS WHO SUCCEEDED IN BOTH TYPES OF TREATMENT AND THOSE WHO FAILED: EARLY ABNORMAL ENVIRONMENTAL EXPERIENCES (PERCENTAGES)

	SUCCESSES	FAILURES
No abnormal environmental experiences	51.8	38.9
Abnormal environmental experiences	48.2	61.1
Total number of known cases	*199*	*90*

TABLE 57. OFFENDERS WHO SUCCEEDED IN BOTH TYPES OF TREATMENT AND THOSE WHO FAILED: HABITS OF OFFENDERS (PERCENTAGES)

	SUCCESSES	FAILURES
No bad habits	29.0	18.5
Bad habits	71.0	81.5
Total number of known cases	*210*	*92*

TABLE 58. OFFENDERS WHO SUCCEEDED IN BOTH TYPES OF TREATMENT AND THOSE WHO FAILED: MENTAL CONDITION (PERCENTAGES)

	SUCCESSES	FAILURES
No mental disease, distortion, marked liabilities of personality, or marked adolescent instability	37.0	26.1
Mental disease or distortion	14.7	18.5
Marked personality liabilities or marked adolescent instability	48.3	55.4
Total number of known cases	*184*	*92*

Chapter XVII

OFFENDERS WHO SUCCEEDED DURING INTRAMURAL TREATMENT AND THOSE WHO SUCCEEDED DURING BOTH FORMS OF TREATMENT

IN our search for the reasons why certain offenders did not behave satisfactorily except behind walls, we now turn to a comparison of this group (214 cases) with the offenders who succeeded at least at times during both supervised freedom and while in peno-correctional institutions (209 cases).

RESEMBLANCES

The two groups of offenders we are considering here—those who succeeded only during intramural treatment and those who succeeded during both extramural and intramural—resembled each other in a number of ways. First, in family background: the boys were of like nativity; the average age of the younger of their parents at the time of marriage was the same, as was the average difference in age between the younger and older of their parents; the families of the two groups were of equal size, they had a like history of mental disease and/or defect, and they were to an equal extent aided by social agencies during the boyhood of our offenders.

Also, certain characteristics of the boys themselves were similar. At the time they were examined at the Clinic of the Judge Baker Foundation the two groups were in about the same condition of health, and an equal incidence of mental disease or distortion or of personality liabilities was discovered among them. They were in equal measure retarded in school. They were of the same average age when they began to work, and they engaged in the same types of occupation. During boyhood they were to an equal extent members of gangs or street crowds of boys, and similar proportions of the two groups had not belonged to any organizations for the constructive use of leisure.

They resembled each other in the age at onset of misbehavior manifestations and in the age of first arrest, and therefore in the length of time that elapsed between onset of first misbehavior and first arrest. And, finally, the two groups were to an equal extent lone offenders, as reflected in the particular offense for which they appeared before the Boston Juvenile Court.

SLIGHT DIFFERENCES

A comparison of the slight differences in the background and characteristics of the offenders who responded satisfactorily only to institutional life and those who behaved well during some or all their extramural and intramural peno-correctional treatments shows that there were in the former group a slightly higher proportion of Negroes, a slightly higher proportion of youths who the offspring of marriages between native-born and fore parents, and a slightly higher proportion of sons of American-born or Irish-born fathers and American-born mothers. Their parents had been in America for a somewhat longer period than had the parents of the youths who responded satisfactorily to both types of treatment.

The offenders who behaved well in institutions but not during extramural supervision were reared in homes of slightly lower economic status than the youths who responded acceptably to both intramural and extramural treatment. They were to a somewhat greater extent the sons of mothers who had been compelled to work in order to supplement a meager family income. The youths who behaved well only in institutions differed from the others in having less affection from their mothers during boyhood, and in being reared in homes in which there was slightly more delinquency among their parents and/or brothers and sisters and where the moral standards were slightly lower. It should be said, however, that they grew up in homes and neighborhoods in which the physical living conditions were slightly better.

The youths who behaved well in institutions but not during periods of extramural supervision had slightly higher intelligence than the youths who adjusted to both extramural and intramural peno-correctional treatment. As children, the former had more bad habits than the latter and had misbehaved in school to a greater extent, particularly as school truants.

It is already evident from the slight differences between the two groups that those who got along well in institutions but not during the freer oversight afforded by extramural treatment were, by and large, less favorably circumstanced than were the youths who showed capacity to behave satisfactorily under all forms of treatment. This finding is substantiated by a comparison of the more marked differences between the groups.

MARKED DIFFERENCES

First, it should be emphasized that there are no marked differences in the personal characteristics of the two groups. The differences which occur are found in their family background.

The youths who behaved well only in institutions were sons of parents who had better schooling than were the youths who adjusted to both intramural and extramural treatment, as is shown in Table 59. This is explained by the fact that they were to a greater extent the sons of native-born parents, who naturally had more opportunity for schooling than the foreign-born parents.

As will be seen from Table 60, the former group were to an appreciably greater extent than the latter the sons of parents whose conjugal relationships were not satisfactory. Also, they were to a greater extent reared in homes that were broken by death, desertion, separation, or divorce (Table 61); and they were subjected to more abnormal environmental experiences, largely as the result of the break-up of their homes but partly also because their homes were for other reasons unsuited to the wholesome rearing of children (Table 62). This last finding is emphasized in Table 63, which shows that fewer of them were held in affection by their fathers than were those who responded well to both types of treatment, and by Table 64, which shows that the disciplinary practices of their parents were poorer.

It would appear, therefore, from the marked differences between the offenders who behaved well only behind walls and those who responded satisfactorily to both extramural and intramural peno-correctional supervision, that the generally poorer parental and parent-child relationships in the former group had something to do with their inadequate response to treatment. There was obviously less security and more unwholesomeness in their early upbringing, which seems to have been reflected in an inability to make good adjustments without the intensive restraint and control offered by a peno-correctional institution. Evidently an insecure and poorly disciplined offender finds in an institutional regime a needed prop to good conduct which is lacking in the freer oversight of extra-mural correctional treatments.

TABLE 59. OFFENDERS WHO SUCCEEDED IN INTRAMURAL BUT FAILED IN EXTRAMURAL TREATMENT, AND THOSE WHO SUCCEEDED IN BOTH TYPES: EDUCATION OF PARENTS (PERCENTAGES)

	INTRAMURAL SUCCESSES, EXTRA-MURAL FAILURES	SUCCESSES IN BOTH TYPES
No formal schooling	44.9	61.9
One or both attended common school	50.6	34.2
One or both entered high school	4.5	3.9
Total number of known cases	*156*	*257*

TABLE 60. OFFENDERS WHO SUCCEEDED IN INTRAMURAL BUT FAILED IN
EXTRAMURAL TREATMENT, AND THOSE WHO SUCCEEDED IN
BOTH TYPES: CONJUGAL RELATIONS OF PARENTS
(PERCENTAGES)

	INTRAMURAL SUCCESSES, EXTRA- MURAL FAILURES	SUCCESSES IN BOTH TYPES
Good	56.1	66.1
Fair	16.1	12.9
Poor	27.8	21.0
Total number of known cases	*155*	*171*

TABLE 61. OFFENDERS WHO SUCCEEDED IN INTRAMURAL BUT FAILED IN
EXTRAMURAL TREATMENT, AND THOSE WHO SUCCEEDED IN BOTH
TYPES: BROKEN HOMES (PERCENTAGES)

	INTRAMURAL SUCCESSES, EXTRA- MURAL FAILURES	SUCCESSES IN BOTH TYPES
Home not broken	47.5	57.0
Home broken	52.5	43.0
Total number of known cases	*202*	*200*

TABLE 62. OFFENDERS WHO SUCCEEDED IN INTRAMURAL BUT FAILED IN
EXTRAMURAL TREATMENT, AND THOSE WHO SUCCEEDED IN BOTH
TYPES: EARLY ABNORMAL ENVIRONMENTAL EXPERIENCES
(PERCENTAGES)

	INTRAMURAL SUCCESSES, EXTRA- MURAL FAILURES	SUCCESSES IN BOTH TYPES
No abnormal environmental experiences	36.4	51.8
Abnormal environmental experiences	63.6	48.2
Total number of known cases	*195*	*199*

TABLE 63. OFFENDERS WHO SUCCEEDED IN INTRAMURAL BUT FAILED IN
EXTRAMURAL TREATMENT, AND THOSE WHO SUCCEEDED IN BOTH
TYPES: AFFECTION OF FATHERS FOR OFFENDERS
(PERCENTAGES)

	INTRAMURAL SUCCESSES, EXTRAMURAL FAILURES	SUCCESSES IN BOTH TYPES
Good	55.4	66.3
Fair	28.5	20.4
Poor	16.1	13.3
Total number of known cases	*130*	*98*

TABLE 64. OFFENDERS WHO SUCCEEDED IN INTRAMURAL BUT FAILED IN
EXTRAMURAL TREATMENT, AND THOSE WHO SUCCEEDED IN BOTH
TYPES: DISCIPLINE BY PARENTS (PERCENTAGES)

	INTRAMURAL SUCCESSES, EXTRAMURAL FAILURES		SUCCESSES IN BOTH TYPES	
	Fathers	*Mothers*	*Fathers*	*Mothers*
Good	.8	–	2.3	–
Fair	15.0	15.1	28.5	29.6
Poor	84.2	84.9	69.2	70.4
Total number of known cases	*127*	*166*	*130*	*159*

Chapter XVIII

OFFENDERS WHO SUCCEEDED DURING EXTRAMURAL TREATMENT AND THOSE WHO SUCCEEDED DURING BOTH FORMS OF TREATMENT

WE now turn to those offenders who did not respond satisfactorily to incarceration but did behave acceptably during at least some of the extramural treatments to which they were subjected (48 cases). As in the previous chapter, a comparison of the background and characteristics of this conduct type will be made with those of the offenders who behaved satisfactorily during both extramural and intramural peno-correctional treatment (91 cases). From such a comparison should emerge some clues to the reasons why certain offenders, though able to get along well under extramural oversight, do not respond to the more severe and persistent restraint of institutional life.

RESEMBLANCES

There are a number of factors in which the youths who were able to get along satisfactorily under extramural supervision but not under intramural control resembled those who responded satisfactorily to both types of treatment.

First of all, the two groups contained like proportions of white and Negro youths. They were of similar nativity and were sons of parents of like nativity; those among their parents who were foreign born had been in America for the same length of time before the boys' appearance in the Boston Juvenile Court. They were offspring of families of equal size, the average difference in age between their parents was the same, and the average age of the younger of their parents at the time of marriage was the same.

The two groups were alike in the limited education of their parents; in the extent to which they were products of broken homes;

and in the degree to which they were subjected to early abnormal environmental experiences, such as placement in foster homes, frequent moving about, commitment to juvenile institutions, and so on. They were to an equal extent denied the care of their mothers, for like proportions of both groups had mothers who were gainfully employed outside the home. They were in equal proportions offspring of families in which there was a history of mental disease or defect; they came from families in which members other than the offenders (parents and/or brothers and sisters) were also delinquents; in equal proportions they were reared in homes in which the moral standards were low; the same proportions of the families were assisted by social agencies during the boyhood of the offenders. The two groups were held in parental affection to a like degree during childhood, and were subjected to similar disciplinary practices by their parents.

As to the youths themselves, they misbehaved in school in like extent, particularly as school truants. They began to work at the same early age, and were to an equal extent engaged in street trades upon entering industrial life. They had a like equipment in physical health, as determined at the time of their examination at the Clinic of the Judge Baker Foundation. The boys were of the same average age at first arrest, and a like period elapsed between the onset of misbehavior and first formal recognition of delinquency. And finally, they resembled each other in the limited extent to which they were in boyhood members of boys' clubs, settlements, and other organizations for the constructive use of leisure.

SLIGHT DIFFERENCES

We now turn to the factors in which the two groups differed slightly, to see whether we can find in them any suggestion of why certain offenders respond well to extramural supervision but not to incarceration.

It will be recalled that for the purpose of our comparisons "slight differences" are those in which the difference in incidence of one or more sub-categories is not more than 4 to 10 per cent. In view of the fact that there were only 48 boys in the group who behaved well under extramural but not under intramural treatment, each of the slight differences may have little if any significance. However, a distinct trend of difference in several factors in combination may suggest, at least, the reasons why the two groups behaved differently during treatment.

A slightly larger proportion of the youths who behaved satisfactorily during extramural treatment but not during intramural than of those who behaved well during both were first-born children. To a slightly greater extent their parents did not live together compatibly even though they were not actually to any greater extent separated or divorced. The boys were to a slightly greater extent reared in homes in which the economic and living conditions were poor, even though the neighborhoods in which they grew up were slightly better.

There are three minor differences in the characteristics of the boys themselves: slightly larger proportions of those who responded well only during extramural treatment than of those who responded well to both types of treatment were of low intelligence, were retarded in school, and had bad habits in boyhood.

Although the differences between the two groups of delinquents are small, it is evident that the trend is essentially in the direction of a poorer early environment and of a slightly worse innate equipment (reflected in their somewhat lower intelligence and in school retardation) among those who got along well during extramural supervision but not behind walls. However, only a comparison of the marked differences between the groups will show whether the trend of difference is really significant.

MARKED DIFFERENCES

Although the two sets of offenders are to a like extent the sons of foreign-born parents, there is a considerable difference in the country of birth of their parents. Table 65 shows that an appreciably greater proportion of the offenders who got along well only during extramural supervision were sons of Italian-born fathers and

TABLE 65. OFFENDERS WHO SUCCEEDED IN EXTRAMURAL BUT FAILED IN
INTRAMURAL TREATMENT, AND THOSE WHO SUCCEEDED IN BOTH
TYPES: BIRTHPLACE OF PARENTS (PERCENTAGES)

	EXTRAMURAL SUCCESSES, INTRAMURAL FAILURES		SUCCESSES IN BOTH TYPES	
	Fathers	*Mothers*	*Fathers*	*Mothers*
United States	19.1	20.0	20.2	20.5
Italy	44.8	46.7	31.8	32.3
Russia, Poland, Lithuania	19.1	17.8	14.1	13.8
Ireland	2.1	6.6	11.6	14.4
Other	14.9	8.9	22.3	19.0
Total number of known cases	*47*	*45*	*198*	*195*

mothers, and that proportionately fewer of them were the sons of
parents born in Ireland. The suggestion may be ventured that possibly the temperament of South European peoples does not adapt
itself so well to the rigid discipline of institutional life.[1]

Three other factors of significant difference in the characteristics of the two groups of offenders may shed further light on the
reasons why certain offenders, though responding satisfactorily to
a less rigid form of peno-correctional treatment, do not get along
well in the more closely supervised life of institutions. As Table 66

TABLE 66. OFFENDERS WHO SUCCEEDED IN EXTRAMURAL BUT FAILED
IN INTRAMURAL TREATMENT, AND THOSE WHO SUCCEEDED
IN BOTH TYPES: EARLY ASSOCIATES
(PERCENTAGES)

	EXTRAMURAL SUCCESSES, INTRA-MURAL FAILURES	SUCCESSES IN BOTH TYPES
Neither crowd nor gang associations	83.3	71.4
Ran about with crowd	14.6	22.2
Member of gang	2.1	6.4
Total number of known cases	*48*	*203*

[1] It should be pointed out also that a larger proportion of youths who behaved well during extramural supervision but not in institutions were sons of Catholic parents. This fact
hinges, however, on the larger proportion of Italian parents in this group and is of no significance in itself, as is shown by the opposite situation in the case of the Irish.

shows, those who responded well only to extramural treatment were, to a less extent than the others, boys who in their childhood belonged to gangs or ran about with crowds of boys; that is, they kept to themselves to a significantly greater degree. Apparently they were to a greater extent of the type who do not like group life than were those who behaved well during both extramural and intramural treatment. Their potentialities for good behavior become evident only in the more individualized treatment offered by extramural supervision, where association between the offender and the probation or parole officer constitutes the major basis of treatment, as contrasted with a multifarious rubbing of shoulders (and temperaments) with many fellow-inmates and officers during intramural control. This finding is further borne out in Table 67, which

TABLE 67. OFFENDERS WHO SUCCEEDED IN EXTRAMURAL BUT FAILED IN INTRAMURAL TREATMENTS, AND THOSE WHO SUCCEEDED IN BOTH TYPES: ACCOMPLICES IN OFFENSE FOR WHICH THEY WERE BROUGHT BEFORE BOSTON JUVENILE COURT
(PERCENTAGES)

	EXTRAMURAL SUCCESSES, INTRAMURAL FAILURES	SUCCESSES IN BOTH TYPES
Offense committed alone	41.5	29.5
Offense committed with one other	19.5	30.6
Offense committed with two or more others	39.0	39.9
Total number of known cases	*41*	*173*

reveals that these youths were lone offenders to a significantly greater degree than were the boys who responded to both types of treatment.

And, lastly, it is evident from Table 68 that the youths who behaved well only during periods of extramural treatment were to a less extent than the others burdened with liabilities of personality. This fact in conjunction with our other findings would indicate that a tendency to withdraw from the company of others or an inability to get along with others, although not necessarily classifiable

TABLE 68. OFFENDERS WHO SUCCEEDED IN EXTRAMURAL BUT FAILED IN
INTRAMURAL TREATMENTS, AND THOSE WHO SUCCEEDED IN BOTH
TYPES: MENTAL CONDITION (PERCENTAGES)

	EXTRAMURAL SUCCESSES, INTRAMURAL FAILURES	SUCCESSES IN BOTH TYPES
No mental disease, distortion, marked liabilities of personality, or marked adolescent instability	49.0	37.0
Mental disease or distortion	14.3	14.7
Marked personality liabilities or marked adolescent instability	36.7	48.3
Total number of known cases	49	184

as mental pathology but merely as a "personality handicap," apparently largely explains why certain offenders do not behave well in confinement, where they must get along with others and make forced adaptations, although they respond satisfactorily to extramural supervision.

*   *   *   *   *

Now that we have discerned very real differences between our four major "conduct types" that indicate what may be the explanation for their divergent responses to extramural and intramural treatment in general, we can turn to the preparation of prediction charts showing the probable behavior of offenders during the various forms of peno-correctional treatment. If certain factors in the constitution, the background, and the foreground of our offenders are found to be sufficiently predictive of the course of their behavior under different forms of peno-correctional treatment, it will be possible to conclude that our conduct types are also representatives of "treatment types," i.e., that the application of different forms of correctional therapy or punishment may be expected to bring about at least roughly definable and predictable results. Such a finding should be of great value to judges, parole board members, and others concerned with the administration of criminal justice.

Chapter XIX

PREDICTING BEHAVIOR DURING VARIOUS FORMS OF PENO-CORRECTIONAL TREATMENT

IN our analyses of the "conduct types" we discovered several clues to the reasons why certain offenders do not respond to certain types of peno-correctional treatment. Our next step is to use this information in such a way that a judge, knowing certain facts about the background and personal characteristics of a prisoner brought before him for sentencing, will be helped in deciding which of the various forms of peno-correctional treatment is likely to produce the best results. For example, we found that offenders who did not like companionship did not behave as well in institutions as on probation or parole; special provision should be made for such offenders to insure more individualized attention than is ordinarily given in institutions. We also found that certain youths who were victims of deep feelings of insecurity engendered by their early environment behaved well in institutions but not during extramural supervision; probation and parole authorities should be guided by this finding in giving closer and more sympathetic supervision to such offenders if it is necessary to place them on probation or parole.

If it is possible to determine to which kind of peno-correctional treatment a particular offender is most likely to respond, and so to subject him only to treatments which will increase his capacity for adjustment and thereby his responsiveness to treatment, the peno-correctional system can be made to function much more smoothly—and to the ultimate advantage of the public as well as the offender.

In our previous works our prediction tables dealt only with the probable behavior of offenders *following* the completion of a particular form of treatment; in 500 *Criminal Careers* and in *Later Criminal Careers* with behavior after treatment in a men's reformatory, in *Five Hundred Delinquent Women* with behavior after treatment in a women's reformatory, and in *One Thousand Juvenile De-*

linquents with behavior after treatment by a juvenile court upon recommendation of a child guidance clinic.[1] We have never before considered the prediction of behavior *during* specific forms of treatment. However, in the present research we have assembled information regarding the behavior of our 1,000 juvenile delinquents during various peno-correctional treatments from the onset of their delinquent careers until they reached an average age of twenty-nine years.

BASIS OF PREDICTION

In Chapter XIII we described how these basic data were gathered and how the behavior of each offender during each period of peno-correctional treatment was carefully analyzed and a summary made of his conduct during each type of treatment.[2] For example, the case of John G (see page 151) was summarized as follows: he failed during three probations; misbehaved during three periods of probation under suspended sentence but behaved satisfactorily in a fourth; failed during three periods on parole; got along well during two correctional school commitments; failed during one stay in a reformatory; and behaved acceptably during two terms in jail. John G therefore had to be regarded as a failure under straight probation, first a failure but later a success on probation under suspended sentence, a failure on parole, a success in a correctional school, a failure in a reformatory, and a success in a jail. We analyzed in this way the history of each of 962 men about whose conduct during peno-correctional treatments information was available.

After the responses to treatment were summarized, correlations were made between 63 factors in the family and personal history of the delinquents and behavior during each particular form of treatment (straight probation, probation under suspended sentence, parole, correctional schools, reformatories, prisons, jails, Army and

---

[1] See *500 Criminal Careers*, Chapter XVIII; *One Thousand Juvenile Delinquents*, Chapter XI; *Five Hundred Delinquent Women*, Chapter XVII; *Later Criminal Careers*, Chapter XII.

[2] See pages 151 ff.

Navy). By our usual method of first inspecting the correlation tables and then applying the coefficient of mean square contingency wherever the degree of relationship was in doubt, five factors were selected from each set of correlations which, with one or two exceptions, showed the highest degree of relationship to behavior during each form of treatment. If more than five factors showed about an equal degree of relationship to behavior during treatment, those five were chosen about which information could be most readily obtained for the court by probation officers or others. If there were a sufficient number of factors upon which to construct the predictive table without utilizing the factor "Mental condition," this factor was omitted because most courts do not go to the expense of subjecting offenders to psychiatric examination.[3] It should be said, finally, that wherever two factors were equally predictive and a choice could be made between them the one which was more objective in character, or about which information could be obtained more easily by officers of the court, was chosen. An examination of the factors selected for each prediction table will indicate, however, that it was not always possible to utilize only highly objective factors.

PREDICTING BEHAVIOR DURING PROBATION

The five factors selected as a basis for predicting behavior during probation are shown in Table 69. The behavior of each offender who had been placed on probation and whose status on each of the five factors was known was scored.[4] As in all our previous prediction tables, score classes were set up between the limits of the lowest and the highest possible failure score—in this instance between 162.7 and 318.4. Then the cases were distributed into their particular failure-score classes in accordance with behavior during probation. When the table was completed it was examined to determine what contraction of the score classes should be made, the process resulting in Table 70.

---

[3] Intelligence of offender was, however, included where it was predictive.

[4] Since this process of scoring was described in Chapter XII there is no need to repeat it here.

TABLE 69. FACTORS PREDICTIVE OF BEHAVIOR DURING STRAIGHT PROBATION

PREDICTION FACTORS AND SUB-CATEGORIES*	COEFFICIENT OF MEAN SQUARE CONTINGENCY	PERCENTAGE INCIDENCE OF FAILURE DURING PROBATION
Birthplace of father	.17	
Poland, Russia, Lithuania		45.4
Italy, Ireland		53.7
United States or foreign countries except Italy, Ireland, Poland, Russia, and Lithuania		65.5
Discipline by father	.22	
Good		16.7
Fair		45.5
Poor		62.9
Discipline by mother	.22	
Good		15.4
Fair		48.6
Poor		65.2
School retardation	.17	
No retardation		43.5
Retarded one year		54.9
Retarded two or more years		62.7
School misconduct	.20	
No misconduct		41.7
Misconduct other than truancy		51.5
Truancy		62.1

* Whatever contractions have been made of the original more detailed sub-categories of the factors are based on an examination of the raw tables, from which it could readily be determined which sub-categories to combine.

From this table a judge can ascertain, for example, that an offender scoring under 240 has six and a half chances in 10 (64 per cent) of behaving well under probation; two chances in 10 (20 per cent) of erratic behavior (that is, sometimes succeeding and sometimes failing, but not progressing consistently from poorer to better behavior); less than half a chance in 10 (4 per cent) of behaving well on probation later though not immediately; and only about one chance in 10 (12 per cent) of failing entirely. In other words,

TABLE 70. TOTAL FAILURE SCORE RELATED TO BEHAVIOR DURING
STRAIGHT PROBATION (CONTRACTED)

TOTAL FAILURE SCORE	ALWAYS SUCCESS		ALWAYS FAILURE		EARLY FAILURE, LATER SUCCESS		ERRATIC BEHAVIOR		TOTAL
	Num-ber	Per cent	Num-ber	Per cent	Num-ber	Per cent	Num-ber	Per cent	Num-ber
Under 240	16	64.0	3	12.0	1	4.0	5	20.0	25
240 to 270	16	33.3	21	43.7	6	12.5	5	10.5	48
270 and over	42	14.4	183	62.9	32	11.0	34	11.7	291
Total	74	20.3	207	56.9	39	10.7	44	12.1	364

$$C = .35$$

the chances of immediate or ultimate good behavior of this offender during probation are almost nine out of 10. Obviously, a judge would readily place such an offender on probation since the likelihood of his good response is so high.

On the other hand, if he has before him an offender who scores 270 or over, he will see from the prediction table that the chances of failure under this form of treatment are more than six out of 10, and he therefore would not be so likely to place this particular offender on probation. However, the important question that would naturally arise in the mind of a reflective judge is whether this offender has a better chance of good behavior under some other form of peno-correctional treatment. The answer to this question will be found in the next chapter.

PREDICTING BEHAVIOR DURING PROBATION UNDER SUSPENDED SENTENCE

The five factors in the family and personal history of our group of offenders which showed the highest relationship to behavior during this form of probation[5] are shown in Table 71. It will be noticed that in all but one factor the predictive elements are the same as for straight probation; in Table 71 the factor "Affection of father for offender" has replaced "School retardation" of Table 69.

By the same methods applied throughout the construction of pre-

[5] Probation under suspended sentence carries a threat of commitment to an institution in case the probationer violates the conditions of probation.

TABLE 71. FACTORS PREDICTIVE OF BEHAVIOR DURING PROBATION
UNDER SUSPENDED SENTENCE

PREDICTION FACTORS AND SUB-CATEGORIES*	COEFFICIENT OF MEAN SQUARE CONTINGENCY	PERCENTAGE INCIDENCE OF FAILURE DURING PROBATION UNDER SUSPENDED SENTENCE
Birthplace of father	.20	
Foreign countries except Italy and Ireland		58.6
Italy		66.2
United States or Ireland		78.4
Discipline by father	.26	
Good		37.5
Fair		55.8
Poor		76.4
Discipline by mother	.20	
Good		33.3
Fair		58.8
Poor		75.0
Affection of father for offender	.17	
Good		64.1
Fair or poor		79.4
School misconduct	.14	
No misconduct		51.1
Truancy or other misbehavior		73.9

* Whatever contractions have been made of the original more detailed sub-categories of the factors are based on an examination of the raw tables, from which it could readily be determined which sub-categories to combine.

diction tables, Table 72 was evolved within the score limits of 244.6 to 383.1, which represents the lowest and highest possible failure scores for this particular form of peno-correctional treatment on the basis of the above five factors.

From this table a judge would see that an offender scoring under 300 has a fifty-fifty chance of success during probation under suspended sentence. If an offender scores 330 or over, however, his chances of failure are almost eight out of 10. A judge would not be likely, therefore, to place such an offender under a suspended sen-

TABLE 72. TOTAL FAILURE SCORE RELATED TO BEHAVIOR DURING
PROBATION UNDER SUSPENDED SENTENCE (CONTRACTED)

TOTAL FAILURE SCORE	ALWAYS SUCCESS		ALWAYS FAILURE		EARLY FAILURE, LATER SUCCESS		ERRATIC BEHAVIOR		TOTAL
	Num-ber	Per cent	Num-ber	Per cent	Num-ber	Per cent	Num-ber	Per cent	Num-ber
Under 300	8	50.0	8	50.0	–	–	–	–	16
300 to 330	17	37.8	19	42.2	3	6.7	6	13.3	45
330 and over	23	13.3	135	78.0	12	6.9	3	1.8	173
Total	*48*	*20.5*	*162*	*69.2*	*15*	*6.4*	*9*	*3.9*	*234*

$$C = .37$$

tence, particularly if the defendant has a better chance of success under some other form of treatment.

PREDICTING BEHAVIOR DURING PAROLE

The five factors found to have the highest predictive value for behavior during parole are shown in Table 73. "Birthplace of mother" is the new factor introduced, taking the place of "School retardation" in the group predictive of behavior on ordinary probation (Table 69) and of "Affection of father for offender" in the prognostic syndrome for probation under suspended sentence (Table 71).

A prediction table was constructed on the basis of these five factors within the score limits of 276.4 to 296.5. Table 74, like the others thus far presented, was contracted from a more refined failure-score classification.

It is evident that an offender in the higher score brackets has less chance of success than one in the lower score brackets. A judge or parole board would not be likely to encourage parole following imprisonment for an offender scoring 350 or over if some other form of treatment were available during which he would be likely to behave more acceptably. If he were placed on parole, he should be subjected to especially strict supervision to prevent the further commission of crimes.

TABLE 73. FACTORS PREDICTIVE OF BEHAVIOR DURING PAROLE

PREDICTION FACTORS AND SUB-CATEGORIES*	COEFFICIENT OF MEAN SQUARE CONTINGENCY	PERCENTAGE INCIDENCE OF FAILURE DURING PAROLE
Birthplace of father	.22	
Foreign countries except Ireland		64.3
United States		77.9
Ireland		89.7
Birthplace of mother	.17	
United States, Italy, Russia, Poland, Lithuania		66.9
Foreign countries except Ireland, Italy, Russia, Poland, Lithuania		72.7
Ireland		86.7
Discipline by father	.17	
Good		40.3
Fair		63.9
Poor		74.1
Discipline by mother	.17	
Good		50.0
Fair		61.7
Poor		73.8
School misconduct	.17	
No misconduct		55.2
Misconduct		72.2

* Whatever contractions have been made of the original more detailed sub-categories of the factors are based on an examination of the raw tables, from which it could readily be determined which sub-categories to combine.

PREDICTING BEHAVIOR IN INDUSTRIAL AND CORRECTIONAL SCHOOLS

Turning now to the various intramural peno-correctional treatments that have been included in this research, we present first, in Table 75, the five factors found to be most highly predictive of behavior in industrial and correctional schools. It will be noted that we have here a different set of factors than for the other forms of treatment considered.

The degree of relationship between these factors and behavior in such schools is not very high, as evidenced by the low coefficients of

TABLE 74. TOTAL FAILURE SCORE RELATED TO BEHAVIOR DURING
PAROLE (CONTRACTED)

TOTAL FAILURE SCORE	ALWAYS SUCCESS		ALWAYS FAILURE		EARLY FAILURE, LATER SUCCESS		ERRATIC BEHAVIOR		TOTAL
	Number	*Per cent*	*Number*	*Per cent*	*Number*	*Per cent*	*Number*	*Per cent*	*Number*
Under 290	1	100.0	–	–	–	–	–	–	1
290 to 350	8	15.4	34	65.4	10	19.2	–	–	52
350 and over	14	8.6	120	73.6	28	17.2	1	.6	163
Total	23	10.6	154	71.3	38	17.6	1	.5	216

$$C = .22$$

mean square contingency,[6] but as they are the five factors showing
the highest association to behavior they had to be used. It will be
noted from Table 76, however, that the coefficient of mean square
contingency representing the degree of association between these
five factors in combination and behavior in correctional schools is
higher than is the coefficient expressing the relationship between
any one of the five individual factors and behavior in correctional
schools.

By consulting Table 76 a judge would see that an offender scoring under 210 has only three chances in 10 of not behaving satisfactorily in an industrial or correctional school at one time or another,
while the chances are almost five and a half in 10 that an offender
scoring as high as 220 or more will not respond satisfactorily to the
regime of such a school either immediately or at a later time. The
judge would be less likely, therefore, to place this offender in such
an institution, but his decision would depend on whether or not
this particular offender has a better chance of good behavior under
some other form of peno-correctional treatment—a point to be en-
larged upon in the next chapter.

[6] The probable reason for this is that "success" in institutional life so often means merely
adherence to rules, compliance with the routine, and the like, and a substantial proportion
of institutional inmates must, by the institution's own standards, be classified as successes.
Therefore the divergencies between the two groups are not as marked, though they are still
consistently in one direction.

TABLE 75. FACTORS PREDICTIVE OF BEHAVIOR IN INDUSTRIAL AND
CORRECTIONAL SCHOOLS

PREDICTION FACTORS AND SUB-CATEGORIES*	COEFFICIENT OF MEAN SQUARE CONTINGENCY	PERCENTAGE INCIDENCE OF FAILURE IN CORRECTIONAL SCHOOLS
Moral standards of childhood home	.08	
Fair or poor		42.3
Good		57.7
Number of children in family	.08	
Two or more children		41.9
Offender only child		57.1
Conjugal relations of parents	.17	
Good		36.9
Fair		48.1
Poor		54.3
Habits of offender	.10	
No bad habits		31.5
Bad habits		45.7
Time between first misbehavior and first arrest	.10	
None		23.1
Some		43.2

* Whatever contractions have been made of the original more detailed sub-categories of
the factors are based on an examination of the raw tables, from which it could readily be
determined which sub-categories to combine.

PREDICTING BEHAVIOR IN REFORMATORIES

We found that the five factors shown in Table 77 bore the highest
relationship to behavior during reformatory treatment. Some of
them are new; for the first time "Intelligence of offender" appears.
On the basis of these five factors we constructed Table 78 within
the score limits of 171.3 to 237.4, derived as always from the lowest
and highest possible percentage incidence of failure on the five
factors involved.

Although the coefficient of mean square contingency is low,
Table 78 has some value; for a judge is at least able to determine
from it which offenders are most likely to succeed under this form
of treatment. For example, an offender scoring under 200 has only

TABLE 76. TOTAL FAILURE SCORE RELATED TO BEHAVIOR IN INDUSTRIAL
AND CORRECTIONAL SCHOOLS (CONTRACTED)

TOTAL FAILURE SCORE	ALWAYS SUCCESS		ALWAYS FAILURE		EARLY FAILURE, LATER SUCCESS		ERRATIC BEHAVIOR		TOTAL
	Number	Per cent	Number	Per cent	Number	Per cent	Number	Per cent	Number
Under 210	11	55.0	6	30.0	2	10.0	1	5.0	20
210 to 220	26	37.1	25	35.7	9	12.9	10	14.3	70
220 and over	23	31.9	39	54.2	6	8.3	4	5.6	72
Total	60	37.0	70	43.2	17	10.5	15	9.3	162

$$C = .24$$

about two chances in 10 of failing consistently if he is placed in a
reformatory; the higher the offender's score the greater the probability of failure under this form of treatment. We shall see from the

TABLE 77. FACTORS PREDICTIVE OF BEHAVIOR IN REFORMATORIES

PREDICTION FACTORS AND SUB-CATEGORIES*	COEFFICIENT OF MEAN SQUARE CONTINGENCY	PERCENTAGE INCIDENCE OF FAILURE IN RE- FORMATORIES
Birthplace of father	.14	
Foreign countries except Italy, Russia, Poland, Lithuania		32.6
United States, Italy, Russia, Poland, Lithuania		45.7
Conjugal relations of parents	.10	
Fair or poor		39.2
Good		48.1
Intelligence of offender	.14	
Not feebleminded		40.0
Feebleminded		55.0
School misconduct	.10	
No misconduct		25.0
Misconduct		40.6
Member of gang or crowd	.17	
Yes		34.5
No		48.0

* Whatever contractions have been made of the original more detailed sub-categories of
the factors are based on an examination of the raw tables, from which it could readily be
determined which sub-categories to combine.

TABLE 78. TOTAL FAILURE SCORE RELATED TO BEHAVIOR IN
REFORMATORIES (CONTRACTED)

TOTAL FAILURE SCORE	ALWAYS SUCCESS		ALWAYS FAILURE		EARLY FAILURE, LATER SUCCESS		ERRATIC BEHAVIOR		TOTAL
	Num-ber	Per cent	Num-ber	Per cent	Num-ber	Per cent	Num-ber	Per cent	Num-ber
Under 200	12	66.7	4	22.2	2	11.1	–	–	18
200 to 210	24	55.8	16	37.2	2	4.7	1	2.3	43
210 to 220	9	40.9	10	45.5	2	9.1	1	4.5	22
220 to 230	8	27.6	19	65.5	1	3.4	1	3.4	29
230 and over	–	–	3	75.0	1	25.0	–	–	4
Total	53	45.7	52	44.8	8	6.9	3	2.6	116

$$C = .14$$

illustrations presented in the next chapter how a judge would determine what alternative treatment to apply if the chances of good behavior in a reformatory are slight.

PREDICTING BEHAVIOR IN PRISONS

It was possible on the basis of the five factors in Table 79 to construct a chart showing probable behavior of offenders in a prison, but since the total number of cases involved is small the resulting predictive instrument can be considered only as tentative and illustrative. Table 80, constructed within the score limits of 94.5 and 214.0, was contracted from a more detailed failure-score classification.

By consulting this table a judge would see that an offender scoring under 120, though having only three chances in 10 of not behaving acceptably in prison, has a like chance of always getting along in prison, two chances in 10 of adjusting himself to a prison regime after a period of failure, and one chance in 10 of behaving well at times. If he scores 120 or over, he has about the same chance of constantly misbehaving in prison as the offender who scores under 120; but he has six and a half chances in 10 of always behaving satisfactorily, as opposed to the three chances in 10 of the offender who scores under 120. The offender with a higher score is more likely, therefore, to be sent to prison than the former.

TABLE 79. FACTORS PREDICTIVE OF BEHAVIOR IN PRISONS

PREDICTION FACTORS AND SUB-CATEGORIES*	COEFFICIENT OF MEAN SQUARE CONTINGENCY	PERCENTAGE INCIDENCE OF FAILURE IN PRISONS
Age of younger parent at marriage	.32	
Twenty-one or over		7.7
Under twenty-one years		41.9
Conjugal relations of parents	.28	
Good or fair		25.8
Poor		61.5
Discipline by father	.17	
Poor		24.0
Good or fair		40.0
Affection of father for offender	.24	
Fair or poor		16.0
Good		34.2
Age of offender at first arrest	.20	
Eleven or older		21.0
Under eleven years		36.4

* Whatever contractions have been made of the original more detailed sub-categories of the factors are based on an examination of the raw tables, from which it could readily be determined which sub-categories to combine.

TABLE 80. TOTAL FAILURE SCORE RELATED TO BEHAVIOR IN PRISONS
(CONTRACTED)

TOTAL FAILURE SCORE	ALWAYS SUCCESS		ALWAYS FAILURE		EARLY FAILURE, LATER SUCCESS		ERRATIC BEHAVIOR		TOTAL
	Number	Per cent	Number	Per cent	Number	Per cent	Number	Per cent	Number
Under 120	3	33.3	3	33.3	2	22.3	1	11.1	9
120 and over	23	65.7	10	28.5	1	2.9	1	2.9	35
Total	26	59.1	13	29.5	3	6.8	2	4.6	44

$$C = .35$$

PREDICTING BEHAVIOR IN JAILS AND OTHER SHORT-TERM INSTITUTIONS

In the prediction of behavior in jails, houses of correction, and other establishments to which short sentences are usually given, we utilized the five factors in Table 81. On the basis of these factors we constructed Table 82 within the score limits of 34.9 to 114.0.

TABLE 81. FACTORS PREDICTIVE OF BEHAVIOR IN JAILS AND OTHER
SHORT-TERM INSTITUTIONS

PREDICTION FACTORS AND SUB-CATEGORIES*	COEFFICIENT OF MEAN SQUARE CONTINGENCY	PERCENTAGE INCIDENCE OF FAILURE IN JAILS
Color of offender	.44	
Negro		6.7
White		17.6
Age at first arrest	.14	
Thirteen or over		12.5
Under thirteen		22.3
Member of gang or crowd	.10	
No		15.7
Yes		24.5
Neighborhood influences in childhood	.17	
Good or fair		0
Poor		19.9
Time between first misbehavior and first arrest	.22	
None		0
One year or less		12.5
Over a year		29.7

* Whatever contractions have been made of the original more detailed sub-categories of the factors are based on an examination of the raw tables, from which it could readily be determined which sub-categories to combine.

TABLE 82. TOTAL FAILURE SCORE RELATED TO BEHAVIOR IN JAILS AND
OTHER SHORT-TERM INSTITUTIONS (CONTRACTED)

TOTAL FAILURE SCORE	ALWAYS SUCCESS		ALWAYS FAILURE		EARLY FAILURE, LATER SUCCESS		ERRATIC BEHAVIOR		TOTAL
	Num-ber	Per cent	Num-ber	Per cent	Num-ber	Per cent	Num-ber	Per cent	Num-ber
Under 70	4	50.0	4	50.0	–	–	–	–	8
70 and over	61	56.0	35	32.1	7	6.4	6	5.5	109
Total	65	55.6	39	33.3	7	6.0	6	5.1	117

$$C = .10$$

It can be seen from a glance at this table that its predictive value is not high, but it suggests the possibility of application of this method to short-term offenders.[7] An offender scoring 70 or over

[7] The superficial standards of satisfactory performance expected of jail inmates are reflected in the low predictive value of the table.

TABLE 83. FACTORS PREDICTIVE OF BEHAVIOR IN ARMY OR NAVY

PREDICTION FACTORS AND SUB-CATEGORIES*	COEFFICIENT OF MEAN SQUARE CONTINGENCY	PERCENTAGE INCIDENCE OF FAILURE IN ARMY OR NAVY
Education of parents	.17	
No formal schooling		34.2
One or both attended common school		41.0
One or both entered high school		60.0
Religion of parents	.20	
Mixed		33.3
Both Catholic or Hebrew		42.2
Both Protestant		58.8
Difference in age of parents	.20	
Five years or less		40.5
More than five years		57.1
Delinquency in immediate family	.20	
Delinquency		38.5
No delinquency		64.7
Neighborhood influences in childhood	.22	
Poor		33.3
Good or fair		58.8

* Whatever contractions have been made of the original more detailed sub-categories of the factors are based on an examination of the raw tables, from which it could readily be determined which sub-categories to combine.

has but little more chance of behaving acceptably in jails than the one scoring under 70. However, the value of Table 82 will be brought out in the next chapter where illustrative cases are given showing how the tables can be used in combination.

Even though all offenders may have about an equal chance of success or failure under a jail routine, a particular offender may have more chance of acceptable conduct in jail than he has under any other form of peno-correctional treatment.

PREDICTING BEHAVIOR IN ARMY OR NAVY

Although enlistment in the Army or Navy is not a peno-correctional treatment, its value in certain types of cases as a supplement to probation or parole cannot be denied. Certain of our offenders responded very well to this type of regime even though they did not behave acceptably under other forms of treatment. Probationers

TABLE 84. TOTAL FAILURE SCORE RELATED TO BEHAVIOR IN ARMY
OR NAVY (CONTRACTED)

TOTAL FAILURE SCORE	ALWAYS SUCCESS		ALWAYS FAILURE		EARLY FAILURE, LATER SUCCESS		ERRATIC BEHAVIOR		TOTAL
	Num-ber	Per cent	Num-ber	Per cent	Num-ber	Per cent	Num-ber	Per cent	Num-ber
Under 230	18	51.4	10	28.6	1	2.9	6	17.1	35
230 and over	3	37.5	5	62.5	–	–	–	–	8
Total	21	48.8	15	34.9	1	2.3	6	14.0	43

C = .26

and parolees have occasionally sought to join the Army or Navy in the belief that such enlistment presented the most promising solution of their behavior problems. For these reasons we have considered it useful to develop a prediction table for this type of discipline.

On the basis of the five factors in Table 83 we evolved Table 84 within the score classes of 179.8 to 299.4. By consulting this table a judge could determine that an offender scoring under 230 has less than three chances in 10 of consistently failing under the regime of the Army or Navy, while one scoring 230 or over has more than six chances in 10 of misbehaving. This information might prove exceedingly useful in determining upon the kind of treatment to be given a particular offender. An institution approaching Army or Navy discipline would probably be more effective than another type for a man with a low score, or, if probation is being considered, the added discipline of the Army or Navy might be indicated.

*   *   *   *   *

We have presented eight prediction tables indicating the probable behavior during each form of peno-correctional treatment of offenders who are or have been juvenile delinquents. The tables clearly indicate that success or failure is relative, for none of them shows a 10-out-of-10 chance of absolute success or failure. This fact should act as a spur to peno-correctional authorities who have perhaps come to feel that certain offenders are not amenable to any known form of treatment. It will be seen that *the right treatment given at the right time to the right criminal is the important factor in the sentencing process. But inventiveness is also called for in experimenting with new forms of character-therapy, habit-training, psychotherapy, and the like.* The chief value in these tables lies in the scientific basis which they provide for the disposition of particular cases, on the sound theory that each offender is essentially typical of some sufficiently definable "treatment type."

Although prediction charts must be used with great discretion, they nevertheless provide the judge with a guide to treatment far more telling than the haphazard method now in use in disposing of cases. Their proper employment is bound to lead to fundamental improvements in present sentencing practices and treatment methods and to a search for other more promising ones. Whether the application of more appropriate treatment will tend to shorten delinquent careers or result in rehabilitating more offenders remains for future research to determine. But at least during treatment a smoother, more effective, and less expensive administration of justice is likely, and the public, which—as much as the offenders themselves—is the victim of an inefficient and haphazard administration of justice, will be safeguarded.

Chapter XX

CASES ILLUSTRATING THE USE OF PREDICTION
TABLES

IN Chapters XII and XIX we presented prediction tables constructed on the basis of the materials of this research, showing the probable recidivism of offenders of the type represented by this group of juvenile delinquents, their probable age at reformation and at change from the commission of serious to minor offenses, and the probable behavior of such offenders during each of seven types of peno-correctional treatment and in the Army or Navy. Although these individual prediction tables are valuable at least in indicating the likelihood of ultimate good behavior or of good behavior during a particular treatment, to make full practical use of them a judge should know not only the type of treatment *during* which an offender is likely to behave well but also the type *following* which he gives the greatest promise of reformation. We are ready, therefore, to illustrate the practical use of prediction charts in improving the disposition practices of the courts within the framework of the present machinery for the administration of criminal justice.[1]

The reader of a work such as this is doubtless familiar with the present haphazard method of disposing of criminal cases. Random, trial-and-error procedures are the rule. Except for efforts to punish the crime—rather than the criminal—by penalties established by statute, there is no consistent approach to the disposition of cases. Courts waver between stringency and leniency, depending on their own or the community's mood or feeling about certain offenses or offenders. A rationale of punishment hardly exists. The typical case history of a criminal career is a series of fines, proba-

---

[1] In *500 Criminal Careers, Later Criminal Careers,* and *Five Hundred Delinquent Women* we presented prediction tables indicating behavior following reformatory treatment, but the use of these charts is limited until we can study the behavior of the same or a like group of offenders during and following other forms of peno-correctional treatment.

tions, commitments, paroles, more fines, recommitments, more probations, and so on and on through a maze of arrests, convictions, releases, nol-prosses. It is evident that offenders are constantly being resubjected to types of treatment to which they have already failed to respond, and until some means are found of subjecting an offender to the form of peno-correctional treatment that is most promising for his particular case, there can be no hope of better results than we are now getting. The disposition of cases by the use of prediction charts, which represent objectified and systematized experience with many cases similar to the particular one appearing before a judge or parole board, offers an efficient method of selecting the treatment to which an offender is most likely to respond; for such charts are based on a consideration of many factors in an offender's history that are much more relevant to the conduct to be expected of him than is the offense itself.[2]

The reader is asked to bear in mind, however, that we are not proposing that judges use prediction charts to the exclusion of any other methods which have already shown themselves to be of value. A prediction table is, after all, only an instrument for the court's use, but it has, at least, a rational foundation and is not the result of vague notions about the presumably deterrent effect of this or that form of punishment, or a whim of the moment on the part of some judge, based on largely irrelevant but seemingly significant considerations—not to speak of pressure on the court for leniency or severity in a given case.

Let us assume that a judge has before him the eleven prediction charts presented in Chapters XII and XIX. These include: one indicating probable behavior of juvenile offenders during a fifteen-year span between the ages of fourteen and twenty-nine (Table 32, page 142), one indicating probable age at change from the commission of serious to the commission of minor offenses (Table 33, page 143), one indicating probable age at reformation (Table 34, page 145),[3] seven showing the probable behavior of offenders dur-

---

[2] See *500 Criminal Careers*, p. 295–296.

[3] As we have shown earlier, this does not mean that arrival at any specific age is in itself

ing specific types of peno-correctional treatment (Tables 70, 72, 74, 76, 78, 80, and 82, all in Chapter XIX), and one indicating probable behavior in the Army or Navy (Table 84, page 214). How would he be aided in disposing of an offender before him for sentence by the application of these predictive devices?

First, for every case appearing before him a judge would have to request a court officer to gather the necessary data on each of the factors used in the construction of the tables, as the basis for figuring the offender's scores. These scores determine his probable behavior during various forms of peno-correctional treatment and the likelihood of his ultimate reform. A glance at the prediction tables indicates that the number of factors about which information has to be gathered for each case is not large, because some of them are used in several tables. There is no doubt that a skilled investigator could assemble the necessary information and verify it in as short a time as is at present required by the court for the usual probation officer's investigation and report preliminary to an offender's sentence.

Once these data have been gathered, each offender can be scored. This process actually takes only a few minutes. With the scores made, the judge can see at a glance not only what the chances are of the particular offender's ultimate reformation, but also at what age he is likely to reform or, if he is not likely to reform, whether he has a reasonable chance at least of becoming a minor offender and at what age; also, he can determine during which form or forms of treatment the particular offender has the best chance of good behavior.

Consider a few illustrations. In Table 85 are shown, for a series of cases, post-treatment failure scores and chances of good behavior (reform) during the age-span fourteen to twenty-nine years under various forms of peno-correctional treatment and in the Army and Navy. Knowing an offender's chances of good behavior during par-

a guaranty of reform, but only that arrival at a certain age by a person possessed of certain traits ("factors") will result in a certain kind of behavior. In these prediction tables, "age" is prognostically significant only as related to other factors. Persons scoring differently on the predictive factors will reform at different ages if at all.

ticular treatments, and the chances of his ultimate reform, a judge examining such individual case charts could arrive rather quickly at a suitable disposition of the case.

Analyzing cases A, B, and C, to whom these tables can be applied because they actually were juvenile delinquents, let us put ourselves back in the juvenile court at the time when, as boys, these offenders first came before the judge, and see how he would have used the prediction tables. By consulting Table 32 in Chapter XII (page 142) he would first ascertain that as the youths score 98.3, 85.5, and 98.3, respectively, they are representative of a "treatment type" in which each has six chances in 10 of ultimate reformation, one and a half chances of remaining a serious offender, one and a half chances of becoming a minor offender, and less than one chance in 10 of erratic behavior (that is, not reforming but being occasionally a serious offender and occasionally minor). He would then ascertain from Table 34 (page 145) that with such scores, A, B, and C have only one and a half chances in 10 of reforming when less than fifteen years of age, five chances in 10 of doing so when between fifteen and twenty-one, and three and a half in 10 when twenty-one or over.

The judge might assume that because A, B, and C have equal chances of reforming, the same treatment is indicated in all three cases. But this is not so, as we shall see from an analysis of their chances of good behavior during various types of treatment. From the scoring made for each form of treatment we see that case A has four chances in 10 of behaving well during straight probation, only two in 10 of behaving well during probation that carries a threat of commitment to an institution, and only three in 10 of behaving well on parole after serving an institutional sentence. Obviously A is too great a threat to the general security to be allowed to remain at large. His chances of responding satisfactorily to treatment in institutions are better than during extramural supervision, for he has four and a half chances of satisfactory behavior in a correctional school, five and a half in a reformatory, six and a half in prison, and seven in jail.

TABLE 85. ILLUSTRATIVE CASES SHOWING CHANCES OF GOOD BEHAVIOR DURING AGE-SPAN FOURTEEN TO TWENTY-NINE AND DURING SPECIFIC TYPES OF PENO-CORRECTIONAL TREATMENT AND IN ARMY OR NAVY

	DURING AGE 14–29	DURING PROBATION	DURING PROBATION UNDER SUSPENDED SENTENCE	DURING PAROLE	IN CORRECTIONAL SCHOOL	IN REFORMATORY	IN PRISON	IN JAIL	IN ARMY OR NAVY
Case A: Score	98.3	287.5	363.3	351.3	221.1	213.5	109.9	89.0	188.7
Chances of good behavior	6	4	2	3	4½	5½	6½	7	7
Case B: Score	85.5	273.1	327.4	341.1	225.4	222.4	128.7	95.4	214.9
Chances of good behavior	6	4	6	6½	4½	3½	7	7	7
Case C: Score	98.3	298.3	348.0	351.3	210.0	222.4	146.9	105.2	214.9
Chances of good behavior	6	4	2	3	6½	3½	7	7	7
Case D: Score	139.2	281.4	335.0	341.1	210.0	222.4	134.3	105.2	214.9
Chances of good behavior	3½	4	2	3½	6½	3½	7	7	7
Case E: Score	132.8	306.6	355.6	351.3	221.2	228.5	146.9	95.4	205.3
Chances of good behavior	3½	4	2	3	4½	3½	7	7	7
Case F: Score	120.0	252.2	296.0	312.0	210.0	206.8	128.7	78.2	188.7
Chances of good behavior	3½	6	5	3½	6½	6	7	7	7
Case G: Score	148.1	310.6	348.0	357.1	221.2	200.4	112.7	105.2	188.7
Chances of good behavior	3½	4	2	3	4½	6½	7	7	7

TABLE 85 (*cont.*)

	DURING AGE 14–29	DURING PROBATION	DURING PROBATION UNDER SUSPENDED SENTENCE	DURING PAROLE	IN CORRECTIONAL SCHOOL	IN REFORMATORY	IN PRISON	IN JAIL	IN ARMY OR NAVY
Case H: Score	145.3	318.4	348.0	371.1	210.0	209.3	127.4	88.0	195.5
Chances of good behavior	3½	4	2	3	6½	6	7	7	7
Case J: Score	168.4	318.4	348.0	351.3	210.0	209.3	162.3	105.2	195.5
Chances of good behavior	3½	4	2	3	6½	6	7	7	7
Case K: Score	184.3	318.4	383.1	364.9	227.4	213.5	130.2	88.0	222.2
Chances of good behavior	3½	4	2	3	4½	5½	7	7	7
Case L: Score	183.2	310.6	370.9	364.9	221.2	213.5	144.1	105.2	262.1
Chances of good behavior	3½	4	2	3	4½	5½	7	7	7
Case M: Score	183.2	310.6	383.1	364.9	195.8	222.4	144.1	68.1	222.2
Chances of good behavior	3½	4	2	3	7	3½	7	5	7

But there is still another matter to be taken into account. Our judge's decision as to the disposition of this case would be determined finally by A's age at the time of the particular court appearance. If he is only thirteen years old, let us say, straight probation might well be indicated, in view of A's reasonably good chances of ultimate reformation and the fact that his antisocial behavior would probably not be serious at that age; if he does not respond satisfactorily to probation he can, on his next appearance in court, be committed to a correctional school. If, however, A, a former juvenile delinquent, is about twenty-one years old at the time of his appearance in an adult court, commitment to a reformatory would be wiser than placement on probation. But in view of the fact that A still has three and a half chances in 10 of reformation after the age of twenty-one too long a sentence is not indicated (see Table 34, page 145). If A is between twenty-five and thirty at the time of court appearance, the judge would choose between prison and jail, depending upon what opportunities A needs for vocational training, health supervision, or psychiatric attention; but subsequent parole would have to be applied with care, because of A's poor chance of good behavior during parole. The parole authorities would have to be particularly admonished to give A close and intensive supervision, or the judge would have to impose a longer sentence in order to avoid parole as long as possible.

As already pointed out, B has the same chance of ultimate reform as A, but his probable behavior during different forms of treatment does not resemble A's in all respects. Like A, he has four chances in 10 of behaving well during probation, but he has six chances (instead of A's two) of good behavior under suspended sentence. Unlike A who has but three chances, B has six and a half chances in 10 of behaving well during parole. Like A, he has four and a half chances of satisfactory behavior in a correctional school, but only three and a half chances of behaving satisfactorily in a reformatory, to A's five and a half. B has seven chances in 10 of behaving acceptably in prison or jail, which is about the same as A's.

In considering the best disposition of B's case, a judge would be likely to place him on probation under a suspended sentence if he was under twenty-one at the time of the particular court appearance; for his chances of good behavior on that form of treatment are greater than under straight probation or in a correctional school or a reformatory. If he is twenty-one or older he might be sent to prison or jail on a sentence which would provide early release on parole, for his score shows that he has six and a half chances in 10 of responding favorably to parole and there is, therefore, no need to keep him behind walls for any considerable length of time. In other words, the judge would see that B would do well on probation under a suspended sentence or under a short sentence to an institution (if commitment is indicated at all for any special reason, such as need of vocational training, medical care, or psychiatric attention) followed by a long period of parole, but that a correctional school or a reformatory should be avoided if possible.

It is of interest at this point to record what actually happened to B under the existing method of disposing of cases. He did finally reform when he was about twenty-six years old, but meanwhile he had been placed on straight probation at the age of fifteen (instead of being given probation under suspended sentence under which, as his prediction chart indicates, his chances of good behavior were much greater than under probation). He soon ran away and when apprehended was committed to a correctional school (the chart indicates that he was not likely to respond well to this form of treatment). There he remained for fifteen months and proved to be very difficult and lazy. At the age of seventeen he was paroled, and for almost four years behaved quite well (his chart indicates a good chance of success on parole). At the age of twenty-two he again appeared in court, this time for non-support, and he was again placed on straight probation. He soon defaulted, however, and joined the Army where he remained for two years; he behaved exceedingly well and was given an honorable discharge (his prediction chart indicates likelihood of good behavior in the Army). Since his honorable discharge from the Army, B has given no trouble whatsoever. Whether he would have reformed earlier if given the kind of treatment during which he had a good chance of behaving well is of course an open question. Obviously, if throughout his career he had been given the kind of treatment during which he was likely to behave reasonably well, he would have avoided friction with the authorities, the public would have had greater protection from his depredations, treatment in his case would have been less wasteful, and possibly good adjustment would have carried over into his life in freedom.

As to case C, the judge would note that his chances of reformation are the same as A's and B's. A glance at his chart indicates that C, like A and B, has four chances in 10 of succeeding under probation; and like A but unlike B, he has very little chance of success either during probation under suspended sentence or during parole. He has, however, a better chance than either A or B of satisfactory conduct in a correctional school but as little chance as B of success in a reformatory, and as good a chance as A and B of adequate adjustment in prison or jail. If C happens to be under seventeen at the time of the particular court appearance, the judge might be inclined to try straight probation in his case. If probation has already been tried and C has not done well, his small chance of succeeding under the more stringent probation accompanied by a suspended sentence to an institution makes it obvious that direct commitment to a correctional school is indicated, for C has six and a half chances in 10 of satisfactory behavior during this type of treatment. A wise judge would avoid sentencing this offender to a reformatory because his chances of satisfactory behavior there are clearly much lower than under the stricter regimes of prison or jail. If he sends C to an institution, it should be on a long rather than a short sentence, in the light of C's probably poor response to parole.[4]

---

[4] The question whether an offender of this type should be released on parole involves a consideration of the entire philosophy of parole and the practical problem of balancing individual and social interests. If parole were implemented by a truly (i.e., wholly) indeterminate sentence the problem would be simple; given so high a risk, it would be the better part of wisdom to keep such an offender under strict institutional control, because the protection of society against aggression comes first and the individual's welfare second. Such a person might be released later in life, when he is no longer actively dangerous. However,

What actually happened to C under the present system of disposing of cases is worth noting. At the age of twelve he was given probation under suspended sentence for the offense of burglary (which his chart indicates should not have been done, for he had but two chances in 10 of success). During this time he was arrested for stealing, the previous sentence was invoked, and he was committed to a correctional school, where his behavior was excellent (as his prediction chart indicates it was likely to be). He was paroled (as the prediction chart indicates he should not have been), and had to be returned to the correctional school because of consistent misbehavior. During a second, third, and fourth stay in the correctional school, C's behavior was excellent (as the chart indicates it was likely to be); while during a second, third, and fourth parole he seriously misbehaved (as the chart indicates he probably would). At the age of eighteen, during parole, he was arrested for larceny and placed on probation, during which he committed larcenies (his chart indicates only four chances in 10 of good behavior on probation). At the age of nineteen he was sent to a reformatory for larceny, and seriously misbehaved there (his chart indicates a very low chance of success in a reformatory). During parole from the reformatory he misbehaved and he was again sent to the reformatory where he again misbehaved; he was again placed on parole and misbehaved, and was again returned to the reformatory and misbehaved. At the age of twenty-three he was transferred from a reformatory to a jail, where he remained for a year and a half, and was then transferred to another jail for a year. While in jail his behavior was satisfactory (reference to the chart indicates that C had a very high chance of good behavior in jail). At the age of twenty-eight

---

existing "indeterminate" sentences are in a sense fixed sentences in that the upper and lower limits of a frequently narrow zone of years are set. As long as this is true, the paroling authority must cope with the puzzling problem of whether it is better, in the long run (a) to release all offenders at some time before the expiration of the maximum limit of sentence thereby affording them some supervision during the transition to absolute freedom but subjecting society to the risk of their committing new crimes during a period when they might have been safely in prison; or (b) to keep them incarcerated for the full term and release them at its conclusion without any supervision.

C is still a serious criminal. Although we cannot, within the present limited state of our knowledge, assert that, given the treatment indicated by the prediction chart, reformation, or minor rather than serious delinquency, would have resulted (it should be remembered that C's chances of ultimate reformation were six in 10), it is certainly reasonable to assume that C would at least have done much less damage along the way, and at less expenditure of public funds for rearrests, retrials, and the like, had he been given the treatment indicated.

It should be evident to the reader by now that although A's, B's, and C's chances of post-treatment reformation are the same, the peno-correctional treatments *during* which they had the best likelihood of good behavior are different.

We turn now to an application of the prediction charts to three other cases, D, E, and F (Table 85). Consultation of Table 32 (page 142) indicates that, unlike cases A, B, and C, who had six chances in 10 of reformation, D, E, and F, scoring 139.2, 132.8, and 120, respectively, have but three and a half chances in 10 of ultimately reforming, a like low probability of ultimately becoming minor offenders, almost two and a half chances of remaining serious offenders, and less than one chance in 10 of being erratic offenders (that is, alternating between serious and minor delinquencies). A glance at Table 33 (page 143) shows further that D, E, and F have but two chances in 10 of becoming minor delinquents while still under twenty-one years of age, almost five in 10 when they are between fifteen and twenty-one, and three in 10 when they are twenty-one and over. In other words, there are about six and a half chances in 10 that they will become minor offenders when they are still under twenty-one, if they do not reform entirely or remain serious delinquents.

Despite the resemblance in the probable ultimate adjustment of cases D, E, and F, an examination of their scores for each form of peno-correctional treatment, as recorded in Table 85, again indicates certain differences in the way a court should dispose of these cases. For instance, F has a much better chance of succeeding on probation than D and E and likewise a much better chance of success on probation under suspended sentence. All three offenders have about a like chance of success on parole; but E has less of a chance of succeeding in a correctional school regime than D and F; while F has a much better chance of behaving well in a reformatory than D and E. All three offenders, however, have an equally good chance of conducting themselves acceptably in prison, in jail, or in the Service.

Examination of the chances of success of each one of these offenders *during* particular forms of peno-correctional treatment indicates that if probation fails in D's case, the correctional school regime gives promise of eliciting good behavior. A reformatory regime should be avoided, if possible, because D's chances of success there are low; prison or jail may be utilized with a good chance of satisfactory behavior, but parole should be avoided unless the strictest kind of supervision can be given, as D's chances of good behavior under this form of treatment are low.

In the case of E, on the other hand, a correctional school regime does not seem very promising, but if E is at the age where prison or jail could be considered, such regimes are more suitable for him. If probation is resorted to and fails and a correctional school is tried and he does not behave well there, this does not mean that E will not adjust himself to later intramural experiences; but if there appears to be no alternative treatment for him, probation and correctional school authorities would have to expend special effort to make the regime work successfully in E's case, and be on guard against his probable misbehavior.

In the case of F, as is readily seen from Table 85, there is a good chance of his success on straight probation or on probation under suspended sentence; not so good a probability of success on parole; but a good chance of adjusting satisfactorily in a correctional school, reformatory, prison, or jail. The judge has a wide variety of choices in prescribing treatment for F, and can be guided by the special facilities of the various institutions, by the call for a "deterrent punishment," or even by F's preferences.

Now a word as to what actually happened to D, E, and F under the present system of disposing of cases. D was placed on probation at the age of ten and did not respond well (his chart indicates four chances in 10 of good adjustment on probation). He was soon placed on probation again, but this time in a foster home where he was closely supervised. Here he behaved well, which would seem to indicate that probation under close supervision outside his home was indicated in his case. At the age of fifteen he was given probation under suspended sentence for the crime of larceny, and violated his probation by again committing larceny (his prediction chart indicates that he had but two chances in 10 of succeeding on probation under suspended sentence). Soon after, still at the age of fifteen, D was placed on probation in the home of an uncle where he was carefully supervised. There his behavior was excellent, as it had previously been while he was on supervised probation in a foster home. D did not ultimately reform (it will be remembered that his chances of reformation were but three and a half in 10), but he did become a minor offender approximately at the age of seventeen. Had the prediction chart been used in his case it is possible that his misconduct during periods of straight probation and probation under suspended sentence would have been avoided; or, if probation had been resorted to, very close extramural supervision, such as was provided in the foster home and in the home of an uncle, would have been given originally.

E and F each had but one period of probation, E at the age of twenty-five and F at the age of fourteen. They both behaved well during these periods. E, who was a minor offender, has remained such, and F reformed approximately at the age of fourteen. The question may well be asked whether the immediate use of the proper treatment for F did not hasten the reformation of this particular offender. This of course remains an academic question for the present. However, in the case of E, who had but one period of probation and then not till he was twenty-five years old, minor delinquencies continued. Is it possible that if probation or some other treatment to which he was likely to respond had been applied much earlier in his career, he might today be a non-delinquent rather than a minor delinquent?

We are now ready to consider the cases of G, H, and J whose probable behavior between the ages of fourteen and twenty-nine and during various peno-correctional treatments is indicated in Table 85. Their chances of ultimate reform, according to Table 85, are the same as of D, E, and F, that is, three and a half in 10; but unlike D, E, and F, who had but two in 10, they have almost four chances in 10 of remaining serious offenders; and further, unlike D, E, and F who had almost four in 10, they have only two chances in 10 of becoming minor offenders. A judge knowing the likelihood of the continuing serious delinquencies of G, H, and J would, for the sake of the public protection, no doubt be inclined to consider either very close extramural supervision or incarceration for them. He would use probation only with extreme caution. In the case of G, however, he might be more inclined at least to try probation during the juvenile court age, because G would have little more chance of successful behavior in a correctional school than on probation, and probation is cheaper; but H and J would have a better chance of adjustment in a correctional school than on probation. If the offenders were of reformatory, prison, or jail age at the time of a particular court appearance, the judge would be likely to resort to commitment to one of those institutions, without even attempting probation.

Under the present system of disposing of cases, G was put on probation when he was eleven years old, and he committed burglaries while on probation. Then commitment to a correctional school was attempted (the prediction chart indicates that G would have very little more chance of good behavior in a correctional school than on probation). He did not behave well during either this or any succeeding commitment to a correctional school, running away several times, committing malicious injury to property, being on one occasion discovered to have a hypodermic needle, assisting in the escape of another boy, and so on. During periods of parole from the correctional school his behavior was equally poor (that it was likely to be is evident from the prediction chart). When G was eighteen years old he was committed to a reformatory where his behavior, though better than in the correctional school, was still not entirely desirable (his chart shows six and a half chances in 10 of good behavior in a reformatory). When on parole from the reformatory, he was arrested several times for assault and battery and for burglary. At the age of twenty-one he was committed to prison where his poor behavior is reflected in several periods of solitary confinement (his chart shows seven chances in 10 of satisfactory behavior in prison). During periods of parole from prison, he was arrested on several occasions for burglary, for larceny, and for keeping and exposing liquor. On a recent commitment to prison, however, G's behavior has distinctly improved. At the present writing he is still incarcerated, but behaving well. He has until very recently seriously misbehaved throughout his career both in extramural and intramural periods, despite the fact that according to his ﹍﹍﹍chart his chances of adjustment *during* certain intramural treatments ﹍﹍﹍﹍ ﹍﹍﹍﹍﹍﹍well be asked, whether, given especially good supervision in certain of the institutions, G might not have gotten along better. However, in a case like this, institutional authorities, guided perhaps by the findings in Chapter XV in which the reasons for failure to behave satisfactorily during intramural treatment are suggested, could determine the reasons in a case like G's, and perhaps give him more telling individualized guidance.

During a long criminal career, H has been placed on probation several times, has had suspended sentences, has been on parole on innumerable occasions, has served many times in correctional schools, and has served several sentences in a reformatory and in jails. Throughout his career, during extramural or intramural treatment and when free, he has committed many serious crimes including theft, burglary, assault to rob. Except during a brief term in jail, he has shown no tendency to good behavior. In view of his low chance of success during extramural treatment, such an of-

behavior in a reformatory). At the age of twenty-three he was sent to prison where his conduct was satisfactory (his chart indicates the high probability of seven chances in 10 of good behavior). Following his release from prison M was placed on parole, and during the next two years his conduct on parole was satisfactory. Is it possible that a substantial period of good behavior in prison contributed to his adjustment on parole, despite the fact that he failed during all previous parole periods and that his chart indicates but three chances in 10 of success on parole?

We want now to consider for a moment the case of K in contrast to L. The likelihood of continuing recidivism on the part of K is as high as L's, and as already indicated, both have exactly the same chances of good behavior during the various forms of peno-correctional treatment. Apparently, therefore, a judge using the prediction charts would handle both of these cases in just the same way. It is of interest at this point, therefore, to see what actually did happen to K and L under the present method of disposing of cases. On the occasion of his first court appearance at the age of sixteen, K was given a suspended sentence to a correctional school, which was imposed in less than a month's time because of failure on probation (his chart shows but two chances in 10 of good behavior on probation under a suspended sentence). He was in the correctional school for almost a year, and his behavior was very good (his chart shows four and a half chances in 10 of good behavior here). He was placed on parole at the age of seventeen and kept under parole supervision until he was twenty-one (his chart shows three chances in 10 of good behavior on parole). During this time his behavior was satisfactory, and he has since been a non-delinquent; and this despite the great probability of his recidivism.

As to L, it will be remembered that four periods on straight probation were attempted from the time he was twelve until he was fifteen years of age, before a correctional school was resorted to. His miserable failure throughout eighteen peno-correctional treatments, terminating in a life sentence to prison where his behavior now at the age of twenty-eight is fairly acceptable, is in sharp contrast to

K's early good adjustment. We again venture the query: May not the fact of proper treatment in K's case almost immediately upon his first court appearance have contributed to his good adjustment not only during treatment but afterwards? Would not the delay in proper treatment in L's case furnish opportunity for the establishment of habits of delinquency which became hard to break?

However, our purpose in this chapter has not been to answer these and related questions, because they are unanswerable within the present state of our knowledge. We have attempted merely to show how treatment becomes more individualized with the use of prediction charts than it is without them.

Chapter XXI

METHOD OF THIS RESEARCH

THE story of our delinquents, from boyhood to manhood, has been told. Before summarizing our findings and attempting any conclusions, we must render account of how we assembled the facts upon which the findings are based. That is the function of this chapter.

The major problems in the present study were: to ascertain whether there had been any change with the passing of the years in the type of delinquency committed by the youths originally investigated in *One Thousand Juvenile Delinquents;* at what stages in their lives they ceased to be criminalistic or, if continuing in their antisocial conduct, when the shift occurred from commission of crimes of major and aggressive character (essentially felonies) to less serious forms of wrongdoing (essentially misdemeanors); and how this group of delinquents responded to the different types of correction to which they were subjected. Whatever investigation was deemed necessary in any case in order to obtain this information and associated detailed data was carried out. The inquiries ranged from merely clearing a case through the court record system of the Massachusetts Board of Probation (where court records of Massachusetts are centralized) to a far-flung, many-sided, and intensive investigation involving the writing of numerous letters to various police and peno-correctional authorities, examination of the records of social agencies and other organizations, combing through various street directories, interviewing the offender himself, his wife, other relatives, family physicians, employers, and others who might have known him during the periods embraced in the research.

PROCEDURES PRELIMINARY TO FIELD INVESTIGATION

In beginning this further follow-up study of the criminal careers of *One Thousand Juvenile Delinquents,* we were of course not completely without knowledge of their doings and whereabouts. We already had certain information about them from the previous study. We knew, for example, where most of them were living at the end of the first five-year follow-up period, and we also had in our files data concerning their criminal records up to the end of that period. In addition we had certain identifying information gathered in connection with the first study, which served as a basis for further investigations. For example, we knew the date and place of birth of the offender, his height, complexion, color of eyes and hair; the names and addresses of his parents and siblings, the names and addresses of other relatives, and even occasionally of some persons having official contact with him, such as doctors, clergymen, representatives of social agencies, and others. With these basic data readily at hand we proceeded to clear all the cases, under the varied spellings of the names and under known aliases, through the criminal record index of the Massachusetts Board of Probation. We were now particularly seeking information about the arrests of the men during a second and a third five-year follow-up period, although we were naturally also concerned with filling in any gaps in the material gathered in connection with the first research.

By this procedure it was possible quickly to eliminate from further investigation about 200 of the 1,000 cases because their criminal records were so continuous as to indicate that the youths had been living in Massachusetts throughout the ten years and it was therefore not necessary to search elsewhere for information about them; also, their official records were of so serious a character that there was no need to make a more personal investigation to determine whether the youths had been committing serious offenses for which they had not been arrested. The following is an illustration of the type of case in which it was not necessary to make a further investigation:

*Court record of John Doe as found in the Massachusetts Board of
Probation covering the second and third five-year follow-up
periods. This record was found to be listed under six
different first names, only two of which turned
out to be true names*

SECOND FOLLOW-UP PERIOD (MAY 1923 TO MAY 1928)

May 3, 1923	Evading taxi fare	Filed
May 16, 1923	Assault and battery	$10 suspended. September 29, 1923, default warrant
May 20, 1923	Drunkenness	Released by probation officer
September 8, 1923	Fornication	September 12, 1923, filed
September 12, 1923	Assault and battery	August 11, 1924, dismissed
October 4, 1923	Drunkenness	Released
October 17, 1923	Surrendered for violation of probation (February 13, 1922)	Six months jail
September 16, 1924	Drunkenness	September 23, 1924, filed
September 16, 1924	Driving without license	$20 appealed September 23, 1924
September 16, 1924	Unlawful appropriation of automobile	September 23, 1924, three months house of correction. Appealed
September 16, 1924	Operating under influence of liquor	Three months house of correction. Appealed
October 10, 1924	Unlawful appropriation of automobile	Three months jail
October 10, 1924	Operating without license	Filed
May 25, 1925	Robbery	June 4, 1925, waived examination
November 2, 1925	Robbery	Not guilty
November 14, 1925	Accosting and annoying	November 18, 1925, default
December 18, 1925	Default removed	Dismissed without prosecution
December 18, 1925	Assault and battery	Three months house of correction. Appealed
December 28, 1925	Appeal withdrawn	Three months house of correction. Committed
March 31, 1926	Drunkenness	Suspended sentence to state farm. Filed October 4, 1926
April 13, 1926	Larceny	April 21, 1926, bound over
May 13, 1926	Larceny	One year house of correction
April 12, 1927	Drunkenness	April 21, 1927, filed
April 12, 1927	Assault and battery on police officer	Six months house of correction. Appealed
May 10, 1927	Assault and battery on officer (2)	Six months jail
November 18, 1927	Larceny	December 9, 1927, discharged
November 28, 1927	Drunkenness	Filed
December 5, 1927	Larceny	Discharged

February 7, 1928	Idle and disorderly	February 15, 1928, six months house of correction. Appealed
February 15, 1928	Keeping and exposing	$50 and one month house of correction. Appealed
March 15, 1928	Keeping and exposing	Two months jail
March 15, 1928	Idle and disorderly	Five months jail

THIRD FOLLOW-UP PERIOD (MAY 1928 TO MAY 1933)

May 25, 1928	Drunkenness	May 29, 1928, filed
May 25, 1928	Breaking and entering	May 29, 1928, "probable cause"
June 13, 1928	Breaking and entering	Two years house of correction
March 26, 1931	Drunkenness	Released by probation officer
April 30, 1931	Drunkenness	Released by probation officer
July 30, 1931	Drunkenness	August 13, 1931, two months house of correction. Appealed
July 30, 1931	Assault and battery	August 13, 1931, not guilty
July 30, 1931	Wanton destruction of property	August 13, 1931, not guilty
October 1, 1931	Assault and battery	October 8, 1931, filed
October 1, 1931	Violating true name law	October 8, 1931, $10. Committed
October 1, 1931	Drunkenness	Two months house of correction
November 16, 1931	Drunkenness	One month house of correction. Suspended May 18, 1932
April 11, 1932	Drunkenness	Filed
April 11, 1932	Surrendered (drunkenness)	Probation October 11, 1932
June 9, 1932	Drunkenness	Filed
June 9, 1932	Surrendered	Probation November 16, 1931
September 9, 1932	Drunkenness	Three months house of correction. Appealed
September 9, 1932	Surrendered	One month house of correction. Appealed
October 4, 1932	Drunkenness	Nol-pros
November 1, 1932	Drunkenness	Defaulted
November 2, 1932	Default removed	10 days house of correction. Suspended May 3, 1933. Defaulted

Since John Doe's record is so continuous and he was convicted of serious offenses in both the second and third five-year periods it was not necessary for us to make any further investigation. His "footprints in the sands of time" told the story completely and eloquently.

The remaining cases (some 800 in all) were then sorted for further study. It was evident, from the nature of the gaps in the criminal records or because no criminal record was revealed through the files of the Massachusetts Board of Probation, that further investigation would be necessary to ascertain whether arrests had occurred in other states or whether the men had been in the Army, Navy, Merchant Marine, or Coast Guard; on boats plying between the United States and foreign countries; in mental hospitals or hospitals for the chronically ill; or, though not arrested, were committing offenses for which they might have come to the attention of the legal authorities at any time; or, though convicted of minor offenses, had committed serious offenses for which they were not arrested. It was necessary also to determine in these cases whether arrests had been recorded under aliases not yet known to us or under a misspelling of the name, or were listed in the record of another person whose name was similar; or, in the absence of an official criminal record, to determine whether a man really was a non-offender.

At this stage in the procedure, street directories were carefully examined for the present or recent addresses of the men in question, and their names as well as those of members of their families were cleared through the Social Service Exchange to determine whether any of them had been known recently to any social agencies that might be helpful in giving us the information needed. No other routine procedure was carried out in all cases, except that an examination was made of the files of the Judge Baker Foundation to see whether, since the first study, the Clinic had received any information about these particular men that would be of any special import at this stage of the investigation.

If a man had already committed a felony in Massachusetts, fingerprints were available in the Fingerprint Division of the Massachusetts State Department of Public Safety. If there was indication that a man lived outside Massachusetts, his case was cleared (with the full cooperation of the fingerprint authorities) not only through the local files but also through the Federal Bureau of Investigation in Washington and the fingerprint department of any other state where he was known to have lived. In this way numerous gaps in the records were filled without a more personal field investigation.

If no fingerprints were available, our task was, of course, greatly complicated; but it was still possible to obtain information occasionally about such cases through police departments, especially if a man's name was rather uncommon and the identifying data were sufficiently distinguishing. Police in some instances even sent us photographs of men whose names were similar to those about whom we were seeking information and we were able to establish identification through relatives.

Through these various procedures, carried out almost entirely by correspondence or by examination of already recorded information in social agencies, police departments, fingerprint files, or street directories, it was possible to eliminate from further field investigation approximately another 200 cases, leaving some 600 who still had to be personally interviewed to determine from the men themselves or from persons knowing them just where they had been living and what they had been doing during the years covered by our study. It was on the basis of such information that we were able to discover their criminal records in cities outside Massachusetts and to determine whether, in the absence of officially recorded delinquency, they had nevertheless been committing offenses for which they might have been arrested. It should be mentioned that this procedure often resulted in proof that the record we had already found through the files of the Board of Probation was a complete record of a man's delinquencies.

The following brief summaries of notes that were given to the field investigators after the preliminary work on the cases had been done indicate the kind of information which it was necessary to seek in each case:

1. PETER committed "serious" offenses (felonies) during the first five-year follow-up period. The Massachusetts Board of Probation records indicate that he was arrested but not convicted for one minor traffic violation during the second five-year follow-up period. There is no further criminal record against Peter in the files of the Board of Probation.

Has he been living outside Massachusetts, and, if so, does he have a criminal record in another state? If he has been living in Massachusetts, has Peter's conduct been such that he might have been arrested?

2. JAMES was convicted of minor offenses in the first five-year period. Clearance of his case through the Board of Probation indicated that he was also convicted of minor offenses in the second and third five-year periods. There is a gap in his criminal record between 1926 and 1931.

Has he been out of Massachusetts during this period, and, if so, where? There is some indication from our previous investigation that he might have gone to New York City as he spent a brief time there during the first five-year period seeking employment. Fingerprints have been sent to the police of New York City but with a negative result. This does not mean, however, that he may not have been arrested there for minor offenses.

3. FRANK was convicted of minor offenses in the first five-year follow-up period. Clearance through the Board of Probation files does not reveal any arrests during the second five-year period but shows that he was arrested once for a serious traffic offense in the third five-year period but not convicted. However, it is known that during most of the second period Frank was in the Army, which accounts for the apparent gap in his criminal record in the second five-year period.

Where was Frank between 1926, when he left the Army, and 1929, when the arrest for a traffic violation is recorded? Does he now admit his guilt on the serious offenses for which he was arrested but not convicted?

4. WILLIAM was a serious offender in the first five-year follow-up period. In the second and third periods he was arrested for serious offenses but not convicted. He was, however, convicted for minor offenses.

As his criminal record is not continuous (there are gaps in it between 1924 and 1928 and between 1928 and 1932), was he arrested or convicted in another state for serious offenses, or was he committing any offenses for which he might have been arrested?

FIELD INVESTIGATION

When a case was turned over to a field visitor, emphasis was placed on the fact that we were particularly interested in ascertaining whether there had been any change with the passing of the years in the type of delinquency committed by the men and at what period in their lives their offenses ceased or, if continuing, changed from a serious and aggressive character to a less serious type of delinquency.

The field investigators always carried with them the identifying

data about an offender, information about his family and environmental background, the date and nature of the offense for which
he originally appeared before the Boston Juvenile Court, the findings of the Judge Baker Foundation Clinic, particularly in regard
to his intelligence and personality traits, a summary of the court
record during the first five-year follow-up period, information as to
whether he is at present married, and any other data which might
prove useful.

For example, in Case 1 the question to be determined by the field
investigator was whether Peter had been living outside Massachusetts and, if so, whether he had a criminal record in another state;
or, if he had been living in Massachusetts, whether his conduct had
been such that he might have been arrested. In this case the investigator added the following bits of information to the more routine
notes given above:

Peter is facetious, lazy, indifferent, has an I.Q. of 81. Soon after he
was placed on probation by the Boston Juvenile Court on recommendation of the Judge Baker Foundation he committed serious delinquencies.
He shortly enlisted, however, in the United States Navy and has apparently not relapsed into misbehavior since then even though he has returned to the same neighborhood in which he lived previously. . . . Ask
Peter why he had not re-enlisted in the Navy as he had been reported to
so intend while he was still in the service. ["This," says the investigator,
"was calculated to give a good talking point, making the interview more
detached and objective and tending in a natural way to bring out the
facts and inferences needed for our study."]

In a general way it may be said that from the point of view of
the technique of the field investigations there is no essential difference between the methods we used in this study and those evolved
and applied in the investigation of ex-inmates of reformatories described in 500 *Criminal Careers, Later Criminal Careers,* and *Five
Hundred Delinquent Women.* We had to cope with the same in-
tricacies of tracing persons whose whereabouts were last known
years ago, and in addition we had to use even greater caution now
than in the first follow-up study of *One Thousand Juvenile Delinquents* (when so few of the youths were married), so that we would

not reveal to wives, who perhaps were unacquainted with their husbands' early misbehavior, that they had been previously known to court or police authorities. We also had to meet the problem of possible hostility to this continuing investigation on the part of the offenders and their families. We appreciate that it is only on the basis of friendliness and a clear understanding of the purposes of our investigations by those interviewed, that we can hope to pursue these studies over the years. It is here that the experience, personality, tact, and patience of the investigators play so crucial a role in the success of the field work.

There are three important phases of the field investigations which therefore had to be stressed: *first,* finding the man or members of his family who are likely to have information about him; *second,* carrying on the interviews in a spirit of friendliness; and, *third,* not revealing to his wife or others who may not know of his delinquency the fact that he had been an offender.

In regard to the tracing of the offenders, it should be recalled that some of this was accomplished before the field worker set out on his quest. What needs to be stressed here is that tracing procedures are complicated because criminals as a class move about a great deal, use aliases, and misspell their names. But no matter how elusive the "game," we persisted in the hunt.

A few illustrations of how we "found the man," or tried hard to find him may help the reader to understand the process.

5. When the case of LEONARD was turned over to the field investigator his address in the West End of Boston was known. It had been readily discovered in the Boston street directory and indicated that he was living with his wife. By the time the field worker was ready to make a visit, Leonard had moved and neighbors did not know his whereabouts. The investigator, knowing that Leonard had previously lived in Watertown, near Boston, decided to go to his former place of residence to see whether any neighbors, who might have kept in touch with him, would know his present address. In this way it was ascertained that Leonard and his wife were now living in East Boston with her family. The field investigator went there but found that neither Leonard nor his wife was at home. By the time he made his next visit, the couple had again moved.

The field agent now called on Leonard's mother, whose address in the

North End of Boston was known. As she spoke practically no English, and claimed to be rarely in touch with Leonard, no help was gotten from her in locating him. The investigator then undertook a more thorough canvass of neighbors in East Boston and was able to learn that Leonard and his wife and her parents had moved "to some other town," but they did not know specifically where. He did ascertain, however, that Leonard's married sister "lives somewhere in the neighborhood." By examining the marriage records he was able to find the name of the sister's husband, and in this way discovered a recent address in East Boston. On calling there he found that the couple had moved, but through a neighbor learned the street on which she now resides in East Boston, and by going from house to house on that street he finally located her. She was not in at his first call but he found her at home later in the day, and through her discovered that Leonard was living in the North End of Boston.

6. When the case of JACOB was turned over to the field investigator, his present address was not known. The court records indicated that as recently as 1926, when we had made the first five-year follow-up study, he had been living in Roxbury with his mother. The field worker proceeded to consult the marriage records to determine whether Jacob had married since our last contact with him. A certificate was found, and the field worker immediately proceeded to look for the wife's parents, through whom he hoped to find Jacob. However, they were not listed in the current street directory. The field worker "on a chance" consulted the divorce records and discovered that Jacob's wife had divorced him and had been allowed to resume her maiden name. From these records he also learned the name of the attorneys in the case and interviewed them. They were willing to give him Jacob's last known address in Jamaica Plain. The field worker visited this address and found that Jacob had moved, but he was able to learn from the present tenant of the apartment that the youth had married again, and that he was working as a chauffeur for a large taxicab company. The investigator immediately communicated with this company without revealing the reason for the inquiry, and they gave Jacob's address in Dorchester. On visiting this address a few days later it was found that Jacob had recently moved to avoid paying rent.

The field worker now had to pursue another course of investigation. He therefore set out to search for the record of Jacob's second marriage but was unable to find it; in view of the fact that Jacob's divorce was not yet absolute it was evident that his alliance was illicit and that he would therefore not welcome an interview at this time. The field worker then determined to find Jacob's first wife, and thinking that she might have married again, he examined the marriage records and found the name of her second husband. He quickly succeeded in locating her through the current directory, and was able to secure sufficient information about Jacob for our purposes without having to see him personally. Obviously, however, the field worker was "hot on the trail" and could have located Jacob, if this had been absolutely necessary.

7. HERBERT, a mulatto, was known to have been living in Boston with his wife as recently as 1931, but there was no trace of the couple in the current Boston directory. It was known that Herbert's parents were both dead. The field investigator tried to locate Herbert's wife's family, whose names he secured from the marriage record, but there was no trace of them in the local directories. From our first follow-up study of Herbert we had an address of Herbert's half brother and his wife, who lived with the wife's parents. The field investigator paid a call at their last known address, found that they had moved, but succeeded in learning from neighbors their present address in Roxbury; from the half brother's parents-in-law he learned Herbert's recent address in the South End of Boston. A visit to this address revealed that Herbert and his wife had moved; neighbors could not give any direct clue to their whereabouts.

The investigator then decided to pay another call on the family of Herbert's half brother in Roxbury, and this time he learned that the half brother had died and that his widow had moved to another city, but that she occasionally returned for a visit. The relatives offered to ask her if she had any knowledge of Herbert's whereabouts. After several weeks, the field investigator received a postcard from the widow of Herbert's half brother saying that she had no knowledge of Herbert but that another brother was living in Roxbury. With this clue, and by examining street directories and poll lists for several years back and interviewing neighbors in the vicinity, the field investigator finally located the estranged wife of this second brother who in turn was able to give him the present address of another brother of Herbert's in the West End of Boston. Through this brother the field worker found Herbert living in the South End of Boston in a rooming house and secured an interview with him.

In the above illustrations we have cited cases in which the offender or members of his family were found. Much effort in tracing was sometimes expended with no result, as in the following instances.

8. When the investigation was begun, it was known that GEORGE had disappeared in 1924, during the first five-year follow-up period; his present whereabouts were unknown to us. Inquiry was made of the Social Service Exchange of Boston to ascertain whether any agencies had known George or any members of his family since 1924, and it was thus learned that in 1932 George had called on one of the local agencies for assistance in finding a job and that another agency had been recently giving assistance to George's father. Through these agencies it was ascertained that George had been drifting back and forth between Boston and California for the past several years. Fingerprints were sent to authorities in California but with negative results. We then tried to locate in a Connecticut city a married sister of George's with whom he had lived prior to 1924, but the town clerk reported that she had moved without trace.

At this point the case was turned over to the field investigator, who succeeded in locating George's father. From him he secured a very superficial story of George's activities. The father, being very elderly and forgetful and rarely in touch with George, knew little about him but was sure that his son had worked mostly on oil-burning ships plying out of New York harbor. With this clue, we wrote to the Seamen's Church Institute in New York City where sailors often receive their mail, but this effort proved abortive. Several months later another visit was paid to George's father in the hope that he might have had some recent word from George or from some other members of the family, but as he claimed not to have, and as his memory was so poor, the tracing of this case was brought to an end.

9. When the investigation of JAMES' case was started it was found that there was no criminal record reported at the Board of Probation, and the Judge Baker Foundation files had no further information about him. We knew only that James' home had been broken by the death of his mother and the disappearance of his father, and that early in the first five-year follow-up period James had drifted away from the home of a woman in Boston who had casually given him a shelter. We knew that James had been in the Navy, and correspondence with the Bureau of Navigation revealed that he had been dishonorably discharged in 1928 on the Pacific Coast. As we knew from our first follow-up study of James that he had been in Highland Park, Michigan, and in Seattle and Spokane, Washington, the directories of those cities were examined, but no trace of James was found. It was then decided to examine old directories of the city of Lynn, Massachusetts, where James' father was known to have

lived after the death of James' mother. He was traced from Lynn to Boston where it was discovered that he had died in 1926.

Through the current Boston directory the woman who had given James shelter in earlier years was located and interviewed. From her the field investigator learned only that James had married and probably settled in California, after receiving a dishonorable discharge from the Navy in 1928. An examination of the street directory of the California city in which James was supposed to be living revealed no clues.

The field investigator then proceeded to verify the marriage in 1935 of James' younger brother, and in this way the brother was located in a town near Boston. He had no information about James, however. The investigator next located James' sister whom he found living near Boston. She was visited, but claimed she had not heard from James since he was in the Navy. She was, however, able to give the name of James' wife who she thought had come from "around Seattle." The Seattle directories were then examined for persons bearing the wife's name; one was found and was written to, but she proved not to be related. The Social Service Exchanges of several cities in California and also of Seattle were communicated with to determine whether they had had any contacts with James and his wife, but none were found. As there remained no other likely source of information to be tapped, nothing further could be done to trace James.

Hundreds of illustrations might be given of tracing procedures. These few are sufficient, however, to indicate that a great deal of time and energy was consumed in tracking down offenders and their families. But it must be kept in mind that our major task began only when the persons whom we wished to interview had been located. Usually the field visitor was able, with a rather simple explanation and a friendly, disarming manner, quickly to win the confidence of the men or their relatives. He first reminded them of his previous visit several years ago, and then explained that we are trying to help those who may "get into trouble" at some future time by learning from those who have "been through the mill" what their experiences have been and how their conduct has changed with the passing of time and varying circumstances. Usually this explanation was sufficient. In fact, of 591 cases in which personal interviews were held with the men or members of their families, the field workers were received with friendliness in 574; in 7 cases there was apparent indifference to the investigation; and in only 10 instances was any real hostility manifested, and in most of these the investigator was able to overcome it.[1]

Let us look in upon a few of these interviews to see how the field worker succeeded in maintaining that friendly spirit so essential to our investigations into criminal careers:

10. As JACK was a traveling musician, it was not possible to see him personally. Jack's mother was therefore located and interviewed, and proved entirely friendly. Soon after the field worker had talked with her, Jack's sister telephoned to express her indignation over our efforts to find out anything about her brother "whose boyish misdemeanors are a thing of the past." The field worker called upon her the very next day and explained at great length the purposes of our studies. She appreciated the courtesy of his visit, and when she clearly understood our purpose she became very friendly and cooperative.

11. When the field worker paid his first visit to TONY he found him already abed. Annoyed at being awakened by his wife to receive a caller, he shouted through the hall door that he did not wish to see anyone. He asked his wife to make an engagement for an interview on the morrow, which was arranged for the next evening. At that time the field worker found that both Tony and his wife were feeling somewhat ashamed of the way in which they had greeted him on the previous day. Sensing their embarrassment he immediately put them at their ease by offering Tony a cigar. Tony's wife then excused herself from the interview and Tony and the field worker were left alone for a comfortable chat.

12. TOM was a chauffeur, and was living with his wife and her parents. In view of the fact that she was not aware of his early escapades, it was not considered wise to run the risk of seeing her, so the field investigator decided to have a talk with Tom's parents. Although his father was friendly, Tom's mother showed decided hostility to any attempt to find out anything about his conduct. The field worker proceeded to make careful explanation to her about the purposes of our inquiry, pointing out that we are trying to determine what benefit youths like Tom actually get from the institutions to which they have been sent. The field worker

---

[1] Appendix B, 1, 2.

was soon able to convert her into a willing talker and a very useful one, because she proved to be a highly intelligent woman.

13. In the case of JAMES, the field worker decided to interview his parents. Here, as in the case of Tom, the father was friendly enough but the mother showed hostility. She deemed the investigator's visit an affront to the family. When he pleasantly agreed with her that James' misdemeanors were merely "boyish affairs," her attitude began to soften, and she finally agreed that it would be useful to all concerned to learn the results of various kinds of peno-correctional procedures in order that wiser modes of treatment might be devised. Her friendliness increased to the point of bringing out a picture album to show the field worker the family photographs, including one of James.

As mentioned above, an important part of the task of maintaining a relationship of friendliness and understanding between the field investigator and the people he interviewed was not to reveal to wives and others that a particular man had had a delinquent career, especially in instances in which such a revelation might create friction in the family. It has been a cardinal principle of our procedure not to create difficulties for the men or their families. Here are a few illustrations of how possible mishaps have been avoided:

14. ALBERT's mother had recently remarried. Her second husband was a police officer, which fact made it especially desirable not to reveal Albert's early delinquencies to the new family connections. Albert himself had recently married and was living with his wife's parents. The field worker therefore planned to avoid Albert and his wife, and to have a talk with Albert's mother. She proved to be extremely appreciative of the fact that the field worker had sought her rather than Albert, and that he had timed his visit when her husband was away from home. She therefore proved unusually responsive and gave a very comprehensive story of Albert's life. She stressed the fact that Albert's wife was of a quarrelsome disposition, which, though not yet causing any serious breach in conjugal relations, might however result in such a break if she were inadvertently given knowledge of his earlier delinquencies. A dangerous interview was thus avoided.

15. Assuming that PASQUALE's wife might not know anything about his earlier history, the field worker was careful not to make any revela-

tion to her. When he called at the home and found that Pasquale was out, he merely explained in a general way to the wife that he wished to see her husband in connection with an old-time interest of people who knew him some years ago. When he finally found Pasquale at home one evening, his three children kept running in and out of the room and Pasquale's wife was within earshot. In order to carry on the interview without arousing her suspicion or that of the children, the field worker avoided the use of any tell-tale words such as "court," "probation," "correctional school," which might cause them to suspect that Pasquale had at one time or another been in the hands of the law. He was able quickly to make Pasquale realize that the utmost care was being taken in carrying on the conversation in the presence of his wife and children. Pasquale was extremely responsive and managed to carry out his side of the interview to the satisfaction of the field worker.

16. In visiting Nicholas' mother, with whom he was not able to carry on much of an interview because of language difficulties, the field investigator learned that the youth had married a few months previously. Special care had to be taken, therefore, to avoid revealing his delinquencies to his newly acquired wife. The field worker left a letter for Nicholas which he asked the mother to give him on his next visit to her. In this letter he explained why he wished an interview with him, and that he wanted to avoid the danger of revealing to Nicholas' wife his career of crime. This resulted in a telephoned invitation from Nicholas to the investigator to visit him. On arriving at the house the field worker found that Nicholas was alone, his wife having gone calling, apparently by prearrangement. Nicholas confirmed the fact that his wife was entirely ignorant of his boyhood delinquencies and that he of course wished her to remain so. He deeply appreciated the field worker's care in approaching him and was extremely cooperative.

COORDINATION OF DATA FROM ALL SOURCES

To avoid any confusion about the status of an investigation at any particular time, a "diary card" of each case was kept on which were entered, day by day in chronological order, any steps taken in the investigation by any member of the staff. The following illustration of this procedure indicates the type of information kept, and how we could determine exactly what had been accomplished up to any point in the investigation.

STEPHEN

June 1, 1937   Office secretary wrote Board of Probation for any record of Stephen since May 1927.

June 5, 1937   Received reply from Board of Probation with record of Stephen since May 10, 1927, and a recent address.

June 16, 1937   Research assistant wrote War Department for exact date of Stephen's enlistment in 1927 and nature of his discharge.

June 24, 1937   Reply received from War Department reporting that Stephen had enlisted November 15, 1927, and was honorably discharged November 14, 1930; reenlisted December 3, 1930, and discharged, not honorably, August 15, 1933, because of conviction by a civil court for breach of peace.

Sept. 25, 1937   Research assistant examined Boston street directory but found no trace of Stephen.

Oct. 15, 1937   Office secretary wrote Boston Social Service Exchange to inquire whether Stephen was known to any social agencies.

Oct. 20, 1937   Reply from Boston Social Service Exchange with registrations for Stephen's parents and his sister.

Nov. 1, 1937   Field investigator located Stephen's sister through street directory.

Nov. 3, 1937   Field investigator interviewed Stephen's sister and her husband and learned that Stephen was living in Brockton, Massachusetts.

Nov. 12, 1937   Field investigator interviewed Stephen.

Nov. 15, 1937   Office secretary wrote War Department for name of town in which Stephen had been convicted for breach of peace.

Nov. 27, 1937   Reply received from War Department stating that Stephen had been convicted of breach of peace in Montpelier, Vermont.

Nov. 30, 1937   Office secretary wrote police of Montpelier for disposition of charge of breach of peace.

Dec. 4, 1937   Reply received from police of Montpelier with information about disposition of Stephen's case.

Dec. 5, 1937   Case studied and found complete. Ready for analysis by research associate.

It must already be evident that the gathering of information on the criminal conduct of a large group of offenders is something of a challenge. The goal is clear enough, but the path to the goal—the securing of a complete record of arrests and convictions and, in the absence of an official record, of sufficient information about the behavior of a man to indicate whether or not he has been committing offenses for which he could have been arrested—is beset with many stumbling blocks. Careful search of the Massachusetts Board of Probation records and the Massachusetts fingerprint files and of official records in other states is likely to produce a good deal of officially recorded information about him, but the completeness of the information is dependent upon the accuracy of our knowledge of a man's whereabouts over a period of years, of his aliases, and of various spellings of his name. The following brief illustrations show how the criminal records were "pieced together" from various sources.

17. Clearance of THEODORE's case through the files of the Board of Probation revealed only a few arrests in the year 1931, so that there were large gaps in his record which had to be filled in. As it was known from the previous investigation that Theodore had been in New York, fingerprints were forwarded to the police department of New York City. In this way it was ascertained that he had a record in Massachusetts under an alias which had been entirely unknown to us, and that he had been arrested in New York City in January 1929 under still another alias, in Hoboken, New Jersey, in September 1932 again under an alias, and in Newark, New Jersey, in August 1933. We now proceeded to clear his record through the Board of Probation under the various newly learned aliases and found several arrests and convictions against him, including a recent sentence to prison.

18. In the case of THOMAS we found no record in the files of the Board of Probation. As there was no trace of him or his family in and around Boston, it was concluded that he had moved out of the state. Fingerprints were therefore sent to the United States Department of Justice, through which a long record of Thomas was revealed in Detroit and New York City. These leads were followed by sending fingerprints to the Michigan State Police and the New York City Police Department

through which a more detailed record was found, including a long prison sentence in Michigan and several additional arrests in New York City.

19. Clearance of the case of FRANCIS through the Board of Probation did not reveal any criminal record for the second five-year follow-up period, and only two arrests for minor offenses during the third period. Through field investigation we learned that Francis had not been living in Massachusetts during most of the second and third five-year periods. Fingerprints were therefore sent to the Department of Justice in Washington, which revealed several arrests in various towns in New Hampshire. This was followed up by writing to the police of these towns, and several additional arrests not reported in the fingerprint files were discovered.

A report from a social service agency in the town in which Francis was finally located provided further details about his criminal conduct. When the record was finally pieced together from these various sources, it was found to be continuous from the end of the first five-year follow-up period until the end of the third five-year period. It might also be mentioned that in the course of this investigation we discovered additional arrests in the first five-year follow-up period which had not been previously known to us, for it now transpired that for part of the first period Francis had been in New Hampshire.

20. In the case of PETER our search for his criminal record led to making an inquiry of the Department of Justice in Belgium. We had known in connection with our previous study that when Peter was paroled from a correctional school in 1924 he returned to Belgium with his parents. Fingerprints were sent to the officials there, with the result that a record of three arrests for assault and battery and "obscene songs" was revealed. As it would have been hardly practicable to have a more detailed investigation made in Belgium, we had to content ourselves with the information already secured, which was at least sufficient to classify Peter as an offender in both the second and third five-year follow-up periods.

Obviously, where there was a long record it was easy enough to determine whether or not a man had been a serious or minor offender during the period in question. However, if no record could be found for one reason or another, or if it was known that there was no record, the method of determining whether a man was, nevertheless, a serious or minor offender or a non-delinquent was much more subtle and dependent upon the experienced judgment of the investigators. For example:

21. Arthur was known to have lived continuously in Boston and was discovered to have a court record of only a few minor offenses. It was necessary to determine, therefore, whether he was committing delinquencies of a serious nature for which he had not been arrested, or whether he was pursuing a continuous course of minor misconduct for which he was not coming to the attention of the police. By a discreet preliminary interview with his mother and sister, the field worker was able to win their confidence. They soon revealed to him that they were greatly discouraged about Arthur because he loafed so continuously, made no effort to get work, allowed his mother and sister to support him, wasted most of his time, and had engaged in various forms of cheap professional gambling. They even asked the field investigator to "give Arthur a talking to" in order to see whether he could not influence him to give up this illicit occupation. When he had a talk with Arthur a few days later, he freely acknowledged habitual gambling.

22. In the case of Frank, it was known that he had been living in Boston throughout the periods under study. The records of the Board of Probation revealed that he had been arrested occasionally for drunkenness, but at long intervals. The question to be determined was how habitual this drinking was. The field investigator, establishing a friendly relationship with Frank's mother, learned from her that Frank was a habitual drinker of the convivial type. As he had never previously committed serious offenses there was no reason to doubt her statement that he had not been doing so.

23. Milton was found to have a record of continuous minor delinquencies (drunkenness and illicit sex indulgence). The question had to be answered whether or not he had committed any unofficial offenses of a serious nature for which he might have been arrested. Milton's mother was visited. A talk with her revealed that she was inclined to be extremely severe with him, and when she told the field visitor that Milton stole a good deal in order to indulge in his drinking and sex habits, he deemed it necessary to check her statements. This he was able to do by consulting a social worker who had had contact with Milton.

An illustration of how we ascertained that a man was really non-delinquent and not merely seemingly so because of the absence of a criminal record is seen in the following case:

24. JOHN had been living continuously in the same house for many years. He was found to be thoroughly acceptable to his landlady and to the neighbors, all of whom were known to be respectable people. Investigation of his life revealed a conscientious attitude toward his wife and his mother, who had been dependent upon him for many years. There was another bit of evidence in the fact that he was a very active member in a club in a neighborhood settlement house. John was very frank in acknowledging his early delinquencies, and in expressing his gratitude for what the Boston Juvenile Court and the Judge Baker Foundation had done in helping him to change his habits. And workers in the settlement house who had known John well over the years further confirmed that he had been non-delinquent.

It should be stressed that in the course of this follow-up study covering a ten-year span, it was necessary to seek certain data about the first five-year period and also about the years preceding the appearance of these offenders before the Boston Juvenile Court, since the present investigation was more detailed than the previous one. In the course of this research, therefore, every effort was made to fill certain gaps in the earlier records, to verify certain data which had not previously been considered important enough to check, and to secure information on cases about which little if anything was previously known or which had been left incomplete because of the dearth of clues. For example:

25. In the first five-year follow-up investigation, VINCENT's whereabouts and behavior were designated as "unknown." In the course of the second follow-up study no record was found in the Board of Probation, but when Vincent's family were interviewed they readily admitted that he had been committed to jail a few years ago. Examination of the institution's records revealed that Vincent had been sent there under the name of James and that his last name had been spelled quite differently from what we had presumed to be the correct spelling. The records of the Board of Probation were then examined under this newly discovered first name and modified spelling of the last name, and a long and continuous record for Vincent (James) was found not only for the first five-year follow-up period but for the second and third.

26. In the first five-year follow-up period, JOSEPH's whereabouts and behavior, like Vincent's, were "unknown." In connection with the second follow-up study, the Judge Baker Foundation files revealed that in 1935 Joseph was living in Athol, Massachusetts, with his wife. When the case was cleared through the Board of Probation files, a criminal record was found for the third five-year follow-up period, but nothing for either the second or the first follow-up period. As the arrests recorded against Joseph were found to be in Boston and not Athol, it was presumed that he was no longer living in Athol. The field investigator easily located him in Boston, and the interview disclosed that during the first five-year follow-up period, when we had to list his whereabouts as "unknown," he was in California, where he had hitch-hiked. He had remained there for several years and been entirely out of touch with his family. He freely acknowledged that he had been in the habit of drinking to excess while in California. "At one time I was so bad that if I had a quarter in my pocket I couldn't get by a saloon nohow." In view of his record in the third five-year follow-up period, it was possible to secure fingerprints, which were then sent to the police of the California city in which Joseph claimed to have lived, and one arrest was revealed for vagrancy early in the second five-year period. Thinking that he might have a criminal record in other cities in California we also sent fingerprints to the state authorities but with negative result. However, there was at least sufficient evidence that he had been a delinquent, not only during the first period, but also during the second and third.

27. In the first five-year follow-up investigation, we were able to learn that BAZ, though having no officially recorded delinquencies against him in the Board of Probation, was known to have admitted the theft of a bicycle. The files of the Board of Probation were examined in connection with the second follow-up study but no criminal record was found. From the files of the Judge Baker Foundation it was learned that Baz had married in 1923. The field investigator immediately proceeded to verify this marriage and thus discovered that Baz had changed his first name to William. The case was immediately cleared through the Board of Probation under this different first name and a long and continuous record for serious offenses was discovered, not only for the second and third five-year follow-up periods but also for the first.

28. In the first five-year follow-up study, HANSON had not been located and the Board of Probation had no record of him. Numerous

efforts to trace his family were unsuccessful, partly because of a very common last name. When the case of Hanson was cleared through the Board of Probation in connection with the second follow-up investigation, again no record was found. As the field worker thought that Hanson might be married, he examined the marriage records. He found a marriage record and then examined the wife's birth record to secure the exact spelling of her rather complicated family name. As a result of this he was able to locate the wife's mother. She was not at home when the investigator called, but a relative was able to give Hanson's address and also that of his mother. The field visitor decided next to call on the mother, who proved to be unusually cordial. She gave a detailed history of Hanson's activities not only during the second and third five-year follow-up periods but during the first which clearly indicated that Hanson had been a non-delinquent during the first five-year follow-up period. Our previous classification of his case as "unknown" was now changed.

WHEREABOUTS OF DELINQUENTS

The range of our investigations is evident from the fact that, at the end of the third follow-up period, 604 of the original group of 1,000 youths were found to be living in Boston and its environs, 33 in other cities in Massachusetts, 112 in other states;[2] 69 were in penal institutions in Massachusetts, 24 in penal institutions in other states;[3] 6 were in hospitals for the mentally diseased, 2 in hospitals for the chronically ill; 11 were in the Army or Navy; 6 were residing abroad (4 in Italy, one in Belgium, and one in the Philippines); 16 were wandering about the United States with no fixed domicile; 7 were on boats at sea; 3 were fugitives from justice. Sixty of the men had died by the end of the third follow-up span. The whereabouts of only 47 of the original group of 1,000 men was unknown at that time, although location of 11 of these was established for part of the period.[4]

[2] Four in Connecticut, one in Maine, 6 in Rhode Island, one in Vermont, 2 in New Hampshire, 51 in New York City, 4 in other parts of New York State, 5 in Pennsylvania, 9 in New Jersey, 9 in Illinois, 3 in Ohio, 4 in Michigan, one in Florida, one in Georgia, 8 in California, one in Oregon, one in Washington, one in Utah.

[3] New Hampshire, Maine, New York, Pennsylvania, Rhode Island, Maryland, Indiana, Illinois, Michigan, Missouri, Kansas, California.

[4] Appendix B, 10.

SAMPLE INVESTIGATION

We have described in detail how the raw materials of this research were gathered. Before closing this account, it will perhaps give the reader a more realistic view of the process of investigation if he accompanies us on our quest for the needed data in one case from beginning to end.

29. When the further follow-up investigation was begun, in the case of JOSEPH, it was known that early in the first five-year period he had enlisted in the Navy and within a few months was dishonorably discharged. Shortly thereafter (and still during the first five-year period) he was arrested for burglary and placed on probation. He made his home with his mother and sisters, idled about a great deal, and made no effort to look for work. It should be noted that the first five-year follow-up period extended from March 1920 to March 1925.

At the beginning of the second follow-up investigation, Joseph's case was cleared through the files of the Massachusetts Board of Probation and it was learned that in November 1928 he had been arrested for assault and battery on wife and placed on probation; in February 1929 he was again arrested for assault and battery on wife and again placed on probation; and in August 1929 he was arrested for neglect of wife and children and for the third time placed on probation; two months later he was surrendered for violating this probation and given three months in the House of Correction. This was the extent of his court record for the second five-year follow-up period, which ended in March 1930.

The Board of Probation files revealed that in the third five-year follow-up period, which extended from March 1930 to March 1935, he was arrested for non-support and given a suspended sentence to the House of Correction; in August 1934 the suspended sentence was revoked and a warrant was issued for his arrest. From the records it was evident that up to the end of the third five-year period in March 1935 the sentence had not been invoked.

No arrests were recorded for Joseph between October 1921 on the first five-year follow-up period after the arrest for burglary, and November 1928 of the second five-year follow-up period when he was arrested for assault and battery on wife. The question immediately raised was whether Joseph had been living in Massachusetts during all this period, and, if so, whether he had been committing any serious offenses during that time. This query was justified in view of the fact that he had been previously arrested for burglary, and had several times been arrested for larceny prior to his appearance before the Boston Juvenile Court.

Closer examination of Joseph's history during the first five-year follow-up period indicated that we had definitely known that at least until the end of that time Joseph had been living in Boston with his mother. Therefore, our concern about his whereabouts was narrowed to the period between March 1925 and November 1928, when he was arrested in Boston for assault and battery on wife. We knew that Joseph had not married up to the end of the first five-year period, but it was now evident from his court record that he had married since. Therefore, the marriage records were examined as well as the divorce and birth records, and in this way the date of Joseph's marriage was ascertained as October 1925. A Boston address was given in the marriage certificate, further establishing the fact that, through the year 1925 at least, Joseph had continued to live in Boston. An examination of the birth records yielded still further evidence of his Boston residence, for a son was born there to Joseph and his wife in August 1926. Further examination of the birth records revealed that in October 1929 another son was born to them at a Boston address.

The divorce records revealed that a decree *nisi* had been granted Joseph's wife in January 1931 for cruel and abusive treatment, and the custody of the two children given her. Joseph was ordered to pay $10 a week toward their support. It is evident from his court record that he did not always fulfil this financial obligation.

Although Joseph's marriage ended in divorce in 1931, the court record revealed later marital trouble. Another examination of the marriage records gave proof of Joseph's second marriage in August 1933. To determine whether there were any offspring of this marriage, the birth records were examined and revealed the birth of a daughter in November 1933, indicating a forced marriage. In the light of the court record, which reported an arrest in February 1934, for non-support, it was evident that Joseph was having difficulty with his second wife. Thinking that this marriage might also have ended in divorce, the field investigator examined the records and found that Joseph's second wife applied for a divorce in August 1934, after the couple had been married only a year. The allegation was cruel and abusive treatment. As Joseph defaulted in December 1934, a decree *nisi* was granted his wife, and the custody of his daughter Florence was given her. Joseph was ordered to pay $5 a week toward the maintenance of the child. The divorce had not yet become absolute at the end of the third follow-up period.

After considering all this evidence, it was still felt that it would be well to interview Joseph or some member of his family. As Joseph's whereabouts were not revealed by an examination of the most recent Boston street directory, the field investigator tried to locate Joseph's mother. He found her and two of Joseph's sisters listed, and paid a call at the address indicated. On the first visit he did not find anyone at home. On the second visit, though finding Joseph's mother, he decided that it would be impossible to interview her as she spoke very broken English. He did not wish to use a neighbor as an interpreter for fear of revealing to anyone not directly concerned anything about Joseph's history. He decided to make another call at a time when one of Joseph's sisters would be in.

One evening a few weeks later the field investigator called on Joseph's mother, and this time found a sister at home who volunteered to act as interpreter. There was also present, however, a young man before whom the field investigator was hesitant to discuss Joseph's affairs. He was assured by the sister that the young man in question (a cousin) knew all about Joseph's difficulties and that there need be no hesitation in carrying on the interview in his presence. The field investigator then proceeded to question Joseph's sister as to his whereabouts between 1926 and 1928 when it would still have been possible that he had been in some other state. However, the mother, sister, and cousin assured the visitor that during this period Joseph had been living in and around Boston.

At the time this particular interview was held, more than a year had elapsed since the end of the third five-year follow-up period. We were not particularly concerned to trace Joseph's history in detail since the end of this period, but it was the field investigator's purpose to locate Joseph in order that he might have a personal interview with him. Joseph's mother and sister, however, were unable to give his address, merely saying that he had been steadily employed for the last few years in a factory in Cambridge, near Boston. They claimed that since his divorce he had been living in rooming houses, moving often, and that they were therefore unable to keep track of him. As the field investigator had not known that Joseph had been living in Cambridge, this opened up a new lead for him. An examination of the Cambridge poll list, however, failed to reveal Joseph's address, even though a search was made under every possible spelling of his name. He might have been quickly located by a telephone call to his place of employment, but this was considered neither wise nor necessary in view of the information which had already been gathered concerning him.

However, the field investigator, having learned from Joseph's mother and sister that a brother of Joseph's was also living in Cambridge (address given by them), decided to call on the brother. At the first visit no one was home. At the second call, the brother was abed and refused to see anyone. On the third visit, however, the field investigator succeeded in interviewing Joseph's brother and his brother's wife. They both said that Joseph had been living in Boston and vicinity (mostly in Cambridge) during the second and third five-year follow-up periods, and that, although he had not been successful in his conjugal relations, he has nevertheless been self-supporting. The brother, like Joseph's mother, stated that Joseph never lived very long in one place. He offered the information that Joseph occasionally spent a few days in his mother's home, and had been working steadily in the factory in Cambridge which the mother and sister had mentioned. Inquiries concerning Joseph's behavior brought an admission from the brother that he was in the habit of drinking, but that his drink habit did not affect his work nor did he lose control of himself sufficiently to be arrested for drunkenness. At this point it was felt that sufficient data had been gathered for our purposes to make further investigation of Joseph's case unnecessary.

A word should be said, however, about the study made in this case of Joseph's behavior under the various forms of peno-correctional treatment to which he had been subjected at one time or another in his career. These experiences were listed chronologically and found to consist of seven probations, one jail commitment, and one probation under suspended sentence. In the case of four of these treatment experiences it was possible quickly to make a judgment concerning his conduct, because he was arrested during the course of each one of them (three probations and one probation under suspended sentence). In the case of the five other treatments it was possible, by examining the court records, to ascertain that Joseph violated the conditions of probation so constantly as to be considered definitely a "failure" while under treatment. In the case of his commitment to a jail where he served three months, correspondence with the jail authorities indicated that he had not committed any infractions of rules during this period.

ANALYSIS OF DATA

When all the necessary information had been gathered from many different sources and the data on a case could be considered complete, the pertinent facts were transcribed to schedule cards especially prepared for the purpose (see page 262). Each one of the factors appearing on this schedule has been carefully defined, several of them originally in connection with *One Thousand Juvenile*

JUVENILE DELINQUENTS
FOLLOW-UP AND TREATMENT STUDY

Name: Birthdate: Date B. J. C. No.
Address: With:
Interview with: (1a) Attitude to investigation: (1b)

Follow-Up Study	Prior Period		Period I	Period II	Period III	
Dates of period						
(2) Dates and cause of death (3)						
Age at end of prd.	(4a)	(4b)	(5a)	(5b)	(6)	
Summary of arrests.	(7)		(21)	(35)	(49)	
Ag. prop.						
Ag. chastity						
Ag. fam. and chn.						
Ag. public hlth.						
Drink						
Drugs						
Ag. person						
Other (stubb. truancy, rnwy, mal. misch.)						
Viol. of prob. (nature of offence unk.)						
Summary of dispositions	(8)		(22)	(36)	(50)	
Commit — new						
Commit — revocation						
Prob.						
S. S. Prob.						
Fine						
Com. for nonp.						
File						
Rest.						
R. P. O.						
Nol Pros						
No Bill						
N. G. or rel.						
Unk. or dft. & no final disp, or other						
No. of arrests	9		23	37	51	No. Arrts.
No. of conv.	10		24	38	52	No. Conv.
No. of pen. exp. (incl. ret. by revoke)	11		25	39	53	No. Pnl.
Nature of penal exp.	12		26	40	54	Ntre. Pnl.
Time spent in penal inst.	13		27	41	55	Time Pnl.
Time spent in Army or Navy						Time Arm.
Mos. in community	14		28	42	56	Mos. Com.
Freq. of arrests	15		29	43	57	Freq. Arrts.
Freq. of conv.	16		30	44	58	Freq. Conv.
Off. recog. of del.	17		31	45	59	Off. rec. del.
Delinquency	18		32	46	60	Delinq.
Pred. offence	19		33	47	61	Pred. off.
Prin. comp. of misconduct	20		34	48	62	Pr. comp.

Treatment Study	Prior Prd.	JBF-BJC Treat. prd.	Period I	Period II	Period III	
Probation	1	4	7	10	14	Prob.
S.S. Probation	1	4	7	11	14	S. S. Prob.
Parole	1	4	8	11	14	Prle.
State Board	1	5	8	11	14	St. Bd.
Foster ho. during prob.	2	5	8	11	15	Fstr. Prob.
Foster ho. during parole	2	5	8	12	15	Fstr. Prle.
Correct'l and truant schls.	2	5	9	12	15	Correct'l
Reformatories	2	6	9	12	15	Refm.
Prisons	3	6	9	12	16	Prisons
Jails, H. of C., farms	3	6	9	13	16	Jails
Schl. F. M.	3	6	10	13	16	F. M.
D. D. D.	3	7	10	13	16	D. D. D.
Army or Navy	4	7	10	13	17	Army
App. rsn. for reformation						
Comments						

Delinquents. Only occasional modifications of these definitions were made so that the facts might be comparable with those of our other researches. Any factors new to this research—that is, which had not been included in the study of *One Thousand Juvenile Delinquents*—were defined in accordance with definitions already in use in our other investigations. The interested reader is referred to Appendix A where these definitions appear in alphabetical order.

All the data concerning the behavior of the delinquents during the period prior to their appearance in the Boston Juvenile Court and during the first, second, and third five-year follow-up periods, as well as the data about their behavior during the various forms of peno-correctional treatment to which they were subjected from the onset of their delinquent careers, period by period, to the end of the third five-year follow-up period, were entered on the schedules and transcribed to code cards.[5] Most of the materials were then tabulated and correlated on the Hollerith machine, although some factors had to be hand-tabulated.

As we have already given account in previous researches of our methods of handling and interpreting social data, there is no need to enter into any discussion of that aspect of the work here. The interested reader is referred to Chapter V of *500 Criminal Careers,* Appendix A of *Five Hundred Delinquent Women,* and Appendix A of *Later Criminal Careers.*

*   *   *   *   *

Upon the accuracy of the basic raw materials of a social research depends the validity of the conclusions and interpretations drawn from it. The building of a statistical structure, simple or elaborate, depends on the groundwork that has been laid to support it. No amount of elaborate statistical treatment based on complicated mathematical formulae can compensate for unreliable raw materials. Sound basic data are particularly difficult to obtain in researches in criminology, where social, economic, psychologic, and other influences—most of them not susceptible to the precise measurement employed in the "pure sciences"—converge in elusive interplay. But this does not mean that there are not readily discernible differences in the degree of reliability of the raw materials entering into social research. It is for this reason that we have rendered account of the methods utilized in gathering and verifying our basic data.

---

[5] The Hollerith 80-column card was utilized for this purpose.

Chapter XXII

SUMMARY AND CONCLUSIONS

BEFORE considering the significance of this research for peno-correctional practice, it is well to summarize the major findings. First, we have noted that with the passing of the years there has been a steady diminution in the number of youths who continued to be offenders, so that by the time our juvenile delinquents had reached an average age of twenty-nine, almost 40 per cent had ceased to be criminals. Furthermore, even among those who continued to commit crimes, significant improvement occurred. The proportion of serious offenders dropped from 75.6 per cent in the period prior to the original contact of the group with the Boston Juvenile Court to 47.8 per cent at the end of the fifteen-year follow-up span.

Second, the internal evidence of the present research as well as a comparison of these juvenile offenders with the ex-inmates of a reformatory who were reported upon in *500 Criminal Careers* and *Later Criminal Careers* has led to the theory that the physical and mental changes that comprise the natural process of maturation offer the chief explanation of this improvement in conduct with the passing of the years. This theory is partially supported by the finding that, regardless of age at the time it begins, delinquency runs a fairly steady and predictable course. Comparison of the former juvenile delinquents with the ex-inmates of the Massachusetts Reformatory showed that although the latter were, on the average, five years older than the former when they first began to manifest delinquent behavior (fourteen and a half and nine and a half years respectively), the two groups most nearly resembled each other in conduct, not at the same age, but rather at a point when they were a like number of years removed from the onset of their delinquent tendencies.[1] This resemblance, twenty years after the first mani-

---

[1] See Chapter VIII. Whether the phenomenon noted above will persist in this group as the years go by can, of course, only be determined by further investigation.

festation of delinquency, is all the more striking in the light of the facts that one group was five years older than the other, that the two groups were drawn from entirely different regions (the younger group being largely Boston residents, the older coming from all over the state of Massachusetts), and that each group had been subjected to many and varied kinds and qualities of peno-correctional treatment. Their marked resemblance in behavior at a point equidistant from the time of onset of delinquency suggests that delinquent tendencies, at least in young persons, are inclined to run a course that is not too readily modifiable by present methods of treatment.

Third, comparison of those among the former juvenile delinquents who had reformed by the end of the fifteen-year follow-up span with those who had not, disclosed that the former were endowed with a better heredity and enjoyed a more wholesome early environment than the men who continued to commit crimes. The normally expectable process of maturation was apparently facilitated by the better equipment of certain offenders and retarded or blocked by the poorer resources of others.

Comparison of the offenders who reformed when still under twenty-one with those who did not abandon criminalistic ways until they were older showed that the former possessed better innate equipment and environmental advantages than those whose reform occurred later, with the result that among the former there was less retarding of the process of maturation.

Comparison of the offenders who continued to be serious criminals throughout the fifteen-year span and those who became minor offenders revealed that the serious offenders had a worse congenital equipment and were reared in even less favorable circumstances and conditions than those who ultimately committed petty offenses only.

Fourth, a prediction table has been evolved covering the behavior of these 1,000 juvenile delinquents during the fifteen years following the end of their treatment by the Boston Juvenile Court and associated agencies. From such a table, juvenile court judges should be able to determine the probable behavior of different types of offenders appearing before them, and approximately the age at which changes in their conduct are likely to occur.[2]

The second half of this work deals with the responses of the former juvenile delinquents to the various kinds of peno-correctional treatment to which they were subjected from the onset of their delinquent careers to the end of the fifteen-year follow-up span. Analysis of distinguishing factors has differentiated the following four conduct types:

1. Those who succeeded during some (not necessarily all) intramural and extramural treatments
2. Those who failed during all intramural and extramural treatments
3. Those who succeeded during intramural treatments but failed during extramural treatments
4. Those who failed during intramural treatments but succeeded during extramural treatments.

The offenders who behaved satisfactorily during extramural treatment as well as intramural (Type 1) were much more favorably circumstanced in their early lives than were those who failed during both forms of treatment (Type 2).

The offenders who behaved satisfactorily during periods of intramural treatment but did not get along well under extramural supervision (Type 3) apparently had an inadequate sense of security in their early upbringing, which seems to have been reflected in an inability to make satisfactory later adjustments without intensive restraint and supervision.

On the other hand, the offenders who could not get along acceptably in the group life of institutions but did behave satisfactorily during periods of extramural oversight (Type 4) had, to a significantly greater extent than the others, already demonstrated their inability to respond well to other group situations in life.

By distinguishing these four conduct types, it has been possible to prepare prediction tables showing the probable behavior of of-

2 See footnote 3.

fenders during extramural and intramural treatment, as well as during specific forms of peno-correctional treatment.

THEORETICAL IMPLICATIONS OF THE FINDINGS

We have ascertained that it is not so much arrival at any particular age-span (at least as far as our analysis of age-spans has thus far gone) as the achievement of a degree of maturity, that makes for social adaptation on the part of former delinquents. Maturity is a complex concept. It embraces the development of a certain stage of physical, mental, and emotional capacity and stability, and a certain degree of integration of the personality. Common experience indicates that as the average person passes through different age-spans there are changes in his development and in the integration or disintegration of his various physical, intellectual, emotional, and volitional-inhibitory powers. Normally, when he reaches chronologic adulthood the development and integration of his physical and mental powers make it easier for him to achieve a capacity for self-control, foresight, planfulness; to postpone immediate desires for later ones; to profit by experience; to develop perseverance, self-respect, regard for the opinion of his law-abiding fellows, and other similar attributes. These enable him to adapt successfully to the demands of society and to avoid drifting into, or persisting in, crime.[3] However, individuals differ in their innate organization and in their early conditioning, so that development and integration of powers sufficient to be designated "maturity" are not always achieved at the expected age-span. If all our offenders had arrived

[3] Not only in the continuance of delinquency already embarked upon, but in the origins of delinquency as well, it is reasonable to assume that uneven rates of development of the physical, mental, and emotional constituents of the organism must lead to stresses and strains which are reflected in personality maladjustment and the kind of behavior that may well turn out to be "delinquent" or "criminal" because it is made so by society's laws. Difference in the age at which delinquency first became manifest and persistent reflects difference in the stage at which the stresses and strains of the organism became too much for the requisite social adaptation. The degree of physical, mental, and emotional-volitional maturity achieved has been so incommensurate with the age reached and the accompanying obligations and expected behavior at that age that, under the stress of certain socio-economic conditions, social adaptation took the form of delinquent behavior.

at the same degree of maturation in any particular age-span, this fact should have been reflected in a similar incidence of improved conduct in each group shortly after arrival at that age. But we have seen that this was not the case.

A psychoanalytic approach to this problem would emphasize that, owing to "fixations" of the "libido" at childhood levels, a clinically well recognized "infantilism," or immaturity of personality, frequently exists in persons who might otherwise (in physique and even in cognition) have attained a maturity commensurate with their age. In fact, from many angles the conduct of not a few offenders, when passed in review over the years, may be regarded as infantile: witness their impulsiveness, their lack of planfulness, their failure to postpone immediate desires for more distant ones, their incapacity or unwillingness to profit by numerous experiences of punishment or correction, the excessive attachment of many of them to their mothers, their inability to assume marital, family, and other responsibilities appropriate to their chronologic age.

As was indicated in *Later Criminal Careers,* the years from about twenty-five to thirty-five seem to be the most crucial in the lives of offenders, since during this age-zone there appears to occur the peak of a sifting-out process which differentiates those who mature normally from those who are inclined never to reach a stage of maturity sufficient to enable them to abandon criminalism, and who will either die as criminals or end their days in almshouses or on the streets. The offenders who are still criminalistic even at the relatively late age of thirty to thirty-five years (the highest age thus far reached by any of our former juvenile delinquents) are those whose pace of maturing is particularly slow, retarded, or otherwise erratic. Our comparison of the make-up and background of the men who have reformed and those who are still criminals confirms the suggestion made in *Later Criminal Careers* that, with the passage of the years, a differentiation seems to occur between the offenders whose delinquency and criminality is due more to adverse environmental and educational influences than to any deep-seated

organismal weaknesses, and those whose inability to conform to
the demands of a complex society is more nearly related to innate
(and, partly, early-conditioned) abnormalities of the kind that set
limits to the achievement of a socially adequate degree of maturity.
The former, sooner or later, acquire the requisite degree of integration of intelligence, impulse, and behavior. The latter never achieve
a stage of maturity requisite to lawful social adaptation. Despite
their arrival at a high chronologic age they continue to be criminalistic until physically and mentally "burned out." Misbehavior
due to *un*integration gives way to misbehavior due to *dis*integration,
until the organism runs down and finally stops.

In discussing "maturation," we should not ignore the slowing
down process which begins to manifest itself after the organism has
reached its peak of maturity. Organismal changes, to which all
flesh is heir, occur regardless of the rate of maturation of the particular individual. With the passage of time, the human being loses
some of his energy and aggressiveness; he tends to slow down and
to become less venturesome. Just as individuals differ in the rate at
which they climb to the maximum maturity of which they are
capable, so they may differ in the rate at which they descend the hill.
But whether the two sets of influences are definitely related or not,
some of our offenders doubtless abandoned criminalistic ways
largely as the result of the settling and disintegrative influences
which were operative, regardless of the tempo of their maturation
or of the maximum stage of maturity that they were finally able to
reach.

Thus, we may conveniently recognize two types of "reformed"
individuals: one type includes youths and men who, having
achieved a socially requisite state of physical, mental, and emotional
maturity and a socially requisite state of personality integration,
have, as psychologic and not merely as physical adults, finally determined or been induced to abandon their criminalistic ways. The
other type are the men whose abandonment of criminalism or drifting into milder, less aggressive, and less daring forms of misconduct

was caused not by mature choice, or reflection on experience or conscious inhibition or adaptation, but rather by the slowing down or deterioration to which they finally succumbed.

The foregoing theory as to the role of maturation will, of course, be subjected to further examination in the light of the results of other follow-up investigations covering later segments of the life cycle of our offenders. The next step in developing the theory of the relationship of maturation to delinquency and criminality is to dissect "maturation" into its components. Such a task must be left to specialists in psychiatry, psychology, physiology, medicine, and related disciplines. The aim should be to develop norms of maturity in every aspect of mental and physical growth at various age-levels—in emotional equipment, in inhibitory powers, in sexual development, and so on. Deviation of individuals from such norms could then be readily determined and an "M.Q." (maturation quotient) could be established.[4]

PRACTICAL IMPLICATIONS OF THE FINDINGS

Turning now to the practical significance of the major findings of this research, we can first point to the feasibility of more refined predictive instruments for the use of courts and parole boards than have heretofore been constructed. Our work in this field has now been extended to include prognostic instruments covering each of the major types of treatment and carries the added feature of predicting conduct at various age-levels.[5] The construction of predic-

---

[4] We are just embarking on a research in which we are comparing 500 delinquent boys with 500 non-delinquents of the same age, nationality, and socio-economic status, and hope that the results will contribute further to a knowledge of the process of maturation and its relation to temperament and behavior.

[5] In this connection, it should be pointed out that the prediction of the various age-levels at which certain changes in the conduct of offenders are most likely to occur is not inconsistent with the more fundamental finding discussed previously, that it is not arrival at any particular age that determines change in conduct but the achievement of an adequate degree of maturity, which in individual instances may occur at one age or another. The prediction tables deal with the age at which those destined to reform are most likely to do so. However, it will be recalled, from Tables 33 and 34, that it is not the relationship of age-spans themselves to conduct that is involved in the predictions, but rather the relationship of certain favorable sub-categories of factors to age at time of change from criminality

tive tables has advanced to a stage where their careful experimental use in juvenile and adult courts and by parole boards would disclose their practical value in the administration of justice. If every second case appearing before a juvenile court were disposed of with the aid of prognostic tables, and a comparison of follow-up results were made between the offenders dealt with under existing methods and those whose disposal rested essentially on prognostication, a great step forward would be taken in the all-too-slow progress of correctional technique. The prediction tables contained in Chapters XII and XIX might serve as the basis for such an experiment, because they have several unique advantages. In the first place, they are based on a large number of former juvenile delinquents; second, they cover a considerable segment in the life cycle; third, they differentiate outcomes under various types of treatment as well as after the close of treatment.

Such prediction tables furnish to courts and parole boards a rational implementation of the indeterminate sentence. They begin to point the way to indeterminate sentences administered not on the basis of "hunches" or of incalculable differences in the seriousness of various crimes, but rather after consideration of the make-up and career of each offender in the light of the recorded conduct, during and after treatment, of many hundreds of similar offenders. "Individualization of justice," which reformers have long claimed to be superior to the fixed-punishment statutes of the Classical period of penology, has not yet proved its superiority in practice; nor can it do so until guesswork as to the needs of each offender is replaced by analyzed experience and this is welded into useful instruments for more accurate and less impressionistic individualization than we have thus far applied. The imposition of sentences with no upper limit, or within a broad zone of time, which would take into account the expectancy of maturation and reform among different

to non-criminality, or from serious to minor criminality. The ages at which these changes occur vary with the incidence of favorable factors in the make-up and background of particular offenders. Until research evolves "maturation ages" analogous to "mental ages" in psychologic testing, the above indirect method must be employed.

"treatment types," is made possible by the use of predictive instruments of the kind here presented.

In this connection it should be pointed out that this study has revealed a sizeable proportion of offenders whose traits and characteristics are such as to make reform difficult if not impossible. They are the kind whose handicaps are so marked and whose behavior under various forms of treatment is so uniformly bad that provision should be made for their permanent segregation from society.[6] The early recognition of this class of offenders and provision for their continuous oversight and study under controlled conditions are basic needs. The waste of money and effort in their unbroken chain of arrests, trials, and futile punishments is tremendous; and the damage they do on the way is large and varied.

Related to the foregoing is another practical implication of this research—the further weight it gives to the suggestion made in *Later Criminal Careers* that experimentation in ways of hastening the maturation process needs to be carried out among certain groups of criminals, to see whether it is possible to shorten the span of criminality.[7] For not only the plant, but the soil, is involved; and even individuals with congenital handicaps can, within limits, be improved through education and therapy. The significant finding, for example, that certain types of offenders have done well during extramural oversight and poorly behind walls, shows that more intelligent decisions regarding the type of treatment best suited to different individuals might bring about the earlier reform of many of them. The devising of new treatment methods might stimulate the maturation process and reduce the average span of criminalism.

But an approach to the crime problem from the point of view of hastening reform of those offenders who are capable of marked changes of conduct presupposes an integrated system of justice instead of the inharmonious congeries of authorities and agencies at

---

[6] Subject, of course, to research in endocrinology, pharmacotherapy, and psychotherapy, whereby persons at present destined to continuing immaturity may some day be enabled to develop more normally.

[7] See *Later Criminal Careers*, pp. 205, 206.

present concerned with each offender. It entails a planned course of treatment for each offender, to be followed over a prescribed and fairly predictable span of years. It cannot succeed if sentencing judge, probation officer, institutional administrator, paroling authority, and parole agent each regards his work as an end in itself and deals with but one piece of what ought to be a unified process. Treatment should be governed by a plan made in the light of the traits, experiences, and predictable progress of the individual offender. Thus we are brought to a reaffirmation of a major conclusion expressed in *Later Criminal Careers*—that a fundamental need in the administration of criminal justice is the integration, or at least the better articulation, of the various parts of the present disconnected "system" of dealing with offenders.

But the fact should be stressed that the best of systems must fail if those who do the work are not adequately equipped in attitude and training. If the business of criminal justice is to be a scientific work of segregating the incurable and, as early as possible, reforming and rehabilitating those offenders who are capable of entering legitimately upon life in society, the attitude of those who carry on the affairs of justice must be that of scientists, not of persons who see the criminal simply in terms of "leniency" and "severity" of punishment. And a "scientific attitude" without requisite equipment in the biologic and social sciences is of little value. If criminal justice is to be more than the dealing out of sentences on principles neither consistent nor effective, judges, probation officers, administrators of correctional institutions, and parole officers must have specialized training, and criminology must be recognized as a profession that is striving to replace guesswork and prejudice with facts and legitimate inferences.

Appendix A

DEFINITION OF TERMS AND SUBJECT INDEX TO

TABLES IN APPENDIX B

THE factors appearing on the schedule are listed in alphabetical order and are defined or explained where necessary. Fuller explanations of the data appear in the text. Beneath each factor appear the numbers of the tables that are concerned with the particular factor. The tables themselves appear in Appendix B.

AGE
- 76 At change from serious to minor offender
- 7 At end of first five-year period
- 6 At end of JBF-BJC treatment period
- 8 At end of second five-year period
- 9 At end of third five-year period
- 77 At reformation
- 5 At time of JBF arrest

ATTITUDE TO INVESTIGATIONS

2

This refers to the attitude of the men personally interviewed, or of their wives or relatives in cases in which the men were not seen.

BEHAVIOR IN ARMY OR NAVY

78

This is of course not a peno-correctional treatment, but it has been included in our study of the response of our group to various forms of treatment because we have noted in previous researches that certain men do well under the rigid discipline and outdoor life in the Army or Navy who do not react so well to peno-correctional discipline. Behavior is determined entirely on the official reports of Army or Navy authorities. Dishonorable discharge or desertion is considered *failure*, honorable discharge, *success*.

BEHAVIOR IN CORRECTIONAL AND TRUANT SCHOOLS

78

Behavior during a period of correctional treatment in a training or truant or disciplinary school was determined from conduct reports kept by the institutional authorities.

A *failure* is one who is a constant disciplinary problem, steals, incites others to misbehavior, runs away from the institution, instructs others in the commission of vice or other offenses, generally disturbs the routine of the institution, or has to be placed in solitary confinement.

A *success* is one who abides by the rules of the institution (not rigidly —occasional minor infringements of the rules are allowable).

BEHAVIOR IN FOSTER HOME DURING PAROLE

78

For definition of success and failure see BEHAVIOR DURING SUPERVISION BY STATE BOARD.

BEHAVIOR IN FOSTER HOME DURING PROBATION

78

For definition of success and failure see BEHAVIOR DURING SUPERVISION BY STATE BOARD.

BEHAVIOR IN INSTITUTIONS FOR DEFECTIVE DELINQUENTS

78

For definition of success and failure, see BEHAVIOR IN CORRECTIONAL AND TRUANT SCHOOLS.

BEHAVIOR IN JAILS, HOUSES OF CORRECTION, STATE FARMS

78

For definition of success and failure, see BEHAVIOR IN CORRECTIONAL AND TRUANT SCHOOLS.

BEHAVIOR ON PAROLE

78

For definition of success and failure, see BEHAVIOR ON PROBATION.

BEHAVIOR IN PRISONS

78

For definition of success and failure, see BEHAVIOR IN CORRECTIONAL AND TRUANT SCHOOLS.

BEHAVIOR ON PROBATION

78

Failure is determined by actual arrests and/or convictions (except for occasional minor traffic violations), by frequent violations of the rules of probation, or by the commission of offenses for which a probationer might be arrested, such as stealing, sex offenses, drunkenness. An occasional minor infringement of the rules of probation (as neglect to report on time or changing jobs without permission) is not considered.

Success is determined by freedom from arrest or conviction (except for occasional minor traffic violations) and from the commission of offenses for which the probationer might be arrested, and by adherence to the rules of probation. As indicated above, occasional minor infringements of the rules of probation are not deemed sufficient to categorize the case as a failure.

BEHAVIOR DURING PROBATION UNDER SUSPENDED SENTENCE
78
For definition of success and failure, see BEHAVIOR ON PROBATION.

BEHAVIOR IN REFORMATORIES
78
For definition of success and failure, see BEHAVIOR IN CORRECTIONAL AND TRUANT SCHOOLS.

BEHAVIOR IN SCHOOLS FOR FEEBLEMINDED
78
For definition of success and failure, see BEHAVIOR IN CORRECTIONAL AND TRUANT SCHOOLS.

BEHAVIOR DURING SUPERVISION BY STATE BOARD
78
This refers to the Massachusetts State Board of Public Welfare, Division of Child Guardianship, under whose care a delinquent child may be placed by a juvenile court for supervisory placement in a foster home. This factor, as well as BEHAVIOR IN FOSTER HOME DURING PROBATION, and BEHAVIOR IN FOSTER HOME DURING PAROLE, refers to behavior in foster homes.

Failure in a foster home is determined by arrests and/or convictions (except for occasional minor traffic violations), or by the commission of any offenses for which one might be arrested such as stealing, illicit sex acts, drunkenness, unmanageableness. Running away from a foster home is also reflective of failure under this form of treatment.

CAUSE OF DEATH
4

DATE OF DEATH
3

DELINQUENCY
26 Prior period
42 Period I
58 Period II
74 Period III
75 Periods I, II, and III combined

Non-delinquent: no police or court record, no dishonorable discharge or desertion from Army or Navy, and no misconduct for which he might be arrested, such as drunkenness, abuse of family, stealing, and so on (i.e., no unofficial misconduct: See OFFICIAL REC-OGNITION OF DELINQUENCY for definition). Technical traffic violations in the absence of any other misconduct are allowable in this category. *Delinquent:* official or unofficial misconduct as above described.

The differentiation between *serious* and *minor* offenders is essentially that between felons and misdemeanants. A man is classified as a serious offender if he has committed property crimes, assault with intent to rob, rape, or murder, or pathological sex offenses. See *500 Criminal Careers*, pp. 141, 354–357, for detailed classification.

FREQUENCY OF ARRESTS

13 Prior period
29 Period I
45 Period II
61 Period III

Frequency is calculated on the basis of the number of months a man was at liberty in the community during the period under study. (See MONTHS IN COMMUNITY for definition.) This total is divided by the number of arrests. If there was only one arrest during a given period, the case is tabulated "incalculable." If a man died before the end of the period, frequency of arrests was calculated on the basis of months in the community to the date of death, minus periods in peno-correctional institutions or mental hospitals.

FREQUENCY OF CONVICTIONS

17 Prior period
33 Period I
49 Period II
65 Period III

See FREQUENCY OF ARRESTS. Method of calculation is the same.

GENERAL SUMMARY OF BEHAVIOR IN EXTRAMURAL AND INTRAMURAL PENO-CORRECTIONAL TREATMENT

80

Extramural peno-correctional treatment includes probation, probation under suspended sentence, parole, and periods in foster homes. *Intramural peno-correctional treatment* includes correctional or truant schools, schools for feebleminded, reformatories, prisons, jails, and institutions for defective delinquents.

INTERVIEW WITH

I

Refers to persons interviewed in connection with field investigation. Categorized in the order indicated in the Code.

MONTHS IN COMMUNITY

22   Prior period
38   Period I
54   Period II
70   Period III

Refers to that portion of each period during which the offender is not under the restraint of a peno-correctional institution or in a mental hospital or in an institution for the chronically disabled.

NATURE OF ARRESTS

12   Prior period
28   Period I
44   Period II
60   Period III

NATURE OF DISPOSITIONS

16   Prior period
32   Period I
48   Period II
64   Period III

NATURE OF PENAL EXPERIENCES, BY TYPE

20   Prior period
36   Period I
52   Period II
68   Period III

NUMBER OF ARRESTS

11   Prior period
27   Period I
43   Period II
59   Period III

NUMBER OF CONVICTIONS

15   Prior period
31   Period I
47   Period II
63   Period III

NUMBER OF PENAL EXPERIENCES

19   Prior period
35   Period I
51   Period II
67   Period III

This includes returns by revocation and transfers from one institution to another. It excludes very brief commitments for non-payment of fine. When a penal experience extends into the next period it is counted in the period in which it started and also in the period following. The actual length of time spent in the institution in each period is recorded under TIME IN PENAL INSTITUTIONS.

OFFICIAL RECOGNITION OF DELINQUENCY

23 Prior period
39 Period I
55 Period II
71 Period III

Official: based on police or court records or on Army or Navy records.

Unofficial: delinquency for which the person has not come to the attention of official agencies of the law.

PLACE OF RESIDENCE AT END OF PERIOD III

10

PREDOMINANT OFFENSE

24 Prior period
40 Period I
56 Period II
72 Period III

This is a social category of offenses which is based on unofficial as well as official misconduct (see OFFICIAL RECOGNITION OF DELINQUENCY). The type of offense most characteristic of the offender during a particular period is designated the predominant offense.

PRINCIPAL COMPONENT OF MISCONDUCT

25 Prior period
41 Period I
57 Period II
73 Period III

Each offender is categorized once in each period, in the order indicated in the tables.

SUMMARY OF ARRESTS, BY TYPE

14 Prior period
30 Period I
46 Period II
62 Period III

SUMMARY OF BEHAVIOR IN ARMY OR NAVY

79

SUMMARY OF BEHAVIOR IN CORRECTIONAL AND TRUANT SCHOOLS

79

Appendix B

ORIGINAL TABLES

For definitions of the factors, see Appendix A, *Definition of Terms and Subject Index of Tables in Appendix B,* in which they are arranged alphabetically.

All tables total 1,000 unless otherwise indicated by the title or by a line appearing either beneath or above a category (as in Table 20, *Nature of Penal Experiences,* beneath the category "inapplicable") which means that, in the categories appearing below the line, a case may have been recorded more than once. Tables like this are designated multiple tables and total more than 1,000. If the sum of the incidence of the categories above or below the line (as the case may be) is subtracted from 1,000, the result is the number of cases actually represented by the remaining categories or sub-classes of the factor.

In Tables 78, 79, and 80, dealing with behavior during peno-correctional treatment, only those cases are categorized in which information about behavior under the particular form of treatment was sufficient to determine success or failure. These tables do not represent, therefore, the actual number of men who had particular treatment experiences in a given period. It will be noted that in some of the tables the figures reported are very small. They are presented in full here but are utilized guardedly in the text.

1. Interview with

175	Offender
404	Relatives
12	Others
409	Information from records only

2. Attitude to investigation

574	Friendly
7	Indifferent
10	Hostile
409	Inapplicable

3. Date of death

    1 In BJC-JBF treatment period
   20 In first five-year period
   18 In second five-year period
   21 In third five-year period
  940 Known to be living

4. Cause of death

   16 Accident
    3 Suicide
    5 Heart ailment
    7 Lung infection
   10 Pneumonia
    3 Meningitis
    1 Convulsions
    4 Result of operation
    2 Electrocution
    6 Other
    3 Cause unknown
  940 Inapplicable as living

5. Age at time of JBF arrest

  316 Under 13 years
  674 13–16 years
   10 17, 18 years

6. Age at end of BJC-JBF treatment period

  703 11–15 years
  294 16–20 years
    2 21–25 years

7. Age at end of first five-year period

   89 Under 16 years
  604 16–20 years
  284 21–25 years
    2 26–30 years
   21 Inapplicable as dead

8. Age at end of second five-year period

88 16–20 years
593 21–25 years
278 26–30 years
2 31–35 years
39 Inapplicable as dead

9. Age at end of third five-year period

85 21–25 years
583 26–30 years
270 31–35 years
2 36–40 years
60 Inapplicable as dead

10. Place of residence at end of period III

604 Boston and environs
33 Other cities in Massachusetts
112 States other than Massachusetts
69 Penal institutions in Massachusetts
24 Penal institutions in other states
3 Fugitive from justice
6 Hospital for mental diseases
2 Hospital for physical diseases
11 Army or Navy
6 Foreign country
16 Wandering about
7 At sea
11 Whereabouts known for part of period but not at end
60 Dead
36 Unknown throughout period

11. Number of arrests (prior period)

294 One arrest
151 Two arrests
80 Three arrests
50 Four arrests
24 Five arrests
11 Six arrests

 10   Seven arrests
  4   Eight or more arrests
374   No arrests
  2   Unknown if arrested, or inapplicable

12. Nature of (1,333) arrests (prior period)

829   Crimes against property
  4   Crimes against chastity
286   Crimes against public welfare
 33   Crimes against person
 14   Violation of probation
167   Other offenses not classifiable above

13. Frequency of arrests (prior period)

 29   One arrest in less than 3 months
 49   One arrest in 3–6 months
 71   One arrest in 6–9 months
 60   One arrest in 9–12 months
 33   One arrest in 12–15 months
 31   One arrest in 15–18 months
 20   One arrest in 18–21 months
 18   One arrest in 21–24 months
 18   One arrest in 24 or more months
668   Frequency incalculable (only one arrest or not arrested)
  3   Unknown if arrested, or frequency unknown

14. Summary of arrests, by type (prior period)

478   Crimes against property (including holdups)
  4   Crimes against chastity
204   Crimes against public welfare
 30   Crimes against person
132   Other (stubbornness, truancy, runaway, malicious mischief)
 15   Violation of probation (nature of offense unknown)

376   Inapplicable, or no arrests, or unknown if arrested

15. Number of convictions (prior period)

 42   None
280   One conviction
138   Two convictions

81 Three convictions
47 Four convictions
11 Five convictions
12 Six convictions
5 Seven convictions
3 Eight or more convictions
7 Unknown if arrested
374 Not arrested

16. NATURE OF (1,333) DISPOSITIONS (PRIOR PERIOD)

77 Commitment—new
20 Commitment—by revocation of sentence
570 Probation
81 Probation under suspended sentence
53 Fine
355 File
14 Restitution
3 Nol-pros
106 Not guilty or released
54 Unknown, or defaulted and no final disposition, or other

17. FREQUENCY OF CONVICTIONS (PRIOR PERIOD)

19 One conviction in less than 3 months
49 One conviction in 3–6 months
67 One conviction in 6–9 months
54 One conviction in 9–12 months
36 One conviction in 12–15 months
31 One conviction in 15–18 months
27 One conviction in 18–21 months
17 One conviction in 21–24 months
26 One conviction in 24 or more months
669 Incalculable (only one arrest, no convictions, or no arrests, or number of convictions unknown, or unknown if convicted)
5 Unknown, or unknown if arrested

18. SUMMARY OF DISPOSITIONS, BY TYPE (PRIOR PERIOD)

70 Commitment—new
18 Commitment—by revocation of sentence
393 Probation
74 Probation under suspended sentence

60 Fine (including commitment for non-payment, and restitution)
202 File
3 Nol-pros
93 Not guilty or released
50 Disposition unknown, or awaiting disposition

---

376 Inapplicable, or no arrests, or unknown if arrested

19. Number of penal experiences (prior period)

930 None
47 One experience
16 Two experiences
5 Three experiences
1 Four experiences
1 Five experiences

20. Nature of penal experiences, by type (prior period)

930 Inapplicable (none, unknown if any, dead)

---

67 Truant and correctional schools
2 Schools for feebleminded
2 Reformatories

21. Time in penal institutions (prior period)

930 None
3 Less than 3 months
4 3–6 months
10 6–12 months
18 12–18 months
11 18–24 months
11 24–30 months
5 30–36 months
4 36–48 months
4 Time unknown

22. Months in community (prior period)

930 Throughout the period
68 Not throughout the period
2 Incalculable, or unknown

23. Official recognition of delinquency (prior period)

7   Non-delinquency
624   Determination of delinquency based on official record
364   Determination of delinquency based on unofficial misbehavior only
5   Unknown if delinquent

24. Predominant offense (prior period)

702   Crimes against property
12   Crimes against chastity
22   Crimes against public welfare
2   Crimes against person
64   Crimes are varied, no one type predominant
186   Not determinable or other
5   Unknown if delinquent
7   Non-delinquent

25. Principal component of misconduct (prior period)

451   Conviction for serious offense
32   Arrest for serious offense, not followed by conviction
264   Unofficial serious offense
74   Conviction for minor offense
10   Arrest for minor offense, not followed by conviction
156   Unofficial minor offense
1   Dishonorable discharge or desertion from Army or Navy
5   Not determinable
7   Non-delinquent

26. Delinquency (prior period)

7   Non-delinquency
241   Delinquency—minor
747   Delinquency—serious
5   Unknown if delinquent

27. Number of arrests (period i)

154   One arrest
167   Two arrests
126   Three arrests
96   Four arrests

78   Five arrests
41   Six arrests
31   Seven arrests
56   Eight or more arrests
190 No arrests
61   Unknown if arrested, or inapplicable

28. Nature of (2,719) arrests (period 1)

1,272 Crimes against property
43   Crimes against chastity
14   Crimes against family and children
580 Crimes against public welfare
242 Drunkenness
1   Drug selling, etc.
115 Crimes against person
110 Violation of probation
342 Other offenses not classifiable above

29. Frequency of arrests (period 1)

16   One arrest in less than 3 months
64   One arrest in 3–6 months
100 One arrest in 6–9 months
74   One arrest in 9–12 months
66   One arrest in 12–15 months
58   One arrest in 15–18 months
81   One arrest in 18–21 months
20   One arrest in 21–24 months
113 One arrest in 24 or more months
343 Frequency incalculable (only one arrest or not arrested)
55   Unknown if arrested, or frequency unknown
10   Inapplicable (non-penal institution, chronic illness, dead)

30. Summary of arrests, by type (period 1)

560 Crimes against property (including holdups)
35   Crimes against chastity
7   Crimes against family and children
327 Crimes against public welfare
100 Drunkenness
1   Drug selling, etc.
93   Crimes against person

237 Other (stubbornness, truancy, runaway, malicious mischief)
93 Violation of probation (nature of offense unknown)

---

251 Inapplicable, or no arrests, or unknown if arrested

31. NUMBER OF CONVICTIONS (PERIOD 1)

16 None
167 One conviction
177 Two convictions
137 Three convictions
99 Four convictions
65 Five convictions
33 Six convictions
18 Seven convictions
36 Eight or more convictions
1 Number of convictions unknown
51 Unknown if arrested
10 Inapplicable (non-penal institution, chronic illness, dead)
190 Not arrested

32. NATURE OF (2,719) DISPOSITIONS (PERIOD 1)

512 Commitment—new
301 Commitment—by revocation of sentence
462 Probation
250 Probation under suspended sentence
366 Fine
1 Commitment for non-payment of fine
442 File
6 Restitution
52 Released by probation officer without court hearing
18 Nol-pros
17 No bill
237 Not guilty or released
55 Unknown, or defaulted and no final disposition, or other

33. FREQUENCY OF CONVICTIONS (PERIOD 1)

14 One conviction in less than 3 months
45 One conviction in 3–6 months
83 One conviction in 6–9 months
72 One conviction in 9–12 months
71 One conviction in 12–15 months

60   One conviction in 15–18 months
79   One conviction in 18–21 months
20   One conviction in 21–24 months
144 One conviction in 24 or more months
347 Incalculable (only one arrest, no convictions, or no arrests, or number of convictions unknown, or unknown if convicted)
55   Unknown or unknown if arrested
10   Inapplicable (non-penal institution, chronic illness, dead)

34. SUMMARY OF DISPOSITIONS, BY TYPE (PERIOD I)

369 Commitment—new
182 Commitment—by revocation of sentence
318 Probation
192 Probation under suspended sentence
201 Fine (including commitment for non-payment, and restitution)
285 File
34   Released by probation office without court appearance
16   Nol-pros
15   No bill
168 Not guilty or released
57   Disposition unknown, or awaiting disposition

251 Inapplicable, or no arrests, or unknown if arrested

35. NUMBER OF PENAL EXPERIENCES (PERIOD I)

518 None
189 One experience
133 Two experiences
58   Three experiences
30   Four experiences
9   Five experiences
2   Six experiences
3   Seven experiences
48   Unknown if any
10   Inapplicable (non-penal institution, chronic illness, dead)

36. NATURE OF PENAL EXPERIENCES, BY TYPE (PERIOD I)

518 Inapplicable (none, unknown if any, dead)

324 Truant and correctional schools

8 Schools for feebleminded
93 Reformatories
22 Prisons
90 Jails, houses of correction, farms
7 Institutions for defective delinquents

37. TIME IN PENAL INSTITUTIONS (PERIOD I)

518 None
19 Less than 3 months
33 3–6 months
89 6–12 months
104 12–18 months
70 18–24 months
36 24–30 months
34 30–36 months
29 36–48 months
10 48–60 months
58 Time unknown or inapplicable

38. MONTHS IN COMMUNITY (PERIOD I)

2 None
2 Less than 3 months
4 3–6 months
6 6–12 months
12 12–18 months
16 18–24 months
31 24–30 months
36 30–36 months
154 36–48 months
164 48–60 months
512 60 months
61 Unknown, or inapplicable (dead)

39. OFFICIAL RECOGNITION OF DELINQUENCY (PERIOD I)

137 Non-delinquency
755 Determination of delinquency based on official record
49 Determination of delinquency based on unofficial misbehavior only
49 Unknown if delinquent
10 Inapplicable (non-penal institution, chronic illness, dead)

40. Predominant offense (period I)

527 Crimes against property
 12 Crimes against chastity
  4 Crimes against family and children
 86 Crimes against public welfare
 34 Drunkenness
  1 Drug selling, etc.
  5 Crimes against person
 60 Crimes are varied, no one type predominant
 75 Not determinable or other
 10 Inapplicable (non-penal institution, chronic illness, dead)
 49 Unknown if delinquent
137 Non-delinquent

41. Principal component of misconduct (period I)

543 Conviction for serious offense
 26 Arrest for serious offense, not followed by conviction
 45 Unofficial serious offense
140 Conviction for minor offense
  7 Arrest for minor offense not followed by conviction
 32 Unofficial minor offense
  9 Dishonorable discharge or desertion from Army or Navy
 58 Not determinable or dead
  1 Inapplicable as in non-penal institution throughout
  2 Inapplicable as in penal institution at least part of the time on sentence imposed in previous period, no other delinquency
137 Non-delinquent

42. Delinquency (period I)

137 Non-delinquency
182 Delinquency—minor
622 Delinquency—serious
 10 Inapplicable (non-penal institution, chronic illness, dead)
 49 Unknown if delinquent

43. Number of arrests (period II)

111 One arrest
118 Two arrests
 75 Three arrests

72 Four arrests
59 Five arrests
40 Six arrests
25 Seven arrests
78 Eight or more arrests
2 Number unknown
297 No arrests
123 Unknown if arrested, or inapplicable

44. Nature of (2,547) arrests (period ii)

613 Crimes against property
59 Crimes against chastity
40 Crimes against family and children
755 Crimes against public welfare
724 Drunkenness
8 Drug selling, etc.
183 Crimes against person
54 Violation of probation
111 Other offenses not classifiable above

45. Frequency of arrests (period ii)

26 One arrest in less than 3 months
63 One arrest in 3–6 months
70 One arrest in 6–9 months
62 One arrest in 9–12 months
47 One arrest in 12–15 months
49 One arrest in 15–18 months
53 One arrest in 18–21 months
4 One arrest in 21–24 months
90 One arrest in 24 or more months
411 Frequency incalculable (only one arrest or not arrested)
88 Unknown if arrested, or frequency unknown
37 Inapplicable (non-penal institution, chronic illness, dead)

46. Summary of arrests, by type (period ii)

295 Crimes against property (including holdups)
46 Crimes against chastity
35 Crimes against family and children
341 Crimes against public welfare
205 Drunkenness

  8 Drug selling, etc.
141 Crimes against person
 83 Other (stubbornness, truancy, runaway, malicious mischief)
 36 Violation of probation (nature of offense unknown)

420 Inapplicable, or no arrests, or unknown if arrested

47. Number of convictions (period II)

 41 None
146 One conviction
105 Two convictions
 83 Three convictions
 61 Four convictions
 54 Five convictions
 32 Six convictions
 15 Seven convictions
 41 Eight or more convictions
  2 Number of convictions unknown
 85 Unknown if arrested
 38 Inapplicable (non-penal institution, chronic illness, dead)
297 Not arrested

48. Nature of (2,547) dispositions (period II)

430 Commitment—new
 76 Commitment—by revocation of sentence
217 Probation
136 Probation under suspended sentence
675 Fine
  8 Commitment for non-payment of fine
347 File
  5 Restitution
113 Released by probation officer without court hearing
 51 Nol-pros
 48 No bill
398 Not guilty or released
 43 Unknown, or defaulted and no final disposition, or other

49. Frequency of convictions (period II)

 16 One conviction in less than 3 months
 42 One conviction in 3–6 months

48 One conviction in 6–9 months
65 One conviction in 9–12 months
47 One conviction in 12–15 months
38 One conviction in 15–18 months
57 One conviction in 18–21 months
9 One conviction in 21–24 months
135 One conviction in 24 or more months
418 Incalculable (only one arrest, no convictions, or no arrests, or number of convictions unknown, or unknown if convicted)
88 Unknown or unknown if arrested
37 Inapplicable (non-penal institution, chronic illness, dead)

50. SUMMARY OF DISPOSITIONS, BY TYPE (PERIOD II)

239 Commitment—new
61 Commitment—by revocation of sentence
153 Probation
92 Probation under suspended sentence
301 Fine (including commitment for non-payment and restitution)
213 File
71 Released by probation officer without court hearing
44 Nol-pros
41 No bill
213 Not guilty or released
43 Disposition unknown, or awaiting disposition

420 Inapplicable, or no arrests, or unknown if arrested

51. NUMBER OF PENAL EXPERIENCES (PERIOD II)

585 None
171 One experience
72 Two experiences
37 Three experiences
15 Four experiences
5 Five experiences
3 Six experiences
1 Seven experiences
3 Eight or more experiences
78 Unknown if any
30 Inapplicable (non-penal institution, chronic illness, dead)

52. Nature of penal experiences, by type (period ii)

693 Inapplicable (none, unknown if any, dead)

---

43 Truant and correctional schools
2 Schools for feebleminded
96 Reformatories
61 Prisons
161 Jails, houses of correction, farms
10 Institutions for defective delinquents

53. Time in penal institutions (period ii)

587 None
48 Less than 3 months
33 3–6 months
52 6–12 months
47 12–18 months
27 18–24 months
18 24–30 months
19 30–36 months
37 36–48 months
18 48–60 months
7 60 months
107 Time unknown, or inapplicable

54. Months in community (period ii)

13 None
2 Less than 3 months
6 3–6 months
7 6–12 months
18 12–18 months
20 18–24 months
25 24–30 months
17 30–36 months
71 36–48 months
138 48–60 months
578 60 months
105 Unknown or inapplicable (dead)

55. Official recognition of delinquency (period ii)

238 Non-delinquency

604 Determination of delinquency based on official record
46 Determination of delinquency based on unofficial misbehavior only
78 Unknown if delinquent
34 Inapplicable (non-penal institution, chronic illness, dead)

56. PREDOMINANT OFFENSE (PERIOD II)

255 Crimes against property
13 Crimes against chastity
17 Crimes against family and children
147 Crimes against public welfare
108 Drunkenness
2 Drug selling, etc.
9 Crimes against person
62 Crimes are varied, no one type predominant
37 Not determinable or other
34 Inapplicable (non-penal institution, chronic illness, dead)
78 Unknown if delinquent
238 Non-delinquent

57. PRINCIPAL COMPONENT OF MISCONDUCT (PERIOD II)

272 Conviction for serious offense
39 Arrest for serious offense, not followed by conviction
28 Unofficial serious offense
215 Conviction for minor offense
27 Arrest for minor offense, not followed by conviction
38 Unofficial minor offense
8 Dishonorable discharge or desertion from Army or Navy
106 Not determinable or dead
2 Inapplicable as in non-penal institution throughout
27 Inapplicable as in penal institution at least part of the time on sentence imposed in previous period, no other delinquency
238 Non-delinquent

58. DELINQUENCY (PERIOD II)

238 Non-delinquency
282 Delinquency—minor
368 Delinquency—serious
34 Inapplicable (non-penal institution, chronic illness, dead)
78 Unknown if delinquent

59. Number of arrests (period iii)

114 One arrest
83 Two arrests
61 Three arrests
60 Four arrests
28 Five arrests
33 Six arrests
30 Seven arrests
71 Eight or more arrests
10 Number unknown
356 No arrests
154 Unknown if arrested, or inapplicable

60. Nature of (2,195) arrests (period iii)

390 Crimes against property
56 Crimes against chastity
71 Crimes against family and children
483 Crimes against public welfare
922 Drunkenness
12 Drug selling, etc.
147 Crimes against person
49 Violation of probation
65 Other offenses not classifiable above

61. Frequency of arrests (period iii)

23 One arrest in less than 3 months
68 One arrest in 3–6 months
52 One arrest in 6–9 months
40 One arrest in 9–12 months
37 One arrest in 12–15 months
37 One arrest in 15–18 months
43 One arrest in 18–21 months
4 One arrest in 21–24 months
63 One arrest in 24 or more months
470 Frequency incalculable (only one arrest or not arrested)
94 Unknown if arrested, or frequency unknown
69 Inapplicable (non-penal institution, chronic illness, dead)

62. Summary of arrests, by type (period iii)

208 Crimes against property (including holdups)
47 Crimes against chastity

43 Crimes against family and children
246 Crimes against public welfare
227 Drunkenness
8 Drug selling, etc.
104 Crimes against person
49 Other (stubbornness, truancy, runaway, malicious mischief)
37 Violation of probation (nature of offense unknown)
510 Inapplicable, or no arrests, or unknown if arrested

63. NUMBER OF CONVICTIONS (PERIOD III)

44 None
138 One conviction
81 Two convictions
61 Three convictions
51 Four convictions
32 Five convictions
21 Six convictions
11 Seven convictions
43 Eight or more convictions
8 Number of convictions unknown
92 Unknown if arrested
62 Inapplicable (non-penal institution, chronic illness, dead)
356 Not arrested

64. NATURE OF (2,195) DISPOSITIONS (PERIOD III)

440 Commitment—new
35 Commitment—by revocation of sentence
134 Probation
150 Probation under suspended sentence
412 Fine
10 Commitment for non-payment of fine
343 File
3 Restitution
198 Released by probation officer without court hearing
44 Nol-pros
33 No bill
352 Not guilty or released
41 Unknown, or defaulted and no final disposition, or other

65. FREQUENCY OF CONVICTIONS (PERIOD III)

9 One conviction in less than 3 months

57   One conviction in 3–6 months
33   One conviction in 6–9 months
28   One conviction in 9–12 months
39   One conviction in 12–15 months
32   One conviction in 15–18 months
46   One conviction in 18–21 months
6   One conviction in 21–24 months
100   One conviction in 24 or more months
487   Incalculable (only one arrest, no convictions, or no arrests, or number of convictions unknown, or unknown if convicted)
94   Unknown, or unknown if arrested
69   Inapplicable (non-penal institution, chronic illness, dead)

66. SUMMARY OF DISPOSITIONS, BY TYPE (PERIOD III)

214   Commitment—new
35   Commitment—by revocation of sentence
104   Probation
99   Probation under suspended sentence
199   Fine (including commitment for non-payment and restitution)
191   File
102   Released by probation officer without court appearance
34   Nol-pros
23   No bill
193   Not guilty or released
33   Disposition unknown, or awaiting disposition

510   Inapplicable, or no arrests, or unknown if arrested

67. NUMBER OF PENAL EXPERIENCES (PERIOD III)

600   None
122   One experience
72   Two experiences
31   Three experiences
16   Four experiences
7   Five experiences
5   Six experiences
2   Seven experiences
2   Eight or more experiences
87   Unknown if any
56   Inapplicable (non-penal institution, chronic illness, dead)

68. NATURE OF PENAL EXPERIENCES, BY TYPE (PERIOD III)

743 Inapplicable (none, unknown if any, dead)

1	Schools for feebleminded
47	Reformatories
97	Prisons
158	Jails, houses of correction, farms
9	Institutions for defective delinquents

69. TIME IN PENAL INSTITUTIONS (PERIOD III)

600	None
32	Less than 3 months
33	3–6 months
30	6–12 months
30	12–18 months
23	18–24 months
19	24–30 months
17	30–36 months
37	36–48 months
22	48–60 months
14	60 months
143	Time unknown, or inapplicable

70. MONTHS IN COMMUNITY (PERIOD III)

18	None
2	Less than 3 months
4	3–6 months
13	6–12 months
23	12–18 months
14	18–24 months
14	24–30 months
26	30–36 months
50	36–48 months
99	48–60 months
598	60 months
139	Unknown or inapplicable (dead)

71. OFFICIAL RECOGNITION OF DELINQUENCY (PERIOD III)

312	Non-delinquency
504	Determination of delinquency based on official record

36 Determination of delinquency based on unofficial misbehavior only
89 Unknown if delinquent
59 Inapplicable (non-penal institution, chronic illness, dead)

72. Predominant offense (period III)

169 Crimes against property
12 Crimes against chastity
20 Crimes against family and children
107 Crimes against public welfare
128 Drunkenness
4 Drug selling, etc.
11 Crimes against person
59 Crimes are varied, no one type predominant
30 Not determinable or other
59 Inapplicable (institution, chronic illness, dead)
89 Unknown if delinquent
312 Non-delinquent

73. Principal component of misconduct (period III)

189 Conviction for serious offense
27 Arrest for serious offense, not followed by conviction
14 Unofficial serious offense
218 Conviction for minor offense
30 Arrest for minor offense, not followed by conviction
34 Unofficial minor offense
145 Not determinable or dead
2 Inapplicable as in non-penal institution throughout
29 Inapplicable as in penal institution at least part of the time on sentence imposed in previous period, no other serious delinquency
312 Non-delinquent

74. Delinquency (period III)

312 Non-delinquency
282 Delinquency—minor
258 Delinquency—serious
59 Inapplicable (non-penal institution, chronic illness, dead)
89 Unknown if delinquent

75. Delinquency in periods I, II, and III combined

226 Serious delinquent throughout

88 Minor delinquent throughout
109 Non-delinquent throughout
27 Unknown throughout
67 Serious in I and II, minor in III
95 Serious in I, minor in II and III
67 Serious in I, non-delinquent in II and III
36 Serious in I, minor in II, non-delinquent in III
46 Serious in I, dead or unknown in II and III
27 Serious in I and II, non-delinquent in III
9 Serious in I and II, dead in III
14 Serious in I, minor in II, dead or unknown in III
14 Serious in I and II, unknown or ill or inapplicable in III
6 Serious in I, minor in II, serious in III
6 Serious in I, unknown in II, minor or non-delinquent in III
2 Serious in I, non-delinquent in II, dead or unknown in III
3 Serious in I, unknown in II, serious in III
4 Serious in I, non-delinquent in II, serious in III
1 Serious in I, non-delinquent in II, minor in III
40 Minor in I, non-delinquent in II and III
23 Minor in I and II, non-delinquent in III
4 Minor in I, dead or unknown in II and III
4 Minor in I and II, dead or unknown in III
2 Minor in I, serious in II, non-delinquent in III
4 Minor in I and II, serious in III
5 Minor in I, serious in II and III
2 Minor in I, unknown in II, serious in III
7 Minor in I, serious in II, minor or unknown in III
3 Minor in I, unknown in II, minor in III
1 Minor in I, non-delinquent in II, minor in III
5 Non-delinquent in I, delinquent in II and III (serious or minor)
5 Non-delinquent in I and II, dead or unknown in III
2 Non-delinquent in I and II, serious in III
4 Non-delinquent in I and II, minor in III
2 Non-delinquent in I, minor in II, unknown or dead in III
1 Non-delinquent in I, minor in II, non-delinquent in III
1 Non-delinquent in I, inapplicable in II and III
5 Non-delinquent in I, serious in II, non-delinquent or minor delinquent in III
1 Non-delinquent in I, unknown in II and III
5 Unknown in I, serious in II and III
2 Unknown in I and II, serious or minor in III

1 Unknown in I, minor in II, serious in III
3 Unknown in I, non-delinquent in II and III
5 Unknown in I, minor in II and III
4 Unknown in I, serious in II, minor in III
2 Unknown in I, died early in II
1 Inapplicable as in non-penal institution throughout
9 Dead before Period I, or very early in I and judgment of conduct impossible

76. Age at change from serious to minor offender

102 Under 17 years
95 17–21 years
63 21–25 years
32 25–29 years
1 29–33 years
707 Unknown or inapplicable

77. Age at reformation

19 Under 12 years
44 12–15 years
75 15–18 years
72 18–21 years
58 21–24 years
41 24–27 years
9 27–30 years
682 Inapplicable, unknown

78. Behavior under various forms of peno-correctional treatment, by periods

	PRIOR PERIOD		JBF-BJC TREATMENT PERIOD		PERIOD I		PERIOD II		PERIOD III	
	Success	Failure	Success	Failure	Success	Failure	Success	Failure	Success	Failure
Probation	74	249	169	281	100	203	38	105	37	57
Probation under suspended sentence	11	51	60	165	50	158	20	72	20	67
Parole	1	39	1	25	56	331	58	170	42	80
Supervision by State Board	–	4	1	10	1	12	1	3	–	–
Foster home during probation	3	2	13	11	4	7	2	–	–	1
Foster home during parole	–	–	–	3	1	2	–	–	1	–
Correctional and truant schools	27	28	50	63	171	155	17	15	1	1
Reformatories	–	2	1	4	31	49	47	41	32	9
Prisons	–	–	–	–	11	2	33	19	68	28
Jails, houses of correction, state farms	–	–	–	–	32	16	72	23	84	23
Schools for feebleminded	1	1	9	17	4	5	2	1	3	–
Institutions for defective delinquents	–	–	–	–	4	4	4	6	4	3
Army or Navy	1	3	2	–	51	49	40	26	14	8

NOTE. In this table and in Tables 79 and 80 only those cases are categorized in which information about behavior under the particular form of treatment was sufficient to determine success or failure. These tables do not represent, therefore, the actual number of men who had particular treatment experiences in a given period.

79. Summary of Behavior Under Various Forms of Peno-Correctional Treatment

	ALWAYS SUCCESS	ALWAYS FAILURE	EARLY SUCCESS, LATER FAILURE	EARLY FAILURE, LATER SUCCESS	ERRATICALLY SUCCESS AND FAILURE
Probation	164	467	65	84	26
Probation under suspended sentence	100	348	19	30	3
Parole	66	334	2	67	3
Supervision by State Board	4	24	–	–	–
Foster home during probation	18	20	1	1	–
Foster home during parole	–	3	1	–	–
Correctional and truant schools	171	180	27	36	6
Reformatories	72	69	4	16	1
Prisons	69	27	5	9	1
Jails, houses of correction, state farms	121	33	7	16	8
Schools for feebleminded	10	17	1	3	–
Institutions for defective delinquents	8	5	–	2	–
Army or Navy	50	56	12	2	1

80. General Summary of Behavior in Extramural and Intramural Peno-Correctional Treatment

16	Success throughout intramural and extramural treatment
91	Failure throughout intramural and extramural treatment
108	Success in intramural treatment, failure in extramural treatment
5	Failure in intramural treatment, success in extramural treatment
104	Success in some intramural treatment, failure in all extramural treatment
125	Failure in all extramural treatment, no intramural treatment
131	Success and failure in extramural treatment, no intramural treatment
137	Success in extramural treatment, no intramural treatment
100	Success in some extramural treatment, success in intramural treatment
10	Failure in most extramural treatment, success in intramural treatment
83	Success and failure in some intramural and extramural treatment

42 Failure in some extramural treatment, failure in intramural treatment

2 Success in intramural treatment, no extramural treatment

2 Success and failure in intramural treatment, no extramural treatment

3 Failure in intramural treatment, no extramural treatment

1 Failure in intramural treatment, failure in some extramural treatment

2 Success in extramural treatment, success in some intramural treatment

38 No treatment experiences, or unknown if any

___

1,000

Appendix C

PERIOD-COMPARISON TABLES

In the following series of tables, which are arranged by subject, we present the status of the 1,000 juvenile delinquents in the period prior to their appearance before the Boston Juvenile Court (designated Prior Period), and during the first, second, and third five-year follow-up spans.

All the tables total 1,000 unless otherwise indicated, except Tables 21 through 28, where the totals refer to the number of cases having a particular treatment experience whose behavior therein was ascertainable.

From the title of each table it is possible to refer to Appendix A, for a definition or explanation of the factor and for the numbers referring to the more detailed tables in Appendix B, from which these have been derived.

1. AGE OF OFFENDER

	AT END OF JBF-BJC TREATMENT PERIOD		AT END OF PERIOD I		AT END OF PERIOD II		AT END OF PERIOD III	
	Number	Per cent	Number	Per cent	Number	Per cent	Number	Per cent
Under 16 years	703	70.4	89	9.1	–	–	–	–
16–20 years	294	29.4	604	61.7	88	9.2	–	–
21–25 years	2	.2	284	29.0	593	61.7	85	9.0
26–30 years	–	–	2	.2	278	28.9	583	62.0
31–35 years	–	–	–	–	2	.2	270	28.7
36–40 years	–	–	–	–	–	–	2	.3
Dead	1		21		39		60	
Average age	14 ± .06		19 ± .06		24 ± .06		29 ± .06	

2. Number of arrests

	PRIOR PERIOD		PERIOD I		PERIOD II		PERIOD III	
	Num-ber	Per cent	Num-ber	Per cent	Num-ber	Per cent	Num-ber	Per cent
Inapplicable, or unknown if arrested	2		61		125		164	
One arrest	294	47.1	154	20.6	111	19.2	114	23.7
Two arrests	151	24.2	167	22.3	118	20.4	83	17.3
Three arrests	80	12.8	126	16.8	75	13.0	61	12.7
Four arrests	50	8.0	96	12.8	72	12.5	60	12.5
Five arrests	24	3.8	78	10.4	59	10.0	28	5.8
Six and more arrests	25	4.1	128	17.1	143	24.9	134	28.0
Total arrested	624	62.5	749	79.8	578	66.1	480	57.9
Not arrested	374	37.5	190	20.2	297	33.9	356	42.1
Average number of arrests of those arrested	$2.28 \pm .04$		$3.42 \pm .05$		$3.76 \pm .06$		$3.78 \pm .07$	

3. Frequency of arrests

	PRIOR PERIOD		PERIOD I		PERIOD II		PERIOD III	
	Num-ber	Per cent	Num-ber	Per cent	Num-ber	Per cent	Num-ber	Per cent
Unknown, inapplicable, or incalculable as only one arrest, or no arrests	671		408		536		633	
One arrest in less than nine months	149	45.3	180	30.4	159	34.3	143	39.0
One arrest in nine to eighteen months	124	37.6	198	33.4	158	34.1	114	31.1
One arrest in eighteen or more months	56	17.1	214	36.2	147	31.6	110	29.9
Average frequency of arrest among those arrested more than once	$10.57 \pm .25$		$14.02 \pm .21$		$13.21 \pm .24$		$12.58 \pm .27$	

4. Nature of Arrests

	PRIOR PERIOD		PERIOD I		PERIOD II		PERIOD III	
	Number	Per cent	Number	Per cent	Number	Per cent	Number	Per cent
Unknown	14		110		54		49	
Crimes against property	829	62.9	1,272	48.7	613	24.6	390	18.2
Crimes against chastity	4	.3	43	1.6	59	2.4	56	2.6
Crimes against family and children	–	–	14	.5	40	1.6	71	3.3
Crimes against public welfare	286	21.7	580	22.2	755	30.3	483	22.5
Drunkenness	–	–	242	9.3	724	29.0	922	43.0
Drug selling	–	–	1	.1	8	.3	12	.6
Crimes against person	33	2.5	115	4.4	183	7.3	147	6.8
Other*	167	12.6	342	13.2	111	4.5	65	3.0
Total arrests	*1,333*		*2,719*		*2,547*		*2,195*	

* Refers in Prior Period and Period I mainly to juvenile offenses such as truancy, stubbornness, running away, unmanageableness, malicious mischief, and in Periods II and III to court appearances on charges of "default."

5. Summary of Arrests, by Type

	PRIOR PERIOD		PERIOD I		PERIOD II		PERIOD III	
	Number	Per cent	Number	Per cent	Number	Per cent	Number	Per cent
Inapplicable, unknown, or not arrested	376		251		420		510	
Crimes against property	478	76.6	560	74.8	295	50.9	208	42.4
Crimes against chastity	4	.6	35	4.7	46	7.9	47	9.6
Crimes against family and children	–	–	7	.9	35	6.0	43	8.8
Crimes against public welfare	204	32.7	327	43.7	341	58.8	246	50.2
Drunkenness	–	–	100	13.4	205	35.3	227	46.3
Drug selling	–	–	1	.2	8	1.4	8	1.6
Crimes against person	30	4.8	93	12.4	141	24.3	104	21.2
Other*	132	21.2	237	31.6	83	14.3	49	10.0

NOTE. Percentages are based on number of men actually known to have been arrested in each period.

* Refers in Prior Period and Period I mainly to juvenile offenses such as truancy, stubbornness, running away, unmanageableness, malicious mischief, and in Periods II and III to court appearances on charges of "default."

6. Number of convictions (summary)

| | PRIOR PERIOD | | PERIOD I | | PERIOD II | | PERIOD III | |
	Num-ber	Per cent	Num-ber	Per cent	Num-ber	Per cent	Num-ber	Per cent
Inapplicable, or unknown if arrested or convicted	7		61		123		154	
No arrests	374		190		297		356	
Arrests but no convictions	42	6.8	16	2.1	41	7.1	44	9.0
Convictions	577	93.2	733	97.9	539	92.9	446	91.0

7. Number of convictions

| | PRIOR PERIOD | | PERIOD I | | PERIOD II | | PERIOD III | |
	Num-ber	Per cent	Num-ber	Per cent	Num-ber	Per cent	Num-ber	Per cent
Inapplicable, or unknown if arrested or convicted	7		61		123		154	
No arrests, or no convictions	416		206		338		400	
One conviction	280	48.5	167	22.8	146	27.2	138	31.5
Two convictions	138	23.9	177	24.2	105	19.6	81	18.5
Three convictions	81	14.0	137	18.7	83	15.5	61	13.9
Four convictions	47	8.1	99	13.5	61	11.4	51	11.6
Five convictions	11	1.9	65	8.9	54	10.0	32	7.3
Six or more convictions	20	3.6	87	11.9	88	16.3	75	17.2
Number unknown	–		1		2		8	
Average number of convictions among those arrested one or more times	$2.18 \pm .03$		$3.12 \pm .05$		$3.3 \pm .06$		$3.24 \pm .06$	

8. Frequency of convictions

	PRIOR PERIOD		PERIOD I		PERIOD II		PERIOD III	
	Number	Per cent	Number	Per cent	Number	Per cent	Number	Per cent
Unknown, inapplicable, or incalculable	674		412		543		650	
One conviction in less than nine months	135	41.4	142	24.2	106	23.2	99	28.3
One conviction in nine to eighteen months	121	37.1	203	34.5	150	33.8	99	28.2
One conviction in eighteen or more months	70	21.5	243	41.3	201	43.0	152	43.5
Average frequency of convictions among those arrested more than once	11.44 ± .25		15.16 ± .21		15.43 ± .25		15.07 ± .29	

9. Nature of dispositions

	PRIOR PERIOD		PERIOD I		PERIOD II		PERIOD III	
	Number	Per cent	Number	Per cent	Number	Per cent	Number	Per cent
Unknown	54		55		43		41	
Commitment—new	77	6.0	512	19.3	430	17.2	440	20.4
Commitment—by revocation	20	1.6	301	11.3	76	3.0	35	1.6
Probation	570	44.6	462	17.4	217	8.7	134	6.2
Probation under suspended sentence	81	6.3	250	9.4	136	5.4	150	7.0
Fine (including commitment for non-payment of fine, and restitution)	67	5.2	373	13.9	688	27.5	425	19.8
File	355	27.8	442	16.6	347	13.9	343	15.9
Released by probation officer	–	–	52	1.9	113	4.5	198	9.3
Nol-pros	3	.2	18	.7	51	2.0	44	2.0
No bill	–	–	17	.6	48	1.9	33	1.5
Not guilty or released	106	8.3	237	8.9	398	15.9	352	16.3
Total arrests	*1,333*		*2,719*		*2,547*		*2,195*	

Note. Percentages are based on total number of known dispositions.

10. SUMMARY OF DISPOSITIONS, BY TYPE

	PRIOR PERIOD		PERIOD I		PERIOD II		PERIOD III	
	Num-ber	Per cent	Num-ber	Per cent	Num-ber	Per cent	Num-ber	Per cent
Inapplicable, unknown, or not arrested	376		251		420		510	
Commitment—new	70	11.2	369	49.3	239	41.2	214	43.7
Commitment—by revocation	18	2.9	182	24.3	61	10.5	35	7.1
Probation	393	63.0	318	42.5	153	26.4	104	21.2
Probation under suspended sentence	74	11.9	192	25.6	92	15.9	99	20.2
Fine (including commitment for nonpayment, and restitution)	60	9.6	201	26.8	301	51.9	199	40.6
File	202	32.4	285	38.1	213	36.7	191	39.0
Released by probation officer	–	–	34	4.5	71	12.2	102	20.8
Nol-pros	3	.5	16	2.1	44	7.6	34	6.9
No bill	–	–	15	2.0	41	7.1	23	4.7
Not guilty or released	93	14.9	168	22.4	213	36.7	193	39.4
Nature of dispositions unknown, or other, or awaiting disposition	50	8.0	57	7.6	43	7.4	33	6.7

11. NUMBER OF PENAL EXPERIENCES (SUMMARY)

	PRIOR PERIOD		PERIOD I		PERIOD II		PERIOD III	
	Num-ber	Per cent	Num-ber	Per cent	Num-ber	Per cent	Num-ber	Per cent
Inapplicable, or unknown if any	–		58		108		143	
None	930	93.0	518	55.0	585	65.6	600	70.0
One or more experiences	70	7.0	424	45.0	307	34.4	257	30.0
Average number of penal experiences among those committed one or more times	$1.72 \pm .06$		$2.06 \pm .04$		$2.02 \pm .04$		$2.14 \pm .05$	

12. NUMBER OF PENAL EXPERIENCES

	PRIOR PERIOD		PERIOD I		PERIOD II		PERIOD III	
	Number	Per cent	Number	Per cent	Number	Per cent	Number	Per cent
Inapplicable, or unknown if any	–		58		108		143	
No penal experiences	930		518		585		600	
One experience	47	67.1	189	44.6	171	55.7	122	47.5
Two experiences	16	22.9	133	31.4	72	23.5	72	28.0
Three experiences	5	7.2	58	13.7	37	12.0	31	12.1
Four or more experiences	2	2.8	44	10.3	27	8.8	32	12.4
Average number of penal experiences	1.72 ± .06		2.06 ± .04		2.02 ± .04		2.14 ± .05	

13. TIME IN PENAL INSTITUTIONS

	PRIOR PERIOD		PERIOD I		PERIOD II		PERIOD III	
	Number	Per cent	Number	Per cent	Number	Per cent	Number	Per cent
None	930		518		587		600	
Less than one year	17	25.8	141	33.3	133	43.5	95	37.0
One to two years	29	44.0	174	41.0	74	24.2	53	20.6
Two to three years	16	24.2	70	16.5	37	12.0	36	14.0
Three or more years	4	6.0	39	9.2	62	20.3	73	28.4
Time unknown	4		58		107		143	
Average months in penal institutions	18.82 ± .85		17.98 ± .39		19.54 ± .61		23.26 ± .74	

14. Months in community

	PRIOR PERIOD		PERIOD I		PERIOD II		PERIOD III	
	Number	*Per cent*	*Number*	*Per cent*	*Number*	*Per cent*	*Number*	*Per cent*
Inapplicable (dead) or unknown	2		61		105		139	
None	–	–	2	.2	13	1.5	18	2.1
Less than one year			12	1.2	15	1.7	19	2.2
One to two years			28	3.0	38	4.2	37	4.3
Two to three years	68	6.8	67	7.1	42	4.7	40	4.6
Three years or more			318	33.9	209	23.3	149	17.3
Throughout	930	93.2	512	54.6	578	64.6	598	69.5
Average number of months in community of those not in community throughout			$41.5 \pm .41$		$39.10 \pm .61$		$35.74 \pm .73$	

15. Nature of penal experiences, by type

	PRIOR PERIOD		PERIOD I		PERIOD II		PERIOD III	
	Number	*Per cent*	*Number*	*Per cent*	*Number*	*Per cent*	*Number*	*Per cent*
Inapplicable (none, unknown if any, dead)	930		576		693		743	
Truant and correctional schools	67	95.7	324	76.4	43	14.0	–	–
Schools for feebleminded	2	2.9	8	1.9	2	.7	1	.4
Reformatories	2	2.9	93	21.9	96	31.3	47	18.3
Prisons	–	–	22	5.2	61	19.9	97	37.7
Institutions for defective delinquents	–	–	7	1.7	10	3.2	9	3.5
Jails, houses of correction, state farms	–	–	90	21.2	161	52.4	158	61.5
Total number of institutional experiences	*71*		*544*		*373*		*312*	

NOTE. Percentages are on basis of number of men known to have penal experiences in each period.

16. Official recognition of delinquency

	PRIOR PERIOD		PERIOD I		PERIOD II		PERIOD III	
	Number	Per cent	Number	Per cent	Number	Per cent	Number	Per cent
Inapplicable (non-penal institutions, dead), unknown	5		59		112		148	
Non-delinquent	7		137		238		312	
Official delinquent	624	63.3	755	93.9	604	92.9	504	93.3
Unofficial delinquent	364	36.7	49	6.1	46	7.1	36	6.7

17. Principal component of misconduct

	PRIOR PERIOD		PERIOD I		PERIOD II		PERIOD III	
	Number	Per cent	Number	Per cent	Number	Per cent	Number	Per cent
Unknown or inapplicable	5		59		108		147	
Non-delinquent	7		137		238		312	
Penal institution at least part of time on sentence imposed in previous period, no other serious delinquency	–	–	2	.2	27	4.1	29	5.4
Conviction for serious offense	451	45.6	543	67.5	272	41.6	189	34.9
Dishonorable discharge or desertion from Army or Navy	1	.1	9	1.1	8	1.2	–	–
Unofficial serious offender	264	26.7	45	5.6	28	4.3	14	2.6
Arrest for serious offense, not followed by conviction	32	3.2	26	3.3	39	6.0	27	5.0
Conviction for minor offense	74	7.5	140	17.4	215	32.9	218	40.3
Unofficial minor offender	156	15.8	32	4.0	38	5.8	34	6.3
Arrest for minor offense, not followed by conviction	10	1.1	7	.9	27	4.1	30	5.5

18. Delinquency (serious and minor)

	PRIOR PERIOD		PERIOD I		PERIOD II		PERIOD III	
	Num-ber	Per cent	Num-ber	Per cent	Num-ber	Per cent	Num-ber	Per cent
Inapplicable, unknown, non-delinquent	12		196		350		450	
Minor offender	241	24.4	182	22.6	282	43.4	282	52.2
Serious offender	747	75.6	622	77.4	368	56.6	258	47.8

19. Predominant offense

	PRIOR PERIOD		PERIOD I		PERIOD II		PERIOD III	
	Num-ber	Per cent	Num-ber	Per cent	Num-ber	Per cent	Num-ber	Per cent
Inapplicable, unknown	5		59		112		148	
Non-delinquent	7		137		238		312	
Crimes against property	702	71.1	527	65.5	255	39.2	169	31.5
Crimes against chastity	12	1.2	12	1.5	13	2.0	12	2.2
Crimes against family and children	–	–	4	.5	17	2.6	20	3.7
Crimes against public welfare	22	2.2	86	10.7	147	22.6	107	19.9
Drunkenness	–	–	34	4.2	108	16.6	128	23.7
Drug selling	–	–	1	.1	2	.3	4	.7
Crimes against person	2	.2	5	.6	9	1.4	11	2.0
Varied	64	6.5	60	7.6	62	9.5	59	10.9
Other or not determinable	186	18.8	75	9.3	37	5.8	29	5.4

20. Delinquency

	PRIOR PERIOD		PERIOD I		PERIOD II		PERIOD III	
	Num-ber	Per cent	Num-ber	Per cent	Num-ber	Per cent	Num-ber	Per cent
Inapplicable (non-penal institution, dead) or unknown	5		59		112		148	
Non-delinquent	7	.7	137	14.6	238	26.8	312	36.6
Minor offender	241	24.2	182	19.3	282	31.8	282	33.1
Serious offender	747	75.1	622	66.1	368	41.4	258	30.3

21. BEHAVIOR DURING PROBATION

	PRIOR PERIOD		PERIOD I		PERIOD II		PERIOD III	
	Number	*Per cent*	*Number*	*Per cent*	*Number*	*Per cent*	*Number*	*Per cent*
Success	74	22.9	100	33.0	38	26.6	37	39.4
Failure	249	77.1	203	67.0	105	73.4	57	60.6
Total whose behavior known	323		303		143		94	

22. BEHAVIOR DURING PROBATION UNDER SUSPENDED SENTENCE

	PRIOR PERIOD		PERIOD I		PERIOD II		PERIOD III	
	Number	*Per cent*	*Number*	*Per cent*	*Number*	*Per cent*	*Number*	*Per cent*
Success	11	17.8	50	24.0	20	21.7	20	23.0
Failure	51	82.2	158	76.0	72	78.3	67	77.0
Total whose behavior known	62		208		92		87	

23. BEHAVIOR DURING PAROLE

	PRIOR PERIOD		PERIOD I		PERIOD II		PERIOD III	
	Number	*Per cent*	*Number*	*Per cent*	*Number*	*Per cent*	*Number*	*Per cent*
Success	1	2.5	56	14.5	58	25.4	42	34.4
Failure	39	97.5	331	85.5	170	74.6	80	65.6
Total whose behavior known	40		387		228		122	

24. BEHAVIOR IN ARMY OR NAVY

	PERIOD I		PERIOD II		PERIOD III	
	Number	*Per cent*	*Number*	*Per cent*	*Number*	*Per cent*
Success	51	51.0	40	60.4	14	63.6
Failure	49	49.0	26	39.4	8	36.4
Total whose behavior known	100		66		22	

25. BEHAVIOR IN CORRECTIONAL AND TRUANT SCHOOLS

	PRIOR PERIOD		PERIOD I		PERIOD II	
	Number	Per cent	Number	Per cent	Number	Per cent
Success	27	49.1	171	52.5	17	53.1
Failure	28	50.9	155	47.5	15	46.9
Total whose behavior known	55		326		32	

26. BEHAVIOR IN REFORMATORIES

	PERIOD I		PERIOD II		PERIOD III	
	Number	Per cent	Number	Per cent	Number	Per cent
Success	31	38.8	47	53.4	32	78.0
Failure	49	61.2	41	46.6	9	22.0
Total whose behavior known	80		88		41	

27. BEHAVIOR IN PRISONS

	PERIOD I		PERIOD II		PERIOD III	
	Number	Per cent	Number	Per cent	Number	Per cent
Success	11	84.6	33	63.4	68	70.8
Failure	2	15.4	19	36.6	28	29.2
Total whose behavior known	13		52		96	

28. BEHAVIOR IN JAILS, HOUSES OF CORRECTION, STATE FARMS

	PERIOD I		PERIOD II		PERIOD III	
	Number	Per cent	Number	Per cent	Number	Per cent
Success	32	66.7	72	75.8	84	78.5
Failure	16	33.3	23	24.2	23	21.5
Total whose behavior known	48		95		107	

INDEX